Henri Nouwen

THE ROAD TO
PEACE

Other Orbis Books by Henri Nouwen

Adam: God's Beloved

A Cry for Mercy: Prayers from the Genesee

Gracias!: A Latin American Journal

Walk with Jesus: Stations of the Cross

With Burning Hearts: A Meditation on the Eucharistic Life

Henri Nouwen

THE ROAD TO
PEACE

Writings on Peace and Justice

edited by John Dear

ORBIS BOOKS

Maryknoll, New York 10545

Third printing, September 2003

The Catholic Foreign Mission Society of America (Maryknoll) recruits and trains people for over-seas missionary service. Through Orbis Books, Maryknoll aims to foster the international dialogue that is essential to mission. The books published, however, reflect the opinions of their authors and are not meant to represent the official position of the society.

Grateful acknowledgment is made to the following publications for permission to reprint the fol-lowing material:

© 1983, 1984 *America* Press, rights reserved.
  – "We Drink from Our Own Wells," October 15, 1983, pp. 205-208;
  – "Christ of the Americas," April 21, 1984, pp. 293-302.

© 1984 HarperCollins, rights reserved.
  – The introduction by Henri Nouwen to the book, *The Church Is All of You: Thoughts of Arch-bishop Oscar Romero,* edited by James Brockman, published by Winston Press, Minneapolis, Minnesota, 1984;
  – © "A Conversation with Henri J. M. Nouwen," in *Living with Apocalypse: Spiritual Resources for Social Compassion,* edited by Tilden H. Edwards, published by Harper and Row, San Fran-cisco, 1984, pp. 15-22.

© 1985 *Maryknoll* magazine,
  – "Prayer Embraces the World," April 1985.

© 1987 *Praying* magazine,
  – "The Journey from Despair to Hope," March-April, 1987.

© 1990 *The Other Side* magazine,
  – "Henri Nouwen: An Interview by Arthur Boers," in the special collection, "Faces of Faith."

The National Catholic AIDS Network:
  – "Our Story, Our Wisdom," talk, June, 1994.

Queries regarding rights and permissions should be addressed to: Orbis Books, P.O. Box 308, Maryknoll, NY 10545-0308.

Manufactured in the United States of America

Library of Congress Cataloging-in-Publication Data

Nouwen, Henri J. M.
     The road to peace : writings on peace and justice/Henri Nouwen ;
   edited by John Dear.
        p.   cm.
     Includes bibliographical references.
     ISBN 1-57075-192-7
     1. Christianity and justice.   2. Peace—Religious aspects—
   Christianity.   3. Social justice.   I. Dear, John, 1959-
   II. Title
   BR115.J8N68   1998
   261.8—dc21
                                                          97-44940
                                                            CIP

For Art Laffin

CONTENTS

ACKNOWLEDGMENTS

I want to offer my thanks to everyone at L'Arche-Daybreak for making this book possible, beginning with Sue Mosteller, Henri's literary executrix, who gave permission for this project, and Kathy Christie, Henri's secretary, who helped me through the editing process.

The staff of the Yale Divinity School Special Collections Department generously assisted me as I studied Henri's archives. Robert Durback sent me a copy of the original manuscript of Henri's book on peacemaking, which, except for excerpts in *The New Oxford Review,* has never been published before. Nancy Forest-Flier translated Henri's account of his journey to Selma, written in Dutch in 1965. Art Laffin, Carolyn Whitney-Brown, Michael Harank, Jim Forest, Jim Wallis, and Laurent Nouwen offered encouragement and suggestions. My Jesuit brothers at New York City's West Side Jesuit Community, especially Daniel Berrigan, Steve Kelly, Don Moore, Bob Keck, Bill McNichols, Ed Zogby, and Joseph Roccasalvo, supported me during this project.

This book would not have been possible without the assistance and friendship of Robert Ellsberg, editor-in-chief of Orbis Books. Special thanks also to Geraldine DiLauro for typing the manuscript.

This collection of Henri's writings on peace and justice is dedicated to Henri's friend and my friend, longtime peacemaker, Plowshares activist and Catholic Worker, Art Laffin.

John Dear, S.J.

INTRODUCTION

In early 1989, a Trappist monk friend of mine sent me a copy of Henri Nouwen's latest book, *In the Name of Jesus*. I was living in Washington, D.C. at the time, working with homeless people in our church's drop-in center and shelter. The weather was bitterly cold, and on my errands I wore a big blue winter coat with deep pockets, so I put this little book in a pocket and carried it around with me.

One day, while attending a demonstration at the mayor's office to protest the latest housing cuts and lack of funding for the homeless, I was arrested by the police. A group of ten homeless people and housing advocates had sat down and blocked the City Council chamber's doorways. I was down the hall speaking to a reporter, explaining our demands. Just then, several police officers approached me, pushed me into an elevator, and placed me under arrest.

When I arrived in the D.C. central cellblock that afternoon, I discovered Henri Nouwen's book in my coat pocket. "I am deeply convinced that the Christian leader of the future is called to be completely irrelevant and to stand in this world with nothing to offer but his or her own vulnerable self," I read. "That is the way Jesus revealed God's love."

I was hooked. I spent that day in jail meditating on the famous spiritual writer's message, which I found both consoling and challenging. "The leader of the future," he continued, "will be the one who dares to claim his or her irrelevance in the contemporary world as a divine vocation that allows him or her to enter into a deep solidarity with the anguish underlying all the glitter of success and to bring the light of Jesus there.

"The long painful history of the church is the history of people ever and again tempted to choose power over love, control over the cross, being a leader over being led. Those who resisted this temptation to the end and thereby give us hope are the true saints."[1]

Right there and then, in our crowded cell, with paper and pencil given to me by other cellmates, I started to write about this book and its implications for Christians. A few days after I was released, I wrote a letter to Henri Nouwen, thanked him for his book, and enclosed a copy of my review written in jail. Henri replied immediately, offering his support and encouragement along with autographed copies of other books.

For the next seven years, until the week he died, Henri corresponded with me regularly, as he did with thousands of people around the world. He sent me copies of each new book, inquired about my interests and adventures, shared his own latest journeys, and encouraged me with his friendship. As I studied his writings, I discovered an underlying, foundational commitment to peace and justice. Most of his readers knew his spiritual themes of prayer, intimacy, solitude, healing, ministry, and Eucharist. But underneath these good reflections on personal spiritual growth lay a definite social spirituality. Henri was a teacher, a preacher, and a writer, but his heart was open to the world and to the possibility of God's reign of justice coming to all people. Henri was a peacemaker.

I heard Henri speak once, at the Sojourners' "Peace Pentecost" gathering in May 1985 at Catholic University in Washington, D.C. He preached for over an hour and a half that Sunday morning, holding over one thousand people spellbound. Several times he interrupted himself to lead us in Taize chants. He reflected on the Pentecost story, the image of Jesus washing the disciples' feet, and the risen Jesus' question to Peter, "Do you love me? Do you love me? Do you truly love me?" That question is the most important question of our lives, especially for those of us concerned about justice and peace, he exclaimed with arms flying back and forth. He quoted Jesus' final words to Peter: "When you were younger, you used to dress yourself and go where you wanted; but when you grow old, you will stretch out your hands, and someone else will put a belt around you and lead you where you would rather not go." Keep your eyes on Jesus, he insisted. Keep working for justice and peace, but do it with heartfelt devotion to the risen Lord.

The day after Henri's powerful Pentecost sermon, I flew to El Salvador, where I met the university Jesuits who were later assassinated, worked for two months in a church-run refugee camp in a war zone, and traveled through the contra-war of Nicaragua and the repression of Guatemala. Throughout those intense months, Jesus' question, asked through Henri's thick Dutch accent, reveberated in my spirit: "Do you love me?" Jesus asked me in my prayer. "Feed my lambs. Do you love me? Tend my sheep. Do you truly love me? Feed my sheep. Someone will put a belt around you and lead you where you would rather not go. Follow me."

After I had spent several months in the Salvadoran war zone of Guasapa, my friends at the Calle Real refugee camp threw a going away party for another young Jesuit and myself. One of the Salvadoran campesinos presented me with a gift—a belt which he had proudly made himself. Suddenly, Jesus' question— and Henri's urgency—took on new meaning: the poor of Central America were putting a belt around me and leading me where I would rather not go—into the struggle of nonviolent resistance against U.S. warmaking. In other words, to the cross.

It was decisive moment in my life. Henri's Pentecost reflections had prepared me to accept that mission, as I later wrote him. I came home broken, shaken, angry, afraid, and determined to speak out against U.S. militarism in Central America and elsewhere.

Over the next few years, my journey led me to four years of theology studies in Berkeley, California; active public resistance to U.S. military aid to El Salvador and the Gulf War massacre; ordination to the priesthood; pastoral work in a small Jesuit parish near the U.S. Capitol; and finally, jail for a Plowshares anti-nuclear demonstration. Throughout those struggles, I received warm letters from Henri, each one an epistle of faith and friendship, filled with stories of his latest travels, spiritual reflections, and concerns for the world and mutual friends.

In the fall of 1990, after I had written Henri with questions about studying theology in the comfortable surroundings of the Graduate Theological Union in Berkeley, California, Henri responded, "I very well understand the doubts you express about studying scripture and theology in the Berkeley setting. I experienced some of the same doubts while I was at Yale and Harvard." Live as if you are a Christian in exile, he wrote. I remember my surprise at this advice from the esteemed spiritual writer. His suggestion would not have been well received by GTU theologians. "I believe that if you live a little bit like an exile," he concluded, "it can be very fruitful and very enriching."

"The Gulf War has certainly been a horrible event," Henri wrote in 1991. "I was in Washington, D.C. on the 14th of January at the National Cathedral to pray with many church leaders in the hope the war could be prevented. Regretfully, the war started the next day and we only lately know how much suffering it has brought. Reaction in Canada was probably a lot less nationalistic than in the United States, but the government decided to support the war militarily even against the desire of the majority of the people. But now it seems that people don't talk about it much anymore. It seems to be, in many ways, a forgotten event, horrible as it was. It certainly caused me a lot of pain and I have become more aware than ever of how hard it is to proclaim radically the peace of Jesus in a world that so quickly gravitates to violent solutions of its problems."

Another exchange stays with me. In October 1992, around the 500th anniversary of Columbus's arrival and the subsequent genocide of the native peoples, I traveled for two weeks with a Pax Christi delegation to Haiti. President Jean-Bertrand Aristide was living in exile in Washington, D.C. at the time. A brutal military regime had taken over the country, killed several thousand people, and threatened the remaining populace with arrest and persecution. We journeyed through Port-au-Prince to Cap

Haitien in the north. Passing through several small villages, we witnessed the grinding poverty and abject misery and listened to dozens of underground priests, sisters, and lay leaders who were in hiding because of their work for justice. At the end, I testified before an Organization of American States committee about the death threats and repressive violence we had heard of in the countryside and called for international pressure against the coup leaders.

I returned home to Oakland, California, devastated by the suffering and violence I had seen in Haiti, inspired by the faith of its courageous people, and shocked once again by our culture's opulence. A package from Henri containing his new book, *Life of the Beloved*, was waiting for me. I decided to spend that first afternoon home reading and praying through Henri's latest book as a way to recenter myself.

But as I finished his little book, I grew more upset. I immediately wrote Henri a letter critiquing the book. I agreed that we are all the beloved of God, but in a world of injustice, we are required to work for justice, and this book neglects this crucial next step. As the beloved of God, we must dedicate ourselves to relieving the suffering of the poor, God's preferential beloved, I wrote. We must seek justice, love our enemies, and oppose war and any form of killing God's other beloved children—or we renounce our belovedness. The life of the beloved children of God, I pointed out, promotes life for all, especially those suffering the brunt of death—the third world poor, the hungry, the homeless, the imprisoned, those on death row, the unborn, children, and the victims of war. We can claim our belovedness, I self-righteously explained to Henri, only if we risk our lives in active love for those marginalized and killed by the world's imperial forces. I described my experience in Haiti, the shock of seeing the poverty and injustice first hand, and the grim truth that most of the repression, while backed by the U.S., was perpetrated by churchgoing Catholic Christians. His book did not urge U.S. Christians to resist the injustice and death inflicted on other Christians, such as the suffering Haitian church, I told him bitterly. It did not encourage us to love our neighbors, beginning with the Haitians at our border, the poorest of the poor in our hemisphere, or for that matter, the Cubans, the Nicaraguans, the Salvadorans, or the Guatemalans. I concluded by asking him to write more about the Gospel's urgent call to seek justice, pursue disarmament, and practice nonviolence.

It is a sign of Henri's compassion and sanctity that he responded as graciously to me as he did. While my letter may have held much truth, the spirit behind it was filled with anger, not compassion or gratitude. I did not know, among other things, that Henri had spent many summers in the previous decades traveling and working in Latin America. I think deep down Henri agreed with me, but felt that North Americans were so despairing, so overwhelmed by the consumeristic culture, that they could not even believe in God, much less that God loves them. He felt a call to announce this simple truth. Years later, as I reread *Life of the Beloved*, I discovered his references to the world's injustice and his belief that the life of faith includes the struggle for justice and peace.

A few months later, on the day before I was ordained, a large package arrived from Henri in Toronto: a beautiful color poster of his favorite painting, Rembrandt's "The Return of the Prodigal Son." Shortly thereafter, I would read his book about the painting and the parable and be moved by his vulnerability and call to compassion.

On December 7, 1993, I was arrested in Goldsboro, North Carolina, with three friends for hammering on an F-16, nuclear-capable, Air Force fighter bomber in an anti-nuclear Plowshares demonstration. It was, for me, a nonviolent way to enact the biblical commands to "beat swords into plowshares" and "love your enemies." We were jailed, indicted, arraigned, tried, and convicted with a felony charge of destruction of government property. During the long eight months in North Carolina county jails, my friends and I never left our cells and never went outdoors. I received many letters of support, but Henri's letters from the L'Arche-Daybreak community were particularly encouraging. He sent me manuscripts and books, and offered repeatedly to help in any way he could. He felt in solidarity with our peace witness, he wrote to me, because he wanted to be an instrument of Christ's peace.

Considering how some of my friends in the church and in the peace movement were angry with us because of our civil disobedience, I was touched by Henri's outpouring of support. He read aloud my hand-written, pencil-scrawled letters at Daybreak's liturgies and community meetings, he wrote, "so that our work for peace and your work for peace will be the same." On May 17, 1994, he wrote: "There was a time in which I thought about prison as a place where I could be quiet, pray, and write, but your story makes it very clear that all of this is pure fantasy. I am deeply aware of the suffering that the noise and the restlessness around you creates. For me that too would be the greatest source of pain. Hopefully you can gradually find some inner silence and inner space in the midst of all the clamor and shouts. It certainly must ask for a generous discipline....I have never spent time in prison but I realize that prison is one of the places where the poor are, and where Jesus is very present. Thank you for your great love for God, for your great love for all those who suffer, and especially for your friendship with me."

After I was released from jail, I was ordered to spend five months under house arrest at the Jesuit community a few blocks from the U.S. Capitol. "I can imagine that it is hard to be so cooped up but I hope that you can make this time a time of inner growth and spiritual fruitfulness," Henri wrote. "I especially hope that you can join St. Paul in writing during your time of house arrest. I still have very good memories of the time I spent with the Trappists, which was sort of a self-imposed house arrest, which proved in the long run to be a very fruitful time, even though when I was living it, it was not very easy."

Our last letters concerned his sabbatical and my work as the executive director of the Sacred Heart Center, a community center for the poor in the projects of Richmond, Virginia. I felt inundated with the needs of the women and children, the administrative and fundraising work, and the Center's demanding programs.

Henri urged me to try "to remain a contemplative in the midst of the whirlwind," by getting away regularly for prayer and rest so that I could be more present to those around me. I wrote back with arrangements to visit him in Toronto, but he never received my letter. He died unexpectedly of a heart attack on September 21, 1996.

Since his funeral, I have met more of his friends and learned more about his amazing life. In a way, our friendship continues. This book carries on that spiritual conversation, his gift to the peacemaking church.

THE JOURNEY FROM ACADEME TO L'ARCHE

Henri Nouwen's journey from Holland to the academic world to L'Arche balanced a deep love for the contemplative life with a passionate concern for the world. The first of five children, he was born on January 24, 1932, in Nijerk, Holland. During his childhood, he and his family had hidden from the Nazis. He was ordained a priest on July 21, 1957, for the Archdiocese of Utrecht, Holland. In 1994, Henri wrote a short synopsis of his life entitled "My History with God" for a class he was teaching in Toronto. It begins with a description of those early years:

> My first twenty-four years of life were basically years to prepare myself for the Catholic priesthood. I was born and raised in a Roman Catholic family, went to Roman Catholic schools, and lived a life in which I related exclusively to Roman Catholics. It was a time in which all the boundaries were clear. I was a Roman Catholic and not a Protestant; I was Christian and not Moslem, Buddhist, or Hindu. I was a believer and not a pagan; I was Dutch and not German, French, or English; I was white and not black, etc. These very clear boundaries gave me a sense of being in the right place, being wholly protected, and being very safe. I never met anybody who was divorced, who had left the priesthood, or who was gay. It was very clear what I was going to do as a priest. I

knew the right teaching and the right way to live the moral life. Six years in the seminary had given me very clear cut guidelines and surrounded me with people who had received the same guidelines. Proclaiming the Gospel and administering the sacraments were challenging, but not complicated, and something I really felt called to do. I was a very happy person, felt very close to God, had a very disciplined prayer life and a very clear-cut vocation.[2]

From 1957 to 1964 Henri studied psychology at the Catholic University of Nijmegen, Holland. In 1964 he moved to the United States for two years of study in psychiatry and religion at the Menninger Clinic in Topeka, Kansas. From 1966 to 1968 he was a visiting professor in the psychology department at the University of Notre Dame, Indiana. From 1968 to 1970 he was a staff member of the Pastoral Institute in Amsterdam and taught at the Catholic Theological Institute in Utrecht. From 1970 to 1971 he finished his doctoral studies in theology at the University of Nijmegen and received his degree in September 1971. Then, he began ten years as a tenured professor of theology at Yale Divinity School in New Haven, Connecticut. Henri's courses included such topics as "The Relationship between Ministry and Spirituality," "The History of Christian Spirituality," "The Ministry of Vincent van Gogh," "The Life and Works of Thomas Merton," and "Prayer."

Henri's writing career began in the late 1960s after he spoke to a conference of priests at the University of Notre Dame. *The National Catholic Reporter* published his remarks, which attracted widespread interest and were quickly put together as his first book, *Intimacy*, in 1969. The forty books that followed provide a record of his passionate search for God and his strong desire to help others to find their way to God's home. His first series of books, including *The Wounded Healer, Creative Ministry, With Open Hands, Out of Solitude*, and *Reaching Out*, focused on the connection between ministry and spirituality and became immediate bestsellers.

In 1974 Henri spent seven months at a Trappist monastery, the Abbey of the Genesee, in Piffard, New York. He later described this experience in *The Genesee Diary*, the first and perhaps the best of his autobiographical/journal writings. In 1976, while he was a fellow at the Ecumenical Institute in Collegeville, Minnesota, he also made the thirty-day silent retreat, the Spiritual Exercises of Saint Ignatius, from June to July. He spent 1978 in Rome as a scholar in residence at the Gregorian University and later at the North American College. In 1979 he spent another six months at the Abbey of the Genesee.

During his 1976 retreat, he began to wonder how much longer he should remain at Yale. He had never intended to stay ten years, and had certainly never felt at home at Yale. In the late 1970s and early 1980s he discerned a possible vocation among the poor in Latin America. He finally resigned his position at Yale and traveled to South America. Between October 1981 and March 1982 he traveled to Bolivia to study Spanish and then moved to Peru to test out this new life.

It was not to be. He returned in March and immediately moved back to the Abbey of the Genesee for his third monastic sabbatical. He published a book called *¡Gracias!*, a journal of his Latin American search. At the suggestion of liberation theologian Gustavo Gutiérrez, he decided to pursue a "reverse mission," to evangelize first world North America from the perspective of third world liberation theology. He still did not know where he could undertake such a mission.

Harvard Divinity School invited Henri to join its faculty, and he decided to give it a try, with the stipulation that he would have to teach only one semester of the academic year. In the spring semester of 1983 he moved to Cambridge, Massachusetts, where he remained a popular speaker and sought-after advisor until the summer of 1985.

In the summer of 1983, Henri flew to Mexico on the way back to Peru for another long stay. But a priest in Mexico urged him to visit Nicaragua instead, and an impromptu two-day visit stretched out over a month. After joining the Witness for Peace delegation on the border of Honduras, he felt a deep responsibility to return to the United States and call the Christian community to oppose the Reagan administration's war. With the support of peace groups and the bishops' conference, he embarked on a grueling six-week national speaking tour, calling the churches to speak out against the U.S.-backed contra war against the poor of Nicaragua. He traveled the country, speaking every day to packed churches in different cities. He recounted his experience in Nicaragua, described the faith-filled, forgiving Nicaraguan *campesinos* he had met, and called for public opposition to the Reagan government's threat of full-scale invasion. Everywhere he went, he gave countless interviews calling for public opposition to the U.S. government's warfare in Central America. His talks were published in local newsletters and stirred widespread debate.

At the end of the tour, just before he was to speak to one last crowded congregation, an anonymous caller left a message that a bomb had been planted in the church and would go off during his speech. Henri was deeply frightened by the bomb threat. When the tour ended, Henri was exhausted, and flew to France at the invitation of Jean Vanier for a period of rest at L'Arche. Afterward, Jean invited him to join L'Arche permanently. In the fall of 1984, after teaching at Harvard in the spring semester, Henri flew back to France and, for the second time, made the thirty-day silent retreat, the Spiritual Exercises. By the time it was over, Henri was ready to take the leap.

When Henri returned to Harvard in January 1985, he knew he could no longer remain in the academic world. At the end of the semester he resigned his position. Later, he told friends and interviewers that Harvard had brought him to the brink of spiritual crisis, that indeed he was "in danger of losing his soul."[3] He wrote:

> During all these years, I learned that Protestants belong as much to the church as Catholics, and that Hindus, Buddhists, and Moslems believe in God as much as Christians do; that pagans can love one another as much as believers can; that the human psyche is multidimen-

tional; that theology, psychology, and sociology are intersecting in many places; that women have a real call to ministry; that homosexual people have a unique vocation in the Christian community; that the poor belong to the heart of the church; and that the spirit of God blows where it wants. All of these discoveries gradually broke down many fences that had given me a safe garden and made me deeply aware that God's covenant with God's people includes everyone. For me personally, it was a time of searching, questioning, and agonizing, a time that was extremely lonely and not without moments of great inner uncertainty and ambiguity. The Jesus that I had come to know in my youth had died. I was traveling in a downcast way to Emmaus, and started hearing the Voice of someone who had joined me on the journey.[4]

Henri began his transitional year by flying to Nevada in August 1985. There he joined a gathering of Christians for four days of prayer and protest at a nuclear weapons test site sixty-five miles northwest of Las Vegas. It was the fortieth anniversary of the U.S. atomic bombings of Hiroshima and Nagasaki. He kept vigil at the entrance as 120 people were arrested in peaceful acts of nonviolent civil disobedience. Because he was a Dutch citizen and feared deportation, Henri did not risk arrest, but he fully supported this campaign to end nuclear weapons testing. Before going to France, he told *The Los Angeles Times,* "I wanted to be here first to make a pilgrimage with peacemaking people."[5] His presence in Nevada, along with his support of demonstrations against the Trident Submarine base in Groton, Connecticut, were part of his ongoing commitment to disarmament.

A few days later, Henri flew to France for a nine-month stay with Jean Vanier and L'Arche. During the year, Henri also visited the L'Arche-Daybreak community in Toronto. Shortly after his arrival, a community member who was disabled was struck by a car. Henri found himself helping the community respond to the sudden crisis. Back in France, he received a letter from Daybreak inviting him to join their community full-time.

In the summer of 1986, at age 54, Henri joined the Daybreak community as an assistant and pastor, and remained there until his death in 1996. "My sense of being called to L'Arche was based more on what I had to receive than on what I had to give. Jean Vanier said, 'Maybe we can offer you a home here.' That, more than anything else, was what my heart desired."[6] For the first time in his life, as he wrote in his journal account, *The Road to Daybreak,* he felt at home.

Henri was assigned the task of caring for Adam, a severely handicapped young man who could not speak, walk, or move. For many long months, Henri spent a good part of each day bathing, dressing, feeding, and attending to Adam. Though Henri could not do anything to change Adam's helplessness, Adam gave Henri a new sense of peace. "Life is harder at Daybreak," he said a year after arriving. "I know that this is where God wants me to be. Here I come in touch with my own brokenness. It's a good struggle for faithfulness. You're working on your salvation for the glory of God, not on your career for the glory of Harvard."[7]

"L'Arche reminds us that a worldwide movement of care for the poor and the oppressed can engender a new consciousness which transcends the boundaries of sex, religion, race, and nation," Henri wrote later. "Such a consciousness can give birth to a world community, a community to celebrate our shared humanity, to sing a joyful song of praise to the God of love, and to proclaim the ultimate victory of life over death."[8]

Shortly after his arrival at Daybreak, a close friendship ruptured and Henri suffered a complete emotional breakdown. He left the community and went to live in a hermitage at a Trappist monstery in Western Canada. From January to June 1987 he underwent regular spiritual direction. Later, in his book *The Inner Voice of Love,* he wrote that those six months were the most painful and difficult of his life, but they opened up new inner freedom and a deeper peace. In the years that followed, he began to share his personal struggles more and more with the community. While he continued to travel, speak, and stay connected with a world-wide network of friends, he clung to his Daybreak friends. From then on, whenever he gave a public lecture, he invited a disabled community member to join him and speak alongside him.

In early 1989, as he was walking along an icy highway on a cold winter morning, Henri was struck in the back by the right side mirror of a passing van. He was taken to the hospital and, while undergoing major surgery, he nearly died. In his book, *Beyond the Mirror*, he described lying in the hospital, feeling "a tremendous sense of the presence of Christ, like I have never felt before."[9] In the years that followed, he spoke often and wrote frequently about the meaning of death, especially in his moving book *Our Greatest Gift*. He cut back on public speaking, spent more time preparing himself for death and reconciling with friends, and continued his prolific writing. He also found joy traveling with trapeze artists. "One day I hope to be able to tell you about a very interesting month I spent recently with a German circus," Henri wrote to me in 1992. "In some ways, life in a circus is not dissimilar to life in a community of nonviolence." Like William Stringfellow, he planned to write a book about circus life, spirituality, and the church.

In the last years of his life, he published a series of smaller books on themes of Christian life and biblical spirituality, such as *The Return of the Prodigal Son*, *Walk With Jesus*, *With Burning Hearts*, and *Can You Drink the Cup?* In notes written in 1994 he summed up this third stage of life, the eight previous years at L'Arche, as an experience of coming home:

> When I joined the l'Arche Daybreak Community in Toronto, I was searching for a new home. I knew it could not be the old home that I had left, but I did not know what the new home would look like. During the last eight years living with people with mental handicaps and their assistants in a very close knit community consisting of people from many different religions, backgrounds, communities, and lifestyles, my heart started to burn, and I started to recognize the presence of Jesus in a radically new way. During this time I have ex-

perienced much loneliness, much confusion, and much
insecurity, but I have experienced all of this sorrow living with poor people who in their simplicity and openness offer me a space that gradually could become a
new home. Since living in community, my spiritual
journey has been radically deepened, the full dimension
of which I am not yet fully able to articulate. But I know
that living with the people of my community is calling
me to be a witness to God in a way that I never could
have been before.[10]

In September 1995 Henri left Daybreak for a year-long sabbatical during which he wrote five new books. He lived with
friends in Canada, Massachusetts, and New Jersey. In January
1996 he returned home for the funeral of Adam, and then returned again to spend Holy Week with his community. Finally,
he arrived back on September 1, 1996, eager to catch up with
everyone, but ready to head off again, this time on a short trip to
St. Petersburg, Russia, to film a documentary about Rembrandt's
"The Return of the Prodigal Son." After a short stay at L'Arche,
he flew to Holland, intending to pay a quick visit to his father,
brothers, and sister before flying to Russia. On Sunday night,
September 15th, Henri called down to the hotel clerk, complain-
ing of chest pains. He was rushed to the hospital, where he en-
dured pain for the next two days. He recovered quickly from two
heart attacks and expected to fly back to Toronto the following
Monday. He prayed the psalms, reminisced with his family, and
called his friends at L'Arche every day. "I am prepared for
death," he told his family. When he died suddenly that Saturday
morning, he was sixty-four years old.

Henri Nouwen's Spirituality of Peace

"At the time of his death," Robert Ellsberg wrote in *The Catholic
Worker* a few months later, "Henri Nouwen was one of the most
popular and influential spiritual writers of his time. Through
dozens of books, he invited countless persons to enter more

deeply into the spiritual life—intimacy with Jesus and solidarity with a wounded world."[11]

Henri wrote beautifully about the personal struggle of faith, spirituality, and intimacy, but he knew that this spirituality of love and hope had social implications. He understood that it required solidarity with the marginalized, steadfast love for our enemies, and reconciliation with all people as our sisters and brothers. Yet everywhere he went, people asked him to help them with their personal faith struggle and he was eager to tell despairing people that God loves them. And so, he focused mainly on the personal, inner work of faith. During his last decade, he led retreats for such diverse groups as Nicaragua's Sandinista leaders, wealthy corporate boards, Congresspeople, and even military personnel. But underlying all his talks, correpondence, and books remained a burning desire to spread the social Gospel of peace with justice. What his readers often failed to grasp was that Henri included the struggle for peace and justice as an integral factor in the spiritual life, if not its very core.

Henri was deeply concerned about injustice, violence, and war. He studied the issues, discussed them with friends, prayed about them, and spoke about them. Foremost among his social concerns was the need for nuclear disarmament. With the support and influence of Art Laffin, Dean Hammer, Jim Wallis, and Daniel and Philip Berrigan, Henri began to denounce U.S. militarism and the U.S. nuclear arsenal as an affront to God. In the early 1980s he spoke to many church conferences and retreats on Gospel peacemaking. "All people who believe that God is a God of life, and especially we who proclaim that Jesus Christ came to live among us to overcome the powers of death, must say 'No' to nuclear arms, a clear and unambiguous 'No,'" Henri announced. "The thought that human beings are considering saving their lives by killing millions of their fellow human beings is so preposterous that the words 'saving life' have lost all of their meaning. One of the most tragic facts of our century is that this 'No' to nuclear weapons has been spoken so seldom, so softly, and by so few."

"Christians should put survival of the planet ahead of national security," Henri once told an interviewer. "Here is the mystery of our global responsibility: that we are in communion with Christ—and we are in communion with all people.... The fact that the people of Nicaragua, Gautemala, El Salvador, Russia, Afghanistan, and Ethiopia are our brothers and sisters is not obvious. People kill each other by the thousands and do not see themselves as brothers and sisters. If we want to be real peacemakers, national security cannot be our primary concern. Our primary concern should be survival of humanity, the survival of the planet, and the health of all people. Whether we are Russians, Iraqis, Ethiopians, or North Americans, we belong to the same human family that God loves. And we have to start taking some risks—not just individually, but risks of a more global quality, risks to let other people develop their own independence, risks to share our wealth with others and invite refugees to our country, risks to offer sanctuary—because we are people of God."[12]

Henri's "spirituality of peacemaking" featured three components which he thought were essential to mature Christian discipleship. First, peacemaking requires a life of prayer, that is, daily meditation on the peacemaking Christ and liturgical intercession for an end to war. Second, peacemaking demands ongoing resistance to the forces of violence, including nonviolent direct action against militarism and public calls for nuclear disarmament. Third, peacemaking necessitates community. Peacemakers need to form, join, and live in communities of active nonviolence, such as Sojourners, The Catholic Worker, and Pax Christi groups. After he joined L'Arche, Henri added a fourth component: peacemaking requires living and working among the poor and the broken. As he wrote in his booklet, *The Path to Peace*, we receive the gift of peace from those who are marginalized and crushed by society, from the powerless and the vulnerable. They reflect the peace of Christ. They teach us how to be peacemakers because they themselves are the true peacemakers.

The spiritual life for Henri, then, far surpassed Sunday Mass obligation or pious devotional practice. It embraced the world. It engaged the principalities and the powers in a nonviolent struggle for peace and justice. Henri taught that participation in church life, Sunday worship, and private prayer were merely outer manifestations of a much more profound life journey. For him, spirituality not only celebrates God's intimate love for each and every one of us, but comprises an active, public love toward every human being on earth, especially our enemies. The inner contemplative life that he encouraged flows out and touches wounded humanity. He knew that if our prayer does not push us to work for nuclear disarmament, to resist war, to abolish the death penalty, to dismantle racism and sexism, to shelter the homeless, to feed the hungry, and to offer compassion to prisoners and those with AIDS, then we have not yet listened closely enough to the Spirit. We have not understood or taken seriously the social implications of Christianity. We might as well start all over again. Go back to the Gospel and figure out how to connect with the peacemaking, crucified Jesus, he would say.

Henri's peace and justice convictions weave in and out of all of his writings. His book on death and dying, *Our Greatest Gift*, for example, begins with the spiritual truth "that we human beings are children of God, brothers and sisters of one another." For the first time in all his books, he describes his experience of marching in Selma for civil rights. The solidarity he felt that day with those struggling against injustice not only sums up the spiritual life, it helps us prepare for death. We have to claim our solidarity with the whole human family, beginning with the poor and oppressed and their struggle, if we want to die well, like Christ on the cross. "In a mysterious way, the people dying all over the world because of starvation, oppression, illness, despair, violence and war become our teachers.... In their immense pain and grief, these people ask for solidarity."[13]

Henri believed that prayer missions us to serve others and transform the world; that all ministries connect together to proclaim prophetically God's reign of justice and peace; and that real openness to Jesus will lead us onto the margins where we will not only befriend Christ in the disenfranchised, we will become, like Jesus, one with them. Henri's spirituality took him out of the classroom into the struggle for peace and the world of the broken. He hoped others might pursue God's presence in the world with the same openness to risk.

Henri was interested in everyone's life, in everyone's spirituality, in the spiritual dimensions underlying every aspect of life itself, including war and injustice. He was political, in the true sense of the word. He passionately desired to know Jesus, to follow him, and to radiate his Gospel message. He wanted humanity to be faithful to the God of peace. He knew that he must denounce nuclear weapons and tour the U.S. calling for public opposition to U.S. warmaking in Central America and continued maintenance of weapons of mass destruction. He understood that Christians cannot merely talk about love, they need to walk among the poor, the ostracized, the disabled, the imprisoned, and the dying, and radiate God's love. Peace and justice were so crucial to his spirituality that they finally drove him away from Yale and Harvard, to Latin America and eventually to L'Arche. There, his spirituality blossomed. He finally experienced personally the peace he sought politically.

The essays on peace and justice gathered here in this collection are not side interests or posthumous footnotes to his great body of writing. They offer some of his most mature spiritual insights. They stand at the center of his thought.

HENRI NOUWEN'S CHALLENGE TO PEACEMAKERS

While Henri firmly embraced the Gospel's social spirituality of peacemaking, he challenged those already engaged in the struggle to deepen the roots of their inner contemplative life. "One of the reasons why so many people have developed strong reservations about the peace movement," Henri wrote, "is precisely that they do not see the peace they seek in the peacemakers themselves. Often what they see are fearful, angry people trying to convince others of the urgency of their protest. Thus the tragedy is that peacemakers often reveal more of the demons they are fighting than of the peace they want to bring."

St. Francis long ago offered the same spiritual advice. "While you are proclaiming peace with your lips," he said, "be careful to have it even more fully in your heart." It is a message echoed by Gandhi, Merton, and Dorothy Day, a wisdom that Henri himself struggled hard to practice.

Henri's writings nourish thousands of readers, but in particular they challenge those concerned with the pressing demands of justice and peace. We are especially susceptible to the world's temptations, he knew. We get trapped into thinking that everything we do depends on ourselves, that real peacemakers produce significant results. We fall prey to the cultural temptations to be successful, powerful, and relevant. Because efforts for peace in a militaristic culture are unsuccessful, humiliating, and dismissed as irrelevant, we quickly fall into despair. Henri's spirituality of peace and justice, and the example of his life journey, invite us to cultivate poverty of spirit, detachment, humility, trust in God, and hope. His writings urge those pursuing a social spirituality of peacemaking to reject the temptation to despair.

First, he challenges us to root our actions for peace and justice in prayer, in the peace that can only come from God. "When our actions against nuclear weapons are not based on the act of prayer, they easily become fearful, fanatical, bitter, and more an expression of survival instincts than of our faith in God and the God of the living," he observes. "Prayer—living in the presence of God—is the most radical peace action we can imagine. Prayer is peacemaking and not simply the preparation before, the support during, and the thanksgiving after....In prayer we undo the fear of death and therefore the basis of all human destruction."

Second, he urges those seeking disarmament and justice to move beyond judgmentalism and self-righteousness and to speak not from anger or fear, but from love. "True peacemaking is based on love, not fear," he wrote. "When peacemaking is based on fear it is not much different from warmaking."

"The words of Jesus go right to the heart of our struggle," Henri wrote. "'Love your enemy, do good to those who hate you, bless those who curse you, pray for those who treat you badly.' The more I reflect on these words, the more I consider them to be the test for peacemakers. What my enemy deserves is not my anger, rejection, resentment, or disdain, but my love. It is essential for peacemakers to be deeply rooted in this all-embracing love of God who 'causes the sun to rise on the bad as well as the good, and the rain to fall on honest and dishonest people alike.' It is only this deep rootedness in God's all-inclusive love that can prevent the peacemaker from being ravaged by the same anger, resentment, and violence that lead to war."

Third, Henri challenges the individualism which plagues our efforts and he calls us to community. He knew that the war-making culture is all-consuming, that we could not seriously resist it for long on our own. He wanted Christians to spend their faith lives seeking justice and making peace, but he knew from his own painful experience that without a community we could not stay committed to the struggle. "As long as we look at resistance as performing individual acts of heroism, there won't be many peacemakers who will survive the enormous pressures put upon them. Resistance that makes for peace is not so much the effort of brave and courageous individuals as the work of the community of faith. Individual people, even the best and the strongest, will soon be exhausted and discouraged, but a community of resistance can persevere even when its members have their moments of weakness and despair. Peacemaking can be a lasting work only when we live and work together. Community is indispensable for a faithful and enduring resistance. Without community we will be quickly sucked back into the dark world of needs and wounds, of violence and destruction, of evil and death."

Fourth, Henri invites Christian peacemakers to seek intimacy with Jesus. "Only by belonging to Christ and Christ alone can we truly resist the devastating powers of evil and work together in this world to avoid collective suicide. Those whose lives are securely anchored beyond the powers and principalities that rule the world can enter that world freely and bring it peace." He recommends regular scripture study, celebration of the Eucharist, and prayerful listening to Jesus' word. He wants us to develop in our quiet prayer a real relationship with our risen Lord.

Finally, he begs us to root our work for justice and peace in our search for God. He points out that our efforts for peace must spring from our inner contemplative life, from our relationship with God. If we want to be Gospel peacemakers, then we will live in Jesus' blessing: we will be sons and daughters of God. As peacemakers, as God's children, we listen attentively to God and do what God wants us to do. "All the issues of the world—from Nicaragua to South Africa—are very, very important and crucial," Henri once told an interviewer. "But I have to learn to enter them from the heart of God. I have to be deeply rooted in God's heart before I can know how to respond faithfully."[14] He suspected that others needed to be just as rooted in God's heart to address these global crises. Trust in God, he recommends. The outcome is in God's hands. God is in charge. The point is to do God's will, to seek peace and resist injustice in God's spirit, in God's way, as God wants.

In one of his earliest works, *The Wounded Healer*, Henri urged both contemplatives and activists, or in his words, "mystics and revolutionaries," each to undergo the personal conversion and public struggle for justice that Jesus lived:

Every real revolutionary is challenged to be a mystic at heart, and one who walks the mystical way is called to unmask the illusory quality of human society. Mysticism and revolution are two aspects of the same attempt to bring about radical change. No mystics can prevent themselves from becoming social critics, since in self-reflection they will discover the roots of a sick society. Similarly, no revolutionaries can avoid facing their own human condition, since in the midst of their struggle for a new world they will find that they are also fighting their own reactionary fears and false ambitions. Mystics and revolutionaries must cut loose from their selfish needs for a safe and protected existence and face without fear their own miserable condition and that of the world around them. The appearance of Jesus in our midst has made it undeniably clear that changing the human heart and changing human society are not separate tasks, but are as interconnected as the two beams of

the cross....Jesus remains for men and women of the
nuclear age the way to liberation and freedom.[15]

Whether we are contemplatives or activists, mystics or revolutionaries, we are all called to explore Gospel nonviolence in
every aspect of life, public or private, globally or locally, in our
hearts and in the world.

HENRI NOUWEN'S WRITINGS ON PEACE AND JUSTICE

After Henri's funeral Mass of the Resurrection in the Slovak
Catholic Cathedral of the Transfiguration in Markham, Ontario,
Art Laffin and I drove through the Canadian countryside to the
small cemetery where Henri was to be buried. As we drove
along, we talked about a way in which we could continue
Henri's ministry, his witness to peace, his testimony to Jesus.

We knew that many people had not yet left the cathedral, but
we did not realize that we would be the first persons to arrive at
the grave. We parked along the country road and walked down a
path, passing the thirty tombstones and crosses in the small, remote cemetery. Up ahead, in the corner, beneath a cluster of pine
trees, stood a pile of dirt. We had expected to find a crowd of
people and a coffin. We walked toward the dirt until we stood together, in silence, looking down into a big hole. We had come
upon an empty tomb!

For a brief moment, I recalled the story of the women arriving at Jesus' tomb on the first morning of the week. They discovered an empty tomb. "Why do you seek the living among the
dead?" an angel asked them. They looked at one another.

As we stood by the empty grave awaiting the funeral procession, I began to understand. Henri lives on with the God of life.
And so, his work continues. I decided then and there to help him
continue his peacemaking work.

This collection gathers for the first time nearly all of Henri's
writings on peace, disarmament and social justice. I have broken
them down into six parts, covering the different themes of Henri's
varied social concerns. Part One begins with Henri's unpublished

manuscript, "A Spirituality of Peacemaking," which Henri wrote in 1984 and later renamed, "Peacework." Excerpts were published in *The New Oxford Review* in the mid-1980s, but it has never before been published in its entirety. A 1985 talk on peacemaking to the General Assembly of the Presbyterian Church plus two anti-war statements given at rallies in the early 1970s are also included, published here for the first time. Part Two records Henri's support of the civil rights movement. In 1964, Henri moved to the U.S. from Holland and immediately identified with Martin Luther King, Jr., and the struggle against racism. He wrote about his experience in Selma for a Dutch journal, and later also felt compelled to record his personal pilgrimage to Atlanta for Dr. King's funeral in April 1968.

Part Three features reflections on Central and South America, particularly the effect of U.S. warmaking against Nicaragua in the 1980s. Part Four focuses on L'Arche with a previously unpublished reflection on the meaning of L'Arche, plus an interview about his work at L'Arche a year after his move to Daybreak. Part Five follows with Henri's 1994 talk to the National Catholic AIDS Network Conference, his first major reflection on AIDS. Part Six concludes with interviews and reflections on social compassion, prayer, and solidarity with the whole human race.

With the publication of these essays on peace, disarmament, and social justice, we catch the full breadth of Henri's vision. This collection rounds out Henri's voluminous spiritual writings because it includes his passionate concerns about the pressing social issues of our times. It fills out the social implications of his spirituality.

"Only those who deeply know that they are loved and rejoice in that love can be true peacemakers," he wrote. The profound love present at his funeral and evident in these writings reveals the depths of Henri's peacemaking life which will go on bearing fruit.

"I leave you with the image of the leader with outstretched hands, who chooses a life of downward mobility," wrote Henri in the concluding words of his book, *In the Name of Jesus*. "It is the image of the praying leader, the vulnerable leader, and the trusting leader. May that image fill your hearts with hope, courage, and confidence as you anticipate the next century."[16] With his stand for peace and justice, as reflected in these writings, Henri became not only an image of the Christian leader, but one of "the true saints," a prophetic voice for truth, a light in dark times, a sign of hope.

May his call for disarmament, justice, and contemplative nonviolence help us to follow Jesus on the road to peace.

John Dear, S.J.
June, 1997

NOTES

1. Henri Nouwen, *In the Name of Jesus* (New York: Crossroad, 1987), 60.

2. Henri Nouwen, "My History with God,"unpublished notes for the class, "Communion, Community and Ministry: An Introduction to the Spiritual Life," Regis College, Toronto, September-December 1994, 1.

3. Bert Witvoet, "Henri Nouwen Has Found a New Peace," *The Calvinist Contact*, October 23, 1987, 10.

4. Nouwen, "My History with God," 1-2.

5. John Dart, "Protesters Mark Atomic Bombings at Nevada Test Site," *The Los Angeles Times*, August 10, 1985.

6. "A Heart's Desire," *Sojourners*, November-December, 1996, 27.

7. Witvoet, 11.

8. "The Henri J.M. Nouwen Memorial Fund," L'Arche-Daybreak brochure.

9. "An Interview with Henri Nouwen," *Catholic Leader*, Toronto, June 11, 1989.

10. Nouwen, "My History with God," 2.

11. Robert Ellsberg, "A Sense of Being Sent," *The Catholic Worker*, January-February 1997, 6-7.

12. "Priest Led from Ivy League to 'Answer Call' at l'Arche," *The Saturday Windsor Star*, October 14, 1988.

13. Nouwen, *Our Greatest Gift* (San Francisco: HarperSan Francisco, 1994), 10, 29, 30.

14. "Priest Sees Love, Not Fear, as Basis for Peacemaking." *Catholic Chronicle*, Bowling Green, May 17, 1985.

15. Nouwen, *The Wounded Healer* (New York: Doubleday, 1972), 19-20; also, Robert Durback, ed., *Seeds of Hope: A Henri Nouwen Reader* (New York: Bantam, 1989), 159-160.

16. Nouwen, *In the Name of Jesus*, 73.

I

THE HOUSE OF PEACE

1

Peace, a Gift We Receive in Prayer

> Long enough have I been dwelling
> with those who hate peace.
> I am for peace, but when I speak,
> they are for fighting.
> (Psalm 120:6-7)

Must it remain this way? Must war drums constantly disturb us? Must we hear over and over that we need more and stronger weapons to safeguard our values and our lives? Must we listen to unsettling speeches saying that 10,000 strategic and 22,000 tactical nuclear weapons, enough to destroy every major Russian city forty times over, are not enough? Must we let our minds be occupied with the destructive possibilities of intercontinental ballistic missiles, B-52 bombers, and Trident submarines? And must we even discuss the acceptability of the death of 15 million people in a limited nuclear war? Must we go on preparing for the greatest mass murder in history?

We have been dwelling with those who hate peace long enough. Long enough have we allowed ourselves to be impressed by "the rulers, the governors and the commanders, the rich people and the men of influence" (Rev 6:15) who try to tell us that the political situation is too complex for us to have an

---

This chapter, and the following two chapters, make up Henri Nouwen's unpublished book, *A Spirituality of Peacemaking,* which was probably written in 1984 and later renamed, *Peacework.*

opinion about the possibility of peace, and who try to convince us that the science of defense is too advanced for us really to understand. Long enough have we been kept silent about those who are for war and are eager to see the demonic products of their intelligence put to use. But when we cry out: "We are for peace, we are for peace," our words sound so incompetent, simplistic, and naive. The sophisticated arguments of those who say the issues of war and peace are too complex for us to understand seduce us into feelings of uselessness.

The truth, however, may be simple after all. Maybe the difficult grammar of warmaking, with terms such as fusion and fission, MAD, MIRV, and MX, is nothing more than an elaborate distraction hiding the face of the One who says: "You must love the Lord your God with all your heart, with all your soul, with all your strength, and with all your mind and your neighbor as yourself" (Lk 10:27). It is a simple but hard truth, requiring constant vigilance, resolution, and practice. This difficult truth, the truth of peace, has to be spoken and lived—directly, courageously, intelligently, gently, lovingly, and repeatedly.

It is far from easy to write on this subject. For a long time, I have sensed within me a strong hesitation to speak or write about peace. I have been dwelling for so long in the houses of those who look at protest and peace movements as expressions of youthful rebellion or antipatriotism that I feel embarrassed to say openly, "I am for peace." Much of this hesitation goes back to my time spent in the Dutch army. Although the seminary had kept me out of military service, I felt that a seminarian should not be exempt from the experience other Dutch men share: two years of uniformed service for their country. So I volunteered to become an army chaplain, took some basic training, and worked as a priest-psychologist on a military mental health team. I have very fond memories of those days. I enjoyed the "team spirit," came to know people I never would have met otherwise, learned a lot about psychology, felt very useful, and made closer friends than during my six years in seminary.

To be a conscientious objector seemed understandable for certain small sects, but unnatural for "normal" Catholics and

Protestants. It was good to defend your country, and no "real man" would try to escape from the duty. Moreover, I liked the uniform: it looked a lot more impressive than my black suit with a Roman collar! But later, during the Vietnam years, I found myself in the United States. A personal friendship with an officer who refused further service and risked going to prison slowly changed my attitude. Those who objected to U.S. involvement in Vietnam no longer seemed selfish cowards or sentimental dreamers, but people who had found the war immoral, illegal, and unjust and dared to act according to their convictions. While counseling war resisters, I received a letter from the chaplaincy office of the Dutch army, announcing that it had pleased Queen Juliana to promote me to major in Her Majesty's Army (on reserve!). When I read that letter, I felt a confusing mixture of embarrassment and pride.

However, it wasn't only my Dutch army experience that made me hesitant to join the peace movement. My observations of the style, language, and behavior often exhibited at anti-war rallies in the 1960s had made me skeptical about the value of much anti-war activity. The many conflicts and divisions among peacemakers evoked an inner distaste in me and renewed my respect for the cleanliness, orderliness, discipline, and single-mindedness of those who served their country in the military. Even today, having become deeply convinced of the immorality of the fabrication, possession, and use of nuclear weapons, I still feel quite nervous about speaking or acting for peace, especially at those times when it brings me into the company of those whose personal style, ideology, and tactics are totally alien to me.

But all these memories and emotions do not diminish the truth that the call to peace is a call for all people regardless of their many differences, regardless of their ideologies, ethnic backgrounds, religious connections, and social conditions, regardless even of "taste and manners." Jesus said: "Happy the peacemakers: they shall be called children of God" (Mt 5:9). These words can no longer remain in the background of our Christian consciousness. These words are breaking into our lives with such urgency that we know that this is the time to say together, "We are for peace."

On August 6, 1945, the day on which the atom bomb was first used in war, peacemaking came to mean what it could not have meant before: the task of saving humanity from collective suicide. On August 6, 1945, while Christians celebrated the Transfiguration of Jesus on Mount Tabor, the nuclear era was inaugurated by a light that incinerated Hiroshima and killed 125,000 of its inhabitants. On that day the blessing on peacemakers became the blessing for our century. The bombing of Hiroshima and the nuclear arms race that followed have made peacemaking the central task for Christians. There are many other urgent tasks to accomplish: the work of worship; evangelization; healing of church divisions; alleviating worldwide poverty and hunger; and defending human rights. But all of these tasks are closely connected with the task that precedes them all: making peace. Making peace today means making it possible to continue our life together on this planet.

Every one of the eight beatitudes that Jesus proclaimed in the Sermon on the Mount is for all people and for all times. But there are times in which one word speaks louder than another. In the thirteenth century St. Francis brought to the foreground the blessing on the poor. In the nineteenth century many saints and visionaries called new attention to the blessing on the pure of heart. Clearly our century is the century of the peacemakers. Qoheleth says: "There is a season for everything... a time for keeping silent, a time for speaking... a time for war, a time for peace" (Eccl 3:1, 7-8). This is the time to speak for peace. If we do not recognize this, there will be no seasons any more for anything, because without peace there will be no life. If this century will be remembered, it will be remembered for those who gave themselves for the cause of peace.

In these reflections I hope to show how peacemaking can no longer be regarded as peripheral to being a Christian. It is not something like joining the parish choir. Nobody can be a Christian without being a peacemaker. The issue is not that we have the occasional obligation to give some of our attention to war prevention, or even that we should be willing to give some of our free time to activities in the service of peace. What we are called to is a *life* of peacemaking in which all that we do, say, think, or dream is part of our concern to bring peace to this world. Just as Jesus' command to love one another cannot be seen as a part-time obligation, but requires our total dedication, so too Jesus' call to peacemaking is unconditional, unlimited, and uncompromising. None of us is excused! It isn't something limited to specialists who are competent in military matters, or to radicals who have dedicated themselves to leafletting, demonstrating, and civil disobedience. No specialist or radical can diminish the undeniable vocation of each Christian to be a peacemaker. Peacemaking is a full-time vocation that includes each member of God's people.

How would the world look if all Christians—in Australia, Asia, Europe, Africa, North and South America—were to commit themselves without reservation to peace? How would the world look if all Christians—young, middle-aged, or old—were to say loudly and clearly in words and deeds: "We are for peace"? And how would the world look if all Christians—Protestants, Catholic, Orthodox—were to witness together for him who is the Prince of Peace, Jesus? What would such a consensus in conscience bring about? Would we still spend billions of dollars every month to build ingenious instruments of death while millions of people are starving? Would we still live with the constant fear of impending holocaust? Would we still hear about parents who question whether it is responsible to bring children into this world and about children who wonder if they will see the turn of the century?

The tragedy is that, in some demonic way, the word *peace* has become tainted. For many people, this most precious word has become associated with sentimentalism, utopianism, radicalism, romanticism, and even irresponsibility. The remark "You are for peace" often seems to mean "You are a dreamer." And when the opportunity presents itself to build a port for the Trident submarine, many are more concerned with creating new jobs than with preventing a new war.

"If I speak of peace, they are for fighting." These words are more real today than ever before. Every day newspapers, radio, and television broadcasts reveal our unashamed desire to show our teeth, fight, and be the strongest superpower. Genuine words of peace are not often heard in our world and when spoken they are mostly distrusted. When said by the enemy they are dismissed as "mere propaganda." While the word *freedom* has become a word uttered with self-confidence, the word *peace* is said timidly and often with the fear of being considered disloyal and untrustworthy.

Christians today, if they want to be Christians, have to find the courage to make the word *peace* as important as the word *freedom*. There should be no doubt in the minds of the people who inhabit this world that Christians are peacemakers.

I say this so simply and directly precisely because I am so aware of the many questions that have often kept Christians divided. Some adopt the just-war theory, others argue for pacifism. Many books and articles have been written on such important issues as nonviolence, conscientious objection, and civil disobedience; I am hopeful that there will be less disagreement among Christians as the discussion develops. But it would be a tragedy if the divergence of opinion on these issues were to prevent the people of God from witnessing clearly and convincingly for peace. The urgency of the need for peacemaking today must allow us to speak and act in spiritual unity, even when many concrete issues of tactics and strategy remain open for further discussion. I therefore am not focusing here on what remains to be worked out, but rather on what gives us the power to speak and act together *now* in preventing a nuclear holocaust.

From the perspective of the Christian tradition I won't say anything that has not been said before. From the perspective of the urgency of the need for peacemaking I will say things that are quite new. These reflections do not ask for involvement in any specific organization or project. But they do ask for a conversion of our whole person so that all we do, say, and think becomes part of our urgent vocation to be peacemakers. Such a conversion can indeed lead to change and to specific actions, but it also can make us live the same life in a totally new way.

✝

There is one thing I ask of the Lord;
    for this I long:
To live in the house of the Lord
    all the days of my life....

For there God keeps me safe in God's tent.
    In the day of evil God hides me.
In the shelter of God's tent on a rock
    God sets me safe....

And now my head shall be raised
    above my foes who surround me.
And I shall offer within God's tent
    a sacrifice of joy.

(Psalm 27:4, 5, 6)

A peacemaker prays. Prayer is the beginning and the end, the source and the fruit, the core and the content, the basis and the goal for all peacemaking. I say this without apology, because it allows me to go straight to the heart of the matter, which is that peace is a divine gift, a gift we receive in prayer.

In his farewell discourse Jesus said to his apostles, "Peace I leave to you, my own peace I give to you; a peace the world cannot give, this is my gift to you" (Jn 14:27). When we want to make peace we first of all have to move away from the dwelling places of those who hate peace and enter into the house of him who offers us his peace. This entering into a new dwelling place is what prayer is all about. The question indeed is: "Where are you staying? To whom do you belong? Where is your home?" Praying is living in the House of the Lord. There "he keeps me safe ... in the day of evil" and there "my head shall be raised above my foes" (Ps 27). We need to prevent ourselves from being seduced by those who prepare for the day of destruction and the end of all things. "Watch yourselves," Jesus said,

> or your hearts will be coarsened with debauchery and drunkenness and the cares of life and that day will be sprung on you suddenly like a trap. For it will come down on every living person on the face of the earth. Stay awake, praying at all times for the strength to survive all that is going to happen and to stand with confidence before the Son of Humanity. (Luke 21:34-36)

"Praying at all times" is the first aspect of peacemaking. What does this mean concretely for us who have barely enough time and space to keep some distance from the cares of life? To answer this question we must be willing to explore critically the ways in which the "cares of life" strangle us. Only then can we see the converting power of prayer and its pervasive role in peacemaking.

As I reflect on our daily human behavior I am overwhelmed by how needy we are. Wherever we look, we see our needs at work: the need for attention, for affection, for influence, for power, and most of all the need to be considered worthwhile. When we explore honestly why we do what we do, say what we say, and think what we think, we discover—to our own horror—that even our most generous actions, words, and fantasies are entangled with these needs.

When we go to comfort a friend we find ourselves wondering if he will appreciate our visit. When we spend time and money to fight hunger and oppression in the world, we find ourselves subtly concerned about recognition and praise. When we listen with great attentiveness to the stories of those who come for help, we find ourselves often caught in the trap of sensationalism and curiosity. And even when we speak with fervor and conviction about the humility and patience of Jesus, we cannot avoid a strong desire to put ourselves at the center of attention. Thus we have to confess that much of our behavior—even our so-called good behavior—is an anxious, though perhaps unconscious, attempt to advance our own cause, to make ourselves known, and to convince our world that we need to be reckoned with. This is the "goodness" of sinners that Jesus so fiercely criticizes.

> If you love those who love you, what thanks can you expect? Even sinners love those who love them. And if you do good to those who do good to you, what thanks can you expect? For even sinners do that much. And if you lend to those from whom you hope to receive, what thanks can you expect? Even sinners lend to sinners to get back the same amount. (Luke 6:32-34)

Why is it so hard to go beyond this strange moral exchange in which every good deed has a price attached to it? Why is it that our needs often spoil even our most altruistic gestures? Our needs for affection, attention, influence, and power are anchored in very old and often deeply hidden wounds. These wounds may have been inflicted by experiences of being disliked, unappreciated, or even rejected. They can be attached to concrete events in the past, to vague memories, or to overheard stories. They can be very specific or very global. But somehow, somewhere, they make us wonder if we are really worth being. It is this fundamental inner doubt about our own value that catapults us into a search for self-esteem so loaded with apprehension that it easily becomes compulsively egocentric and even destructive.

When I listen to the sounds of greed, violence, rape, torture, murder, and indiscriminate destruction, I hear a long sustained cry coming from all the corners of the world. It is the cry of a deeply wounded humanity that no longer knows a safe dwelling place but wanders around the planet in a desperate search for love and comfort.

Needs that are anchored in wounds cannot be explained simply. Even though we can point an accusing finger at someone whom we consider the cause of our problem and even though we can make ourselves believe that things could have been different if only that someone had done or said something differently, we are part of a chain of wounds and needs that reach far beyond our own memories and aspirations. Our unquenchable need to be loved may be connected with an experience of rejection in our early months of life. Still, weren't our parents subject to wounds and needs too, wounds and needs that go back to their parents and grandparents and through them far into the most hidden recesses of the past? And we, in turn, may have a strong desire to be blameless in the eyes of our children and friends, to not hurt them, and to keep the pain that we have suffered far from them. Yet we will come to the painful realization that they too will feel wounded and carry on in their lives a search for a love we could not provide, a search stretching out into the far reaches of the future. This is the pervasive tragedy of humanity, the tragedy of an experience of homelessness that winds through history and is passed by each generation to the next in a seemingly unending sequence of human conflicts with ever more destructive tools of rage in our hands. The vicious repetition of wounds and needs creates and sustains the milieu of "those who hate peace." It is the dwelling place of demons. And it is a place that lures us precisely because we all are wounded and needy.

It can indeed come as a great shock to realize that what we consider works of service in the name of God may be motivated to such a degree by our wounds and needs that not peace, but resentment, anger, and even violence become their fruits. The great irony is that Satan finds his safest hiding place where we are most explicitly involved in the work of God's kingdom. The "enemy...prowling round like a roaring lion, looking for someone to eat" (1 Pt 5:8) is often very successful when and where we least expect him. The name of God is used for many demonic actions. It is the safest mask of Satan and we have continually to tear it off it if we want to be peacemakers. Though it might be easy to recognize the forces of darkness around us, it is very hard to recognize these same forces in our own "good works." Self-doubt, inner restlessness, fear of being left alone, need for recognition, and desire for fame and popularity are often stronger motives in our actions for peace than a true passion for service. These are the motives that bring elements of war into the midst of our action for peace.

Only when we are willing repeatedly to confess that we do have dirty hands even when we work for peace can we fully understand the hard task of peacemaking.

The great spiritual tragedy is that many cruel and inhuman acts are committed in the name of serving God. After the atom bomb was successfully exploded over Hiroshima, President Truman wrote: "We thank God that it [the bomb] has come to us ...and we pray that he may guide us to use it in his ways and for his purposes." Events in Guatemala offer another hideous example. When General Rios Montt came to power in March 1982, he presented himself as an ardent follower of Jesus. Seven months later, 2,600 Guatemalan peasants—men, women, and children—had been killed. We cannot assume that those who dropped the bomb or murdered innocent Indians were psychopaths. Most of them were normal men born and raised in Catholic families. They had been brought up to believe that what they were doing was a holy duty in the service of their country, a task of obedience to their God-fearing president, and even a mission given them by God.

Thus we come to the painful realization that our so-called good works and the works of those who drop bombs and commit genocide are not necessarily opposites. They might all have a place on the large spectrum of evil. Our wounds and needs and those of the men who dropped the bomb on Hiroshima and kill and torture in Guatemala are not as different as we might like to think. Thus we cannot dismiss the horrendous cruelties about which we read in the papers as "things we would never do." The wounds and needs that lie behind the wars we condemn are the wounds and needs that we share with the whole human race. We too are deeply marked by the dark forces that make one war emerge after another. We too are part of the evil against which we protest.

Here we catch a glimpse of the true sinfulness of our humanity. It is a sin so deeply anchored in us that it pervades all of our lives. And when it is possible for "normal" human beings of our time to kill men, women, and children indiscriminately, why then would it not be possible for us to become accomplices in a worldwide mass murder in which the incineration of millions of people is considered acceptable? We too act in "obedience" and claim that what we do is in defense of our Christian values.

What then is the dwelling place of those who hate peace? It is our own familiar world in which peace is still ridiculed and in which the interlocking wounds and needs of individuals, groups, and nations continue to make war a more likely choice than peace.

Against this dark and fearful background I want to express the urgency of prayer as the first characteristic of the work of peacemaking.

The invitation to a life of prayer is the invitation to live in the midst of this world without being caught in the net of its wounds and needs. The word "prayer" stands for a radical interruption of the vicious chain of interlocking dependencies that leads to violence and war, and for an entering into an entirely new dwelling place. It points to a new way of speaking, of breathing, of being together, of knowing—truly, to a whole new way of living.

It is not easy to express the radical change that prayer represents, since for many the word *prayer* is associated with piety; talking to God; thinking about God; attending morning and evening worship; going to Sunday service; saying grace before meals; and many other things. All of these have something to do with prayer, but when I speak about prayer as the basis for peacemaking I speak first of all about moving away from "the dwelling place of those who hate peace" into the house of God. Prayer is the center of Christian life. It is living with God, here and now.

As I read the Gospels I am struck how often images connected with a new dwelling place are used. These images bring me to think of the peacemaker as one who has found a new home where peace resides and from which peace is brought into the world. John the Evangelist describes Jesus as the Word of God who came into the world and pitched his tent among us (Jn 1:14). He also tells us how the first disciples asked Jesus when they first met him, "Teacher, where do you live?" and were invited to stay in his home (Jn 1:38-39). Here we are already made aware that following Jesus means changing places, entering into a new milieu, and living in new company. The full meaning of this gradually unfolds in the Gospels. We come to see that Jesus not only invites his followers to live with him in the same house, but that he himself *is* the house.

On the evening before his death he says to his friends: "Make your home in me, as I make mine in you.... Whoever remains in me, with me in him, bears fruit in plenty" (Jn 15:4-5). This divine dwelling place enables us to live as peacemakers in a hostile world like sheep among wolves. In his words of farewell Jesus leaves no doubt about the nature of the world his followers have to live in, but he also assures them that they can live in the world with peace.

> They will expel you from places of worship, and indeed the hour is coming when anyone who kills you will think he is doing a holy duty for God. They will do these things because they have never known either the Father or myself.... But I have told you all this so that you may find peace in me. In the world you will have trouble, but be brave: I have conquered the world. (John 16:2-3, 33)

These words powerfully express how prayer is the basis and core of peacemaking. Even while being surrounded with conflict, wars, torture, and death, while being threatened by individual and collective destruction, we are not obliged to live in the dwelling place of those who hate peace. Prayer is the new language that belongs to the new house.

I would like to explore in more detail what these biblical images of a new dwelling place can say to us who live in a world threatened by total extinction. It is not hard to see that the house of those who are for fighting is a house ruled by fear. One of the most impressive characteristics of Jesus' description of the end-time is the paralyzing fear that will make people senseless, causing them to run in all directions, so disoriented that they are swallowed up by the chaos that surrounds them: "There will be signs in the sun and moon and stars; on earth nations in agony bewildered by the clamor of the ocean and its waves; people dying of fear as they await what menaces the world, for the power of heaven will be shaken" (Lk 21:25-26). The advice that Jesus gives his followers for these times of turmoil is to remain quiet, confident, peaceful, and trusting in God. He tells them not to follow those who sow panic, nor to join those who claim to be saviors, nor to be frightened by rumors of wars and revolution, but "to stand erect and hold your heads high" (Lk 21:28).

Panic, fear, and anxiety are not part of peacemaking. This might seem obvious, but many who struggle against the threat of a world war not only are themselves motivated by fear, but also use fear to bring others to action. Fear is the most tempting force in peacemaking. The stories about nuclear weapons and descriptions of what would happen if a nuclear war were to take place are so terrifying that we are easily inclined to use that fear to bring ourselves as well as others to be advocates of peace. Many films, slide shows, and picture books are made with the explicit intention of shocking people into a change of mind and heart. We need to be reminded in very concrete ways of the demonic power at work in our world, but when an increase of fear is the main result we become the easy victims of these same powers. When peacemaking is based on fear it is not much different from warmaking. Although peacemakers might use words that are different from those used by warmakers, they may still be speaking the same language. They remain captive to the strategies of those who want to fight.

Peacemaking is the work of love, and "in love there can be no fear, but fear is driven out by perfect love" (1 Jn 4:18). Nothing is more important in peacemaking than that it flow from a deep and undeniable experience of love. Only those who know deeply that they are loved and rejoice in that love can be true peacemakers. Why? Because the intimate knowledge of being loved sets us free to look beyond the boundaries of death and to speak and act fearlessly for peace. Prayer is the way to that experience of love.

Prayer means entering into communion with the One who loved us before we could love. It is this "first love" (1 Jn 4:19) that is revealed to us in prayer. The more deeply we enter into the house of God, the house whose language is prayer, the less dependent we are on the blame or praise of those who surround us, and the freer we are to let our whole being be filled with that first love. As long as we are still wondering what other people say or think about us and trying to act in ways that will elicit a positive response, we are still victimized and imprisoned by the dark world in which we live. In that dark world we have to let our surroundings tell us what we are worth. It is the world of successes and failures, of trophies and expulsions, of praise and blame, of stars and underdogs. In this world we are easily hurt and we easily act out of these hurts to find some satisfaction of our need to be considered worthwhile. As long as we are in the clutches of that world, we live in darkness, since we do not know our true self. We cling to our false self in the hope that maybe more success, more praise, more satisfaction will give us the experience of being loved, which we crave. That is the fertile ground of bitterness, greed, violence, and war.

In prayer, however, again and again we discover that the love we are looking for has already been given to us and that we can come to the experience of that love. Prayer is entering into communion with the One who molded our being in our mother's womb with love and only love. There, in the first love, lies our true self, a self not made up of the rejections and acceptances of those with whom we live, but solidly rooted in the One who called us into existence. In the house of God we were created. To that house we are called to return. Prayer is the act of returning.

Prayer is the basis of all peacemaking precisely because in prayer we come to the realization that we do not belong to the world in which conflicts and wars take place, but to him who offers us his peace. The paradox of peacemaking is indeed that we can speak of peace in this world only when our sense of who we are is not anchored in the world. We can say, "We are for peace" only when those who are for fighting have no power over us. We can witness for the Prince of Peace only when our trust is in him and him alone. In short, we can be in this world only when we no longer belong to it. This moving out of the world of warmakers in order to be in it as peacemakers is the Way of the Cross, which Jesus shows us. It is the long process of conversion in which we die to our old identity that is rooted in the ups and downs of worldly praise for all we do in the service of peace. Only by living in the house of peace can we come to know what peacemaking will mean.

This might sound very remote from the concrete down-to-earth daily problems we have to deal with. But the opposite is true. Only by opening ourselves to the language and way of prayer can we cope with the interruptions, demands, and ordinary tasks of life without becoming fragmented and resentful. Prayer—living in the presence of God—is the most radical peace action we can imagine.

Most people think of prayer in contrast to action. They think: "Maybe prayer can prepare for action, maybe it can offer the right context for action, maybe it can be a way of expressing thanks for a successful action, but prayer itself is something different from action." This kind of thinking is built on the conviction that in prayer nothing much really happens and therefore prayer is at best of secondary importance, if not a complete waste of time and an evasion of reality. But if we are willing to see prayer as belonging to the essence of peacemaking and to consider the possibility that prayer itself *is* peacemaking and not simply the preparation before, the support during, and the thanksgiving after, we will have to struggle hard against the secular "dogma" of pragmatism. This is a crucial struggle, because it opens a new way of thinking that is especially important at a time when the nuclear threat makes peacemaking such an urgent necessity. Awareness of such urgency can easily lead us to a desperation that says: "There is now really no time for prayer; we must act." But such an attitude contrasts sharply with Jesus' advice: "Stay awake, praying at all times for the strength to survive all that is going to happen, and to stand with confidence before the Son of Humanity" (Lk 21:36).

If we can come to the realization that it is in and through prayer that we find our true self, we already have a glimpse of its peacemaking quality. When we pray, we break out of the prison of blame and praise and enter into the house of God's love. In this sense prayer is an act of martyrdom: in prayer we die to the self-destroying world of wounds and needs and enter into the healing light of Christ.

I found a very moving example of the power of prayer as an act in the way Floris Bakels describes his experiences in German concentration camps. Bakels, a well-educated Dutch lawyer, simply states that prayer saved him not only spiritually, but also mentally and physically. Why? Because prayer for him was a process of death and rebirth that enabled him to live as a hopeful and caring person even though hundreds of people around him were dying of hunger, being tortured and executed.

Bakels had never considered himself religious. Yet to his own surprise he found himself responding to his dying friends by speaking to them about "God, Jesus, and the Gospel" and discovering a peace in himself and others that was not of this world. It was hard for Bakels to grasp fully what was happening to him. But thirty-four years later he writes:

> I had an idea... hard to articulate.... Being born again presupposes also for me a dying, a dying however of the old man, the birth of a new man.... But this departure of the old man... was an ultimate sorrow, a "sorrow towards God," a world sorrow, a sorrow for what is passing, for the vanishing world, for the letting go of all things.... I started to realize my strong attachment to this world, but to the degree that this process of detachment developed itself, my adoration of the... beauty of this world increased. It was heartrending, it was one great birth pang. What to do? What about love, love for a woman, my wife, my family, the butterflies, the waters and the forests?... All the attractiveness of that great rich life on earth... was I too attached to it? Under the shimmering of eternity I started a new process, a laying down

of the old man, a saying farewell, a departing, even an attempt to be no longer so attached to life itself...and then...a wanting to take up the new man, to be a quiet flame, a reaching upwards...a wanting to come home to the Power out of which I was created....couldn't articulate it well...I only knew one thing to do: to surrender everything to Him.

Floris Bakels expresses here the core of prayer as an act. It is the act of dying and being born again, of leaving the familiar house and coming home to the Power out of which we are created. The concentration camps of the Second World War opened Bakels to this experience. Today, as our world is threatened by a new and even greater holocaust, such acts of prayer are more crucial than ever. By radically breaking through the boundaries between life and death, prayer makes us free to stand in the midst of this world without being overwhelmed by fear.

In a situation in which the world is threatened by annihilation, prayer does not mean much when we undertake it only as an attempt to influence God, or as a search for a spiritual fallout shelter, or as simply a source of consolation in stress-filled times. In the face of a nuclear holocaust, prayer makes sense only when it is an act of stripping oneself of everything, even of our own lives, so as to be totally free to belong to God and God alone.

This explains why, although we often feel a real desire to pray, we experience at the same time a strong resistance. We want to move closer to God, the source and goal of all peace, but the closer we come to him, the more intimately and urgently we experience his demand to let go of the many familiar ways in which we organize our lives. Prayer is such a radical act because it asks us to criticize our whole way of being in the world, to lay down our old selves, and to accept our new self, which is Christ.

This is what Paul has in mind when he calls us to die with Christ so that we can live with Christ. It is to this experience of death and rebirth that Paul witnesses when he writes: "I live now not with my own life, but with the life of Christ who lives in me" (Gal 2:20).

What has all this to do with actions to end the arms race? I think that the most powerful protest against destruction is the laying bare of the basis of all destructiveness: the illusion of control. In the final analysis, isn't the nuclear arms race built upon the conviction that we have to defend—at all costs—what we have, what we do, and what we think? Isn't the possibility of destroying the earth, its civilizations, and its peoples a result of the conviction that we have to stay in control—at all costs—of our own destiny?

In the act of prayer, we undermine this illusion of control by divesting ourselves of all false belongings and by directing ourselves totally to the God who is the only one to whom we belong. Prayer, therefore, is the act of dying to all that we consider to be our own and of being born to a new existence which is not of this world.

Prayer is indeed a death to the world so that we can live for God.

The great mystery of prayer is that even now it leads us into God's house and thus offers us an anticipation of life in the divine Kingdom. Prayer lifts us up into the timeless immortal life of God.

There the meaning of the act of prayer in the midst of a world threatened by extinction becomes visible. By the act of prayer we do not first of all protest against those whose fears drive them to build nuclear warheads, missiles, and submarines. By the act of prayer we do not primarily attempt to stop nuclear escalation and proliferation. By the act of prayer we do not even try to change people's minds and attitudes. All this is very important and much needed, but prayer is not primarily a way to get something done.

No, prayer is the act by which we appropriate the truth that we do not belong to this world with its warheads, missiles, and submarines; we have already died to it so that not even a nuclear holocaust will be able to destroy us. Prayer is the act in which we willingly live through in our own being the ultimate consequences of nuclear destruction and affirm in the midst of them that God is the God of the living and that no human power will ever be able to "unmake" God. In prayer we anticipate both our individual death and our collective death and proclaim that in God there is no death but life. In prayer we undo the fear of death, the basis of all human destruction.

Is this an escape? Are we running away from the very concrete issues that confront us? Are we "spiritualizing" the enormous problems facing us and thus betraying our time, so full of emergencies? This would be true if prayer became a way to avoid all concrete actions. But if prayer is a real act of death and rebirth, then it leads us right into the world where we must take action.

To the degree that we are dead to the world, we can live creatively in it. To the degree that we have divested ourselves of false belongings, we can live in the midst of turmoil and chaos. And to the degree that we are free of fear, we can move into the heart of danger.

Thus the act of prayer is the basis and source of all action. When our actions against war are not based on the act of prayer, they easily become fearful, fanatical, bitter, and more an expression of survival instincts than of our faith in God.

When, however, our act of prayer remains the act from which all actions flow, we can be joyful even when our times are depressing, peaceful even when we are constantly tempted to despair. Then we can indeed say in the face of the overwhelming nuclear threat: "We are not afraid, because we have already died and the world no longer has power over us." Then we can fearlessly protest against all forms of human destruction and freely proclaim that the eternal, loving God is "not the God of the dead but of the living" (Mt 22:32).

What is the concrete day-to-day implication of this view of prayer? It is that we often have to take time to pray, and recognize prayer as the first and foremost act of resistance against militarism. By allowing ourselves quiet time with God we act on our faith that the peace we want to bring is not the work of our hands or the product of movements we join, but the gift of Christ. Entering the special solitude of prayer is a protest against a world of manipulation, competition, rivalry, suspicion, defensiveness, anger, hostility, mutual aggression, destruction, and war. It is a witness to the all-embracing, all-healing power of God's love. By not acting under the pressures of those who live their lives as victims of a series of emergencies, but standing quietly "with confidence before the Son of Humanity" (Lk 21:36), we act for peace. It certainly is not an easy act, since nearly everyone around us opposes it. The predominant voice says: "Keep moving. Keep working. Keep pushing. Keep talking, writing, organizing.... Be sure to get things done... and done as soon as possible." But this voice is not the voice of the Lord of peace. Every time Jesus appears to his friends he calms their hearts and minds, saying: "Don't be afraid, don't be agitated, don't be so doubtful" (Luke 24:38).

When we enter into solitude we will often hear these two voices—the voice of the world and the voice of the Lord—pulling us in two contrary directions. But if we keep returning faithfully to the place of solitude, the voice of the Lord will gradually become stronger and we will come to know and understand with mind and heart the peace we are searching for.

What do we do in our solitude? The first answer is nothing. Just be present to the One who wants your attention and listen! It is precisely in this "useless" presence to God that we can gradually die to our illusions of power and control and give ear to the voice of love hidden in the center of our being.

But "doing nothing, being useless," is not as passive as it sounds. In fact it requires effort and great attentiveness. It calls us to an active listening in which we make ourselves available to God's healing presence and can be made new. The way to develop this attentive listening will vary with different people, but it always includes some type of meditation on scripture. By quietly reading the psalms, reflecting on a scripture passage, or simply repeating a short prayer, we will find that the restless voices of our demanding world lose some of their power. We will feel more and more that solitude offers us a home where we can listen to our Lord, where we can find the strength to be obedient to God's Word, and in which we can act freely and courageously.

If we truly want to die to the old warmaking self and take up lodging in the house of peace, we must take a hidden meditative stand in the presence of God. This is the great spiritual challenge of the peacemaker.

By describing prayer as an act I have tried to re-emphasize the direct connection between the inner and the outer work of peacemaking. Although the remark "Change the world, begin with yourself" has often been used to individualize or spiritualize the urgent task of bringing peace to our planet, it points to the undeniable truth that peace in the world cannot be made without peace in the heart.

This is beautifully illustrated by a little story found in the tales of the Desert Fathers.

> There were three friends who were eager workers, and one of them chose to devote himself to making peace between people who were fighting in accordance with "Blessed are the peacemakers." The second chose to visit the sick. The third went off to live in tranquility in the desert. The first toiled away among the human quarrels of men, but could not resolve them all, and so he went to the one who was looking after the sick, and he found him flagging too, not succeeding in fulfilling the commandment. So the two of them agreed to go and visit the one who was living in the desert. They told him of their difficulties and asked him to tell them what he had been able to do. He was silent for a time, then he poured water into a bowl and said to them, "Look at the water." It was all turbulent. A little later he told them to look at it again, and see how the water had settled down. When they looked at it, they saw their own faces as in a mirror. Then he said to them, "In the same way a person who is living in the midst of people does not see his own sins because of all the disturbance, but if he becomes tranquil, especially in the desert, then he can see his own shortcomings." (Benedicta Ward, *The Wisdom of the Desert Fathers*)

This story leaves little doubt that tranquility of the heart is not a way to "feel good" while the world is ripped apart by violence and war, but a way to come in touch with our being part of the problem. Prayer leads to spiritual tranquility and spiritual tranquility leads us to the confession of our sins, the sins that lead to war. Making peace between people and visiting the sick are important, but doing these things without a repentant heart cannot bear fruit. When we can see our own sinful self in a tranquil mirror and confess that we too are warmakers, then we may be ready to start walking humbly on the road to peace.

2

Resisting the Forces of Death

When the Second World War came to an end, I was only thirteen years old. Although my parents had skillfully protected me and my brother from the horror of the Nazis in my native Holland, they couldn't prevent me from seeing how our Jewish neighbors were led away, and from hearing about concentration camps to which they were deported and from which they never returned. Only in the years after the war did I become aware of the demonic dimensions of the Jewish persecution and learn the word *holocaust.* And now, forty years later, I often ask myself: "Why was there not a massive popular uprising? Why weren't there marches of thousands of people protesting the genocide that was taking place? Why did the millions of religious people not invade the camps and tear down the gas chambers and ovens that were being built to annihilate the Jewish people? Why did those who pray, sing hymns, and go to church not resist the powers of evil so visible in their own land?"

It is important to find answers for these questions. But today I am no longer a thirteen-year-old boy who does not fully understand what is going on. Today I am an adult living only a few miles from the place where the Trident submarine is being built, a weapon able to destroy in one second more people than were gassed in Nazi Germany during the long years of the Hitler regime. Today I am a well-informed person fully aware of the genocide in Guatemala and the murderous terror in El Salvador. Today I am a well educated teacher who is able to show clearly and convincingly that the costly arms race between the superpowers means starvation for millions of people all over the globe. Today I am a Christian who has heard the words of Christ many times and knows that the God of Israel and Jesus Christ is the God of the living in whom there is no shadow of death.

Today I am asking myself the question: "Does my prayer, my communion with the God of life become visible in acts of resistance against the power of death surrounding me? Or will those who are thirteen years old today raise the same question about me forty years from now that I am raising about the adult Christians of my youth?" I have to realize that my silence or apathy may make it impossible for anyone to raise any questions forty years from today. Because what is being prepared is not a holocaust to extinguish a whole people, but a holocaust that puts an end to humanity itself—that will make not only giving answers but also raising questions a total impossibility.

These thoughts are constantly on my mind. These concerns keep me wondering how to be a peacemaker today and every day of my life. I will never be able to say: "I didn't know what was going on." I do know with frightening accuracy what will happen when nothing is done. Being a peacemaker today requires that my prayer become visible in concrete actions.

As I travel through life from day to day, I meet so many fellow travelers who see what I see, hear what I hear, and read what I read, and who are torn in their innermost selves by the same concerns that have come to me during the last decades. They, as I, are tempted to say: "We can't do much else but pray because we have our jobs, our families, our social obligations, and there is just no time left to work for peace. You can only do so much, and you have to accept your limitations." But in the face of nuclear weapons that threaten the very existence of jobs, family, and social obligations, they, as well as I, know that these excuses are groundless. Peacemaking is not an option any longer. It is a holy obligation for all people whatever their professional or family situation. Peacemaking is a way of living that involves our whole being all the time.

The word that I want to make central in these reflections on the daily life of the peacemaker is the word "resistance." As peacemakers we must resist resolutely all the powers of war and destruction and proclaim that peace is the divine gift offered to all who affirm life. Resistance means saying "No" to all the forces of death wherever they may be and, as a corollary, saying a clear "Yes" to all of life in whatever form we encounter it.

To work for peace is to work for life. But, more than ever before in history, we are surrounded by the powers of death. The rapidly escalating arms race has created a death-mood that pervades our thoughts and feelings in ways that we are only vaguely aware of. We try to live and work as if all is normal, but we hardly succeed in keeping the voice of death away from us. It is the voice that says: "Why work when all you create may soon be destroyed? Why study when you doubt that you ever will be able to use your gifts? Why bring forth children when you cannot promise them a future? Why write, make music, paint, dance, and celebrate when existence itself is in doubt?"

We know that in the case of a full-scale Russian nuclear attack 140 million Americans will probably die within days, and a U.S. retaliatory attack would take the lives of at least 100 million Russians. The fact that we can even think about such an event already does great harm to our minds and hearts. That human beings are considering saving their lives by killing millions of their fellow human beings is so preposterous that the words "saving life" have lost their meaning.

One of the most tragic facts of our century is that the "No" against the nuclear arms race has been spoken so seldom, so softly, and by so few. As I try to explain to myself my own lack of resistance against these dark forces of evil, it strikes me that I have always thought of the United States as the land of refuge for those who are persecuted—as the land of freedom, endless opportunity, democracy, and the land that came to the help of the victims of Nazism. Yes, as the land that liberated my own country. These perceptions are so strong that even after the sinister assassinations of John F. Kennedy, Robert Kennedy, and Martin Luther King, Jr., the misery of Vietnam, and the scandal of Watergate, I have kept thinking of the United States as a country in which such events are painful exceptions. While such events are signs of an increasing betrayal of the ideals this country proclaims, I still have a very hard time believing that anything similar to what happened during the Hitler years in Germany can possibly take place here. After all, the United States won a crusade against Nazi tyranny. How could such a tyranny move to this side of the ocean?

Yet many of my friends who have gone to prison for saying "No" to the arms race that causes millions of people to spend their lives in the service of destructive weapons and other millions to suffer starvation are slowly opening my eyes to another America that I do not really want to see, but that can no longer be ignored. It is the America that prepared itself for "first-strike capability," the ability not simply to prevent a nuclear attack by the threat of counterattack, but the ability to strike first and thus kill before being killed.

These friends have reminded me that the plans to fight and win a nuclear war are so completely contrary to Jesus' commandment of love and his own disarmed death on the cross that not saying "No" is a sign of faithlessness. They have made me see that those who prepare for the death of millions of people and are willing to start a nuclear war are doing nothing illegal, while those whose conscience calls them symbolically to hammer down these present-day Auschwitzes and Dachaus are put in prison as criminals.

It is very hard for me to convert my thoughts and feelings to such a degree that I am willing to defend those who "break the law" in order to proclaim the higher law—a commandment of love to which I have dedicated my life. But if I truly believe in Jesus Christ as the man of peace who did not choose to appeal to his Father "who would promptly send more than twelve legions of angels to his defense" (Mt 26:53-54), but who chose to die on a cross in total disarmament, how can I not be a man of peace? How can I allow the power of death to destroy the physical and moral life of millions, now as well as in the future, while remaining a passive and thus guilty bystander? Non-resistance makes us accomplices of a nuclear holocaust.

The nuclear threat has created a situation that humanity has never faced before. History is filled with violence, cruelties, and atrocities committed by people against people. Cities, countries, and whole civilizations have been erased from this planet and millions of people have become the victims of hatred and revenge. But never before has it been possible for humanity to commit collective suicide, to destroy the whole planet and put an end to all of history. This awesome capability was not even within our reach during the Second World War. The bombing of Hiroshima and Nagasaki at the end of the war gave us an inkling of what a next war might look like. But a future world war cannot be compared with any previous war. It will be a war that not only ends all war but also all peace.

It is this totally original situation that makes a "No" to war a universal necessity. It can no longer be seen as a necessity only for certain people at certain times. Because the being or not-being of humanity itself is at stake, the nuclear threat overarches all other threats as cause for resistance. The small groups of "disobedient" people who jump the fences around nuclear weapons facilities, climb on board nuclear submarines, or put their bodies in front of nuclear transports are trying to wake us up to a reality we continue to ignore or deny. Their small numbers should not mislead us.

Throughout history the truth has seldom been spoken by majorities. Statistics are not the way truth becomes known. The prophets of Israel, Jesus and his few disciples, and the small bands of holy men and women throughout history are there to make us wonder if "these crazy peaceniks" might after all not be as important for our conversion today as St. Francis and his followers were seven centuries ago. Their loud, clear, and often dramatic "No" has to make us wonder what kind of "No" we are called to speak.

When I try to come to terms with the effect of the nuclear threat on me, I realize that it not only brings me face to face with a completely new—and original—situation, but also makes me see in a new way the old and all-pervasive fascination with death that is an integral part of our daily lives. The confrontation with universal death has forced me to wonder about the more subtle ways in which death has us in its grip.

The Trident submarine, whose missiles can destroy many cities and countless people in one attack, is indeed the most insidious death machine human beings have ever created. But if we start saying "No" to this monster of destruction made by human hands, don't we also have to say "No" to the much less spectacular ways in which we play our death games? We are not simply victims of the power of death, for we are making Trident submarines and other nuclear weapons systems. The powers of death are far more intimate and pervasive than we are willing to confess.

Our ability to entertain even the possibility of a nuclear war is part of a much wider and deeper domination by death. We will never become true peacemakers until we are willing to unmask these death forces wherever and whenever they operate. An honest "No" against the nuclear arms race requires a "No" to the death hidden in the smallest corners of our minds and hearts. Peace in the world and peace of heart can never be separated. We need not answer the question: "Which is more important, peace in your heart or peace in the world?" Nor should we be distracted by arguments as to whether peace starts within or without. Inner and outer peace must never be separated. Peace work is a spectrum stretching from the hidden corners of our innermost selves to the most complex international deliberations.

Not long ago I visited an exclusive American preparatory school. Most of the boys and girls came from well-to-do families, most were well educated, and all were very bright. They were friendly, well-mannered, and ambitious; it was not hard for me to imagine many of them eventually holding important positions, driving big cars, and living in large homes.

One evening I joined these students in watching a movie in the school's auditorium. It was *The Blues Brothers*. I could not believe what I was seeing and hearing. The screen was filled with the wild destruction of supermarkets, houses, and cars, while the auditorium was filled with excited shouts coming from the mouths of these well-mannered, bright young people. While they were watching the total devastation of all the symbols of their own prosperous lives, they yelled and screamed as if their team had won a championship. As cars were being smashed, houses put on fire, and highrises pulled down, my excited neighbor told me that this was one of the most expensive "funny" movies ever made. Millions of dollars had been spent to film a few hours of what I considered to be death. No human beings were killed. It was supposed to bring a good laugh. But nothing human beings had made was left untouched by the destructive activities of *The Blues Brothers*.

What does it mean that ambitious young Americans are being entertained by millions of dollars worth of destruction in a world in which many people die from fear, lack of food, and ever-increasing violence? Are these the future leaders of a generation whose primary task is to prevent a nuclear war and stop the arms race?

I report this seemingly innocent event to point to the fact that much contemporary entertainment is designed to feed our fascination with violence and death. Long hours of our lives are spent filling our minds with images not only of disintegrating skyscrapers and cars, but also of shootings, torture scenes, and other manifestations of human violence. Once I met a Vietnam veteran on an airplane. He told me that as a youngster he had seen so many people being killed on TV that once he got to Vietnam it had been hard for him to believe that those whom *he* killed would not stand up again and act in the next program. Death had become an unreal act. Vietnam woke him up to the truth that death is real and final and very ugly.

When I am honest with myself I have to confess that I, too, am often seduced by the titillating power of death. I bite my nails in fascinated excitement when I see trapeze artists making somersaults without a safety net beneath them. I look with open eyes and mouth at stunt pilots, motorcyclists, and race car drivers who put their lives at risk in their desire to break a record or perform a dazzling feat. In this respect, I am little different from the Romans who were entertained by the death games of the gladiators, or from the crowds who in the past and even the present are attracted to places of public execution.

Any suggestion that these real or imagined death games are healthy ways to deal with our "death-instincts" or "aggressive fantasies" needs to be discarded as unfounded, unproved, or simply irresponsible. Acting out death wishes either in fact or in the imagination can never bring us any closer to peace, whether it is peace of heart or peace in our life together.

Our preoccupation with death, however, goes far beyond real or imagined involvement in physical violence. We find ourselves engaged over and over again in much less spectacular but no less destructive death games. During my visit to Nicaragua and my subsequent lectures and conversations in the U.S. about the Nicaraguan people, I became increasingly aware of how quick judgments and stereotypes can transform people and nations into distorted caricatures, thus offering a welcome excuse for destruction and war. By talking one-dimensionally about Nicaragua as a land of Marxist-Leninist ideology, totalitarianism, and atheism we create in our minds a monster that urgently needs to be attacked and destroyed. Whenever I spoke about the people of Nicaragua, their deep Christian faith, their struggles for some economic independence, their desire for better health care and education, and their hope that they might be left alone to determine their own future, I found myself confronted with deadening stereotypes. People would say: "But shouldn't we be aware that Russia is trying to get a foothold there and that we are increasingly being threatened by Communism?" Such remarks made me see that long before we start a war, kill people, or destroy nations, we have already killed our enemies mentally, by making them into abstractions with which no real, intimate human relationship is possible. When men, women, and children who eat, drink, sleep, play, work, and love each other as we do have been perverted into an abstract Communist evil that we are called—by God—to destroy, then war has become inevitable.

The Nazis were able to make the concrete human beings we call Jews into abstractions. They made them into "the Jewish problem." And for abstract problems there are abstract solutions.

The solution to the Jewish problem was the gas chamber. And on the way to the gas chamber, there were many stages of dehumanizing abstraction: isolation from non-Jews, labeling with yellow stars, and deportation to faraway concentration camps. Thus the Jew became less and less one-of-us and more and more the stranger, the xxx, and finally, simply, "the problem."

As I reflect on the horrors of the Second World War, I realize how much violence was mental before it was physical. Today, again, it seems that a similar process is taking place. We have "made up our mind" about the Nicaraguans, the Cubans, the Russians, and these abstract creations of the mind are the first products of the powers of death.

Saying "No" to death therefore starts much earlier than saying "No" to physical violence, whether in war or entertainment. It requires a deep commitment to the words of Jesus: "Do not judge" (Mt 7:1). It requires a "No" to all the violence of heart and mind. I personally find it one of the most difficult disciplines to practice.

Constantly I find myself "making up my mind" about somebody else: "He cannot be taken seriously. She is really just asking for attention. They are rabble-rousers who only want to cause trouble." These judgments are indeed a form of moral killing. I label my fellow human beings, categorize them, and put them at a safe distance from me. By judging others I take false burdens upon myself. By my judgments I divide my world into those who are good and those who are evil, and thus I play God. But everyone who plays God ends up acting like the demon.

Judging others implies that somehow we stand outside of the place where weak, broken, sinful human beings dwell. It is an arrogant and pretentious act that shows blindness not only toward others but also toward ourselves. Paul says it clearly: "...No matter who you are, if you pass judgment you have no excuse. For in judging others you condemn yourself, since you behave no differently from those you judge. We know God condemns that sort of behavior impartially" (Rom 2:1-2).

I am moved by the idea that the peacemaker never judges anybody—neither his neighbor close by, nor his neighbor far away; neither her friend nor her enemy. It helps me to think of peacemakers as persons whose hearts are so anchored in God that they do not need to evaluate, criticize, or weigh the importance of others. They can see their neighbors—whether they are North Americans or Russians, Nicaraguans or South Africans—as fellow human beings, fellow sinners, fellow saints, men and women who need to be listened to, looked at, and cared for with the love of God and who need to be given the space to recognize that they belong to the same human family as we do.

I vividly remember encountering a man who never judged anyone. I was so used to being around people who are full of opinions about others and eager to share them that I felt somewhat lost at the beginning. What do you talk about when you have nobody to discuss or judge? But, discovering that he also did not judge me, I gradually came to experience a new inner freedom within myself. I realized that I had nothing to defend, nothing to hide, and could be myself in his presence without fear. Through this true peacemaker, a new level of conversation opened up, based not on competing or comparing but on celebrating together the love of the One who is "sent into the world not to judge the world, but so that through him the world might be saved" (Jn 3:17). Through this man I came to realize that for Jesus, to whom God has entrusted all judgment (see John 5:22), the other name of judgment is mercy.

This encounter continues to change my life. For a long time I had simply assumed that I needed to have opinions about everyone and everything in order to participate in ordinary life. But this man made me see that I am allowed to live without the heavy burden of judging others and can be free to listen, look, care, and fearlessly receive the gifts offered to me. And the more I become free from the inner compulsion to make up my mind quickly about who the other "really" is, the more I feel part of the whole human family stretched out over our planet from east to west and from north to south. Indeed, saying "No" to the violence of judgments leads me into the nonviolence of peacemaking which allows me to embrace all who share life with me as my brothers and sisters.

But there is more. As peacemakers we must have the courage to see the powers of death at work even in our innermost selves because we find these powers in the way we think and feel about ourselves. Yes, our most intimate inner thoughts can be tainted by death.

When I reflect on my own inner struggles I must confess that one of the hardest struggles is to accept myself, to affirm my own person as being loved, to celebrate my own being alive. Sometimes it seems that there are evil voices deeply hidden in my heart trying to convince me that I am worthless, useless, and even despicable. It might sound strange, but these dark inner voices are sometimes most powerful when family and friends, students and teachers, and supporters and sympathizers cover me with praise. Precisely then there are these voices who say: "Yes, but they really do not know me, they really cannot see my inner ugliness. If they could know and see they would discover how impure and selfish I am and they would withdraw their praise quickly." This self-loathing voice is probably one of the greatest enemies of the peacemaker. It is a voice that seduces us to commit spiritual suicide.

The central message of the gospel is that God sent his beloved Son to forgive our sins and make us new people, able to live in this world without being paralyzed by self-rejection, remorse, and guilt. To accept that message in faith and truly believe that we are forgiven is probably one of the most challenging spiritual battles we have to face. Somehow we cannot let go of our self-rejections. Somehow we cling to our guilt, as if accepting forgiveness fully would call us to a new and ominous task we are afraid to accept. Resistance is an essential element of peacemaking, and the "No" of the resisters must go all the way to the inner reaches of their own hearts to confront the deadly powers of self-hate.

I often think that I am such a hesitant peacemaker because I still have not accepted myself as a forgiven person, a person who has nothing to fear and is truly free to speak the truth and proclaim the kingdom of peace. It sometimes seems to me that the demonic forces of evil and death want to seduce me into believing that I do not deserve the peace I am working for. I then become self-accusing, apologetic, even self-defeating, always hesitant to claim the grace I have been given and say clearly: "As a forgiven person I call forth the peace which is the fruit of forgiveness!"

My own inner struggles are not just my own. I share them with millions of others. Underneath much self-assured behavior and material success, many people think little of themselves. They might not show it—since that is socially unacceptable— but they suffer from it no less. Feelings of depression, inner anxiety, spiritual lostness, and (most painfully) guilt over past failures and past successes are often constant companions of highly respected men and women. These feelings are like small rodents slowly eating up the foundations of our lives.

Personally I believe that the battle against these suicidal inner powers is harder than any other spiritual battle. If those who believe in Jesus Christ were able to believe fully that they are forgiven people, loved unconditionally, and called to proclaim peace in the name of the forgiving Lord, our planet would not be on the verge of self-destruction.

It might seem contrived to extend the "No" of the peacemakers against nuclear war to a "No" against violent public entertainment, destructive stereotyping, and even self-loathing. But when we are trying to develop a spirituality of peacemaking we cannot limit ourselves to one mode of resistance. All levels need to be considered, even when it might seem that we are stretching things too far. I am deeply convinced that we have to keep all these forms of resistance together as parts of the great work of resistance. Peace activists who are willing to risk their freedom to prevent a nuclear holocaust, but who at the same time feed their imaginations with violent scenes, stereotype their fellow human beings, or nurture an inner disgust for themselves cannot be witnesses to life for very long. Full spiritual resistance requires a "No" to death wherever it operates.

Wherever there is life there is movement and growth. Wherever life manifests itself we have to be prepared for surprises, unexpected changes, and constant renewal. Nothing alive is the same from moment to moment. To live is to face the unknown over and over again. We never know exactly how we will feel, think, and behave next week, next year, or in a decade. Essential to living is trust in an unknown future that requires a surrender to the mystery of the unpredictable.

At a time such as ours, in which everything has become unhinged and there is little to hold onto, uncertainty has become so frightening that we are tempted to prefer the certainty of death over the uncertainty of life. It seems that many people say in words or actions: "It is better to be sure of your unhappiness than to be unsure of your happiness." Translated into different situations this reads: "It is better to have clear-cut enemies than to have to live with people of whose lasting friendship you cannot be sure"; or, "It is better to ask people to accept your weaknesses than to be constantly challenged to overcome them"; or, "It is better to be defined as a bad person than to have to be good in constantly changing circumstances." It is shocking to see how many people choose the certainty of misery in order not to have to deal with the uncertainty of joy. This is a choice for death, a choice that is increasingly attractive when the future no longer seems trustworthy.

As I reflect on my childhood experiences of fear, I remember a time in which I was tempted to fail even before I had seriously tried to succeed. Somewhere I was saying to myself: "Why not run back from the diving board and cry so that you can be sure of pity, since you are not so sure of praise." Such childhood memories offer me an image of the temptation that faces all of us on a world-wide scale. It is the temptation to choose the satisfaction of death when the satisfaction of life seems too precarious. When the future has become a dark, fearful unknown that repulses me more and more, isn't it then quite attractive to opt for the satisfactions that are available in the present, even when these satisfactions are very partial, ambiguous, and tainted with death?

The nuclear situation in which the future itself has become not only dark and fearful but also uncertain has made the temptation to indulge ourselves in brief pleasures of the present greater than ever. It is therefore quite possible that we will see an increasingly death-oriented self-indulgence going hand-in-hand with increasing doubt about a livable future. Fascination with death and hedonism are intimately connected, because both lust and death keep our eyes away from the anxiety-provoking future and imprison us in the pleasurable certainties of the moment.

Peacemaking requires clear resistance to death in all its manifestations. We cannot say "No" to nuclear death if we are not also saying "No" to the less visible but no less hideous forms of death, such as abortion and capital punishment. As peacemakers we have to face the intimate connection between the varied forms of our contemporary fascination with death and the deaths caused by a nuclear holocaust. By recognizing in our own daily lives our many "innocent" death games, we gradually come to realize that we are part of that complex network of war making that finds its most devastating expression in a nuclear holocaust.

Real resistance requires the humble confession that we are partners in the evil that we seek to resist. This is a very hard and seemingly endless discipline. The more we say "No," the more we will discover the all pervasive presence of death. The more we resist, the more we recognize how much more there is to resist. The world—and we are an intimate part of the world—is indeed Satan's territory. When the demon shows Jesus all the kingdoms of the world and their splendor, he says: "I will give you all these, if you fall at my feet and worship me" (Mt 4:9). Jesus never disputes that these kingdoms are Satan's; he only refuses to worship him. The world and its kingdoms are under the destructive power of the evil spirit, the spirit of destruction and death. The nuclear threat reveals the ultimate implication of this truth. It is not that God—who created the world out of love—will destroy it, but that *we* will destroy it when we allow the satanic power of death to rule us. This is what makes saying "No" to death in all its manifestations such an urgent spiritual task.

3

Celebrating Life

Resisting the forces of death is meaningful only when we are fully in touch with the forces of life. What is finally important is not that we overcome death but that we celebrate life.

I have found that total concentration on fighting the forces of destruction is dangerous and can be very damaging. When I allow my mind and heart to experience what a nuclear holocaust will do to our planet, it often seems that a deep darkness starts to surround me and pull me into a pit of depression and despair. When I try to confront the powers of death that already have a hold on me, I often feel so powerless that I lose contact with the source of my own life. How easy it is to become a victim of the very forces I am fighting against! When all my attention goes to protesting death, death itself may end up receiving more attention than it deserves. Thus my struggle against the dark forces of death becomes the arena of my own seduction.

There is a very old piece of wisdom that comes from the fourth-century monks of the Egyptian desert: "Do not combat the demons directly." The desert fathers felt that a direct confrontation with the forces of evil required so much spiritual maturity and saintliness that few would be ready for it. Instead of paying so much attention to the prince of darkness, they advised their disciples, focus on the Lord of light and thus, indirectly but inevitably, undo the power of the demon. The desert fathers thought that a direct confrontation with the demon would give the demon precisely the attention he is trying to get. Once he has our attention he has the chance to seduce us. That is the story of the fall.

Eve's first mistake was to listen to the serpent and consider him worthy of a response.

This early Christian wisdom is very important for peacemaking. As a peacemaker, my temptation is to underestimate the power of the forces of death and thus attack them directly. Precisely because I am such a sinful, broken person, these forces have many handles on me and can easily pull me into their network. Only the sinless Christ was able to overcome death. It is naive to think that we have the strength to face death alone and survive.

Here we touch one of the greatest dangers that face peacemakers: that peacemakers themselves become the victims of the evil forces they are trying to overcome. The same fear of "the enemy" that leads warmakers to war can begin to affect the peacemaker who sees the warmaker as "the enemy." Words of anger and hostility can gradually enter into the language of the peacemaker. Even the sense of urgency and emergency that motivates the arms race can become the driving force behind the peacemaker. Then indeed the strategy of war and the strategy of peace have become the same, and peacemaking has lost its heart.

One of the reasons why so many people have developed strong reservations about the peace movement is precisely that they do not see the peace they seek in the peacemakers themselves. Often what they see are fearful and angry people trying to convince others of the urgency of their protest. The tragedy is that peacemakers often reveal more of the demons they are fighting than of the peace they want to bring about.

The words of Jesus go right to the heart of our struggle: "Love your enemies, do good to those who hate you, bless those who curse you, pray for those who treat you badly" (Lk 6:27-28). The more I reflect on these words, the more I consider them to be the test for peacemakers. What my enemies deserve is not my anger, rejection, resentment, or disdain, but my love. Spiritual guides throughout history have said that love for the enemy is the cornerstone of the message of Jesus and the core of holiness.

What has all this to do with the work of resisting the forces of death? It means that only a loving heart, a heart that continues to affirm life at all times and places, can say "No" to death without being corrupted by it. A heart that loves friends and enemies is a heart that calls forth life and lifts up life to be celebrated. It is a heart that refuses to dwell in death because it is a heart always enchanted with the abundance of life. Indeed, only in the context of this strong loving "Yes" to life can the power of death be overcome. I therefore want to say here as clearly as I can that the first and foremost task of the peacemaker is not to fight death but to call forth, affirm, and nurture the signs of life wherever they become manifest.

Death is solid, uniform, unchangeable. It is also big, boisterous, noisy, and very pompous. A military parade in which tanks and missiles are proudly displayed, preceded and followed by disciplined, uniformed soldiers, is a typical manifestation of the death force. Life is different. Life is very vulnerable. Life, when first seen, needs protection—a plant slowly opening its flowers, a bird trying to leave its nest, a little baby making its first noises. It is very small, very hidden, very fragile. Life does not push itself to the foreground. It wants to remain hidden and only hesitantly reaches out. Life is soft-spoken. The sounds of life come gently and often seem part of the silence in which they are heard. Life moves moderately: no quick, brisk steps but a growth so imperceptible that we never really see it, only recognize it. Life touches gently. It does not slap or beat, but caresses and strokes. It makes us speak a tender language: "Be still, she is asleep." And then later: "You can come now and look. Isn't she beautiful? Do you want to hold her for a moment? Be careful."

Those who resist the power of death are called to search for life always and everywhere. The search for this tender and vulnerable life is the mark of the true resister. I have learned this from friends who have dedicated themselves to resistance. They have helped me appreciate anew the beauty of life. One of them spends an afternoon every week visiting cancer patients, another works with the mentally disabled, a third spends time with lonely people in a psychiatric institution. Somehow their direct contact

with the powers of death has made them aware of the precious-
ness of life and given them the desire to affirm life precisely
where it is weak and very tender.

This has opened my eyes to life in a new way. Having a
baby seems such a natural, obvious, and rather unspectacular
event. But for those who are deeply aware that we are living on a
planet that is being prepared for total destruction, in a time that
can be sure only of the past and the present but not of the future,
giving life to a new human being becomes an act of resistance.
Bringing into the world a little child totally dependent on the
care of others and leading it gradually to maturity is true defiance of the power of death and darkness. It is saying loudly: For
us life is stronger than death, love is stronger than fear, and hope
is stronger than despair.

I still remember vividly how my friend Dean Hammer spoke
about the baby he and his wife, Katie, were expecting. Dean had
just spent several months in prison for civil disobedience, for a
Plowshares disarmament action, and was faced with the possibility of another sentence that might put him behind bars for several
years. But in the midst of all the worries about their personal future as well as their deep concern for the future of the world,
waiting for this baby felt to them like another type of disobedience, a disobedience of the powers that could only give birth to
death. When Hannah was born, she was received as a sign of the
divine victory of life over death.

Having known Dean and Katie for many years, and having
followed their agonizing struggle against the nuclear arms race, I
was able to see Hannah in ways I had never seen a baby before.
This small and fragile new child, looking trustfully at me with
her beautiful dark eyes, told me something new about resistance
that I had not known before. She told me that there is hope even
when optimism seems absurd; there is love even when people
die of fear; and there is reason to celebrate even in a civilization
dressed in mourning for its own rapid decline.

When I held little Hannah and saw the intense joy of Dean
and Katie, I knew that the "No" to death that had led Dean to go
to prison was such a hopeful "No" because it was undergirded by

a strong and fearless "Yes" to life. And with little Hannah in my arms, I could easily make the connection between resisting nuclear weapons and protecting the unborn child, caring for the severely mentally and physically disabled, offering support to the elderly, defending the life of the prisoners on death row, and reaching out to all people whose life is precarious. The Lord of life is the Lord who does not "break the crushed reed, nor quench the wavering flame" (Is 42:3). In our utilitarian, pragmatic, and increasingly opportunistic society, however, there is less and less room for the weak, the unborn, the prisoners, the broken, and the dying. The crushed reed is easily discarded and the wavering flame easily quenched.

Reflecting on the affirmation of life as an act of resistance, I gradually came to see three aspects of life that are in stark contrast to the powers of death. They are humility, compassion, and joy. These three aspects of life, therefore, must also characterize the "Yes" of the resister. I would like to explore a little more now how a humble, compassionate, and joyful "Yes" is the way to true peace.

The "Yes" to the life of the peacemaker is first of all a humble "Yes." The word *humble* comes from the Latin word *humus* which means soil. Humble people are close to the soil and thus able to experience their lives as deeply connected with all other lives. If I learned anything during my visits to Latin America it was the humility of the poor. Their humility had nothing to do with self-depreciation or self-rejection, but everything to do with their connectedness with the land and its people. In our modern civilization so much emphasis is placed on being different, unique, and special, that it is very hard to remain truly connected. For us the most important question is: "How am I distinct from others?" This question often makes us lose sight of our basic sameness as created human beings. As long as our distinctiveness is our major concern, we put ourselves on the dangerous road of comparing and competing. When countries and continents follow this road, violence, war, and even global suicide are real possibilities. But when we are willing to acknowledge and even celebrate our intimate connectedness as human beings, we are on the road to peace. Being older or younger, smarter or more attractive, stranger or friend, Russian or American becomes less important than being a member of the human race. Humility is this always-deepening awareness of human solidarity. It is the freeing affirmation: "I am like all other people and I am grateful for it!"

It is important that the "Yes" of the peacemaker be a humble "Yes." It is humility that allows us to consider a quiet afternoon with a distressed friend just as important as any spectacular peace action. Visible and publicized peace actions are important for raising people's awareness of the sinister consequences of human arrogance and pride, but "passing" an afternoon with a friend in pain is a humble celebration of our common humanity. Such a simple act is indeed like the sowing of a mustard seed.

Visiting the sick, feeding the hungry, consoling the dying, or sheltering the homeless may not catch the public eye and are often perceived as irrelevant when put in the perspective of a possible nuclear holocaust. There are many voices that say: "These little acts of mercy are a waste of time when we consider the urgency of stopping the arms race." But the peacemaker knows that true peace is a divine gift that has nothing to do with statistics or measures of success and popularity. Peace is like life itself. It manifests itself quietly and gently. Who can say that a "lost afternoon" with a sick friend is in truth not much more than an interruption of "true" peace work? It might be the most real contribution to peace. Who knows? Jesus' way is the humble way. He calls out to us: "Learn from me for I am gentle and humble of heart" (Mt 11:29). A humble "Yes" to all forms of life—even the less noticed—affirms the deep interconnection between all people and forms the true basis of peace.

The "Yes" of the peacemaker also has to be a very compassionate "Yes," a "Yes" that constantly keeps the concrete, unique suffering of individual people in mind. During the past few years I have become increasingly aware of the real temptation to focus more on issues than on people. But when our peace work is primarily issue-oriented it easily loses heart and becomes cold, calculating, and very impersonal. When we fight for issues and no longer see concrete people with their unique personalities and histories, competition will dominate compassion and winning the issue may mean losing the people. There are endless problems in the world, such as poverty, exploitation, and corruption, that urgently beg for solutions. But people are not problems. They smile and cry, work and play, struggle and celebrate. They have names and faces to be remembered.

When I went to Peru for the first time I was strongly motivated by the burning issues of Latin America. I had heard and read about illiteracy, malnutrition, poor health, infant mortality, and many other problems. I was so overwhelmed by my own privileged position that I could no longer tolerate my "splendid isolation" and wanted to do something to alleviate the suffering of my fellow human beings. But when I arrived in Peru and began living there, what I came to know first of all were not issues but people: Sofia who struggled with back pain; Pablo who lost his job over and over again; Maria who dreamt about having her own doll; Pablito who wanted to go to the library and read books; and Juanito who loved playing practical jokes on me. They certainly suffered from poverty, oppression, and exploitation, but what they asked of me more than anything was not to solve their many problems, but to become their friend, share my life with them, mourn with them in their sadness, and celebrate with them in their gladness.

When our "Yes" remains compassionate, that is, people-oriented, the complex issues of our time will not drag us down into despair and our hearts will burn with love. We cannot love issues, but we can love people, and the love of people reveals to us the way to deal with issues. A compassionate resister always looks straight into the eyes of real people and overcomes the human inclination to diagnose the "real problem" too soon.

There is no question about the need for critical analysis of the world we live in. We have to try constantly to identify the dynamics that create poverty, hunger, homelessness, oppression, and war. Helping individual people in need is not the final answer. But when we become so overwhelmed by the abstract problem that we no longer consider the concrete, daily pain of men, women, and children worthy of our attention, we have already been seduced by the demon of death. Jesus understood the problems of the world in the most radical way, but wherever he went he responded to the concrete needs of people. A blind man saw again; a sick woman was healed; a mother saw her dead son come back to life; an embarrassed wedding host was given the wine he needed; thousands of hungry people received bread and fish to eat. Jesus left no doubt that the help he offered was only a sign of a much greater renewal. However, he never let that truth prevent him from responding to the concrete and immediate concerns of the people he met.

Finally, the "Yes" of the peacemaker is a joy-filled "Yes." The fruit of humility and compassion is joy. When we resist the powers of death and destruction with a sad heart we cannot bring peace. Joy is one of the most convincing signs that we work in the Spirit of Jesus. Jesus always promises joy; a joy like the joy of a mother after childbirth (see John 16:21); a joy no one can take from us (see John 16:22); a joy not of this world but a participation in the divine joy; a joy that is complete (see John 15:11). There is probably no surer sign of a true peacemaker than joy.

Sadness, bitterness, anger, and melancholy are dark experiences that show how close to the powers of death we have come. Where there is joy there is life. When Elizabeth heard the greeting of her cousin Mary, the child in her womb leapt for joy (see Luke 1:44). New life always leaps for joy—parents welcoming a child, children discovering the world, young people falling in love, men and women standing in admiration of the beauty of nature, North Americans who celebrate Thanksgiving and Russians who celebrate Easter. Joy is a free leaping toward the unexpected, a lifting up of what is new, a reaching out to heaven in hope, a touching of the Kingdom, an expectant tiptoeing. Sadness is always stagnant, heavy, and old. There is no old joy. Joy is always moving, light, and new.

Affirming life always brings joy. I have been amazed by the joy that radiates from the faces of those who work with the poorest of the poor. When I first saw the miserable and seemingly hopeless conditions in which many of these men and women have to live and work I expected depression and despair. But what I found among the most committed was joy. While teaching little children to read and write, feeding the hungry, visiting the sick, and caring for the dying, they spoke to me about the immense joy that had grown in their hearts. Some would say: "I love to be here with these poor people. Here I come to know Jesus and he has given me joy I never knew before."

When I heard these words for the first time, I felt a deep jealousy. I wanted that joy so much for myself, but had not found it among the scholars, teachers, and students with whom I have spent most of my time. I was suddenly struck by how somber and sad my friends and I are. We have enough food and shelter and more than enough health care and education, but are we living joyful lives? Why are we so serious all the time, so intense, so preoccupied with the next thing to accomplish, so disappointed after a small setback, so apprehensive when we are not being noticed, so angry when we are rejected, and so deeply sad when life is not going as we had planned it? When we are entangled in many complex issues, sadness can indeed imprison us and further remove us from the joy we so much desire.

Many peacemakers, overwhelmed by the great threats of our time, have lost their joy and have become prophets of doom. Yet anyone who grimly announces the end of the world and then hopes to move people to peace work is not a peacemaker. Peace and joy are like brother and sister; they belong together. I cannot remember a moment of peace in my life that wasn't also very joyful. In the Gospels, joy and peace are always found together. The angel who announces the birth of Christ, the prince of peace, to the shepherds says: "Listen, I bring you news of great joy to be shared with the whole people" (Lk 2:10). And when Jesus has completed his work of peace on earth and is lifted up to heaven, the disciples return to Jerusalem "full of joy" (Lk 24:25). Thus the Gospel of peace is also a Gospel of joy. Thus peace work is joyful work.

This joy does not necessarily mean happiness. In the world we are made to believe that joy and sorrow are opposites and that joy excludes pain, suffering, anguish, and distress. But the joy of the Gospel is a joy born on the cross. It is not the sterile happiness of victory parties, but the deep joy hidden in the midst of struggle. It is the joy of knowing that evil and death have no final power over us, a joy anchored in the words of Jesus: "In the world you will have trouble, but be of good cheer; I have conquered the world" (Jn 16:33).

Thus the "No" to death can be fruitful only when spoken and acted out in the context of a humble, compassionate, and joyful "Yes" to life. Resistance becomes a truly spiritual task only when the "No" to death and the "Yes" to life are never separated.

Increasing starvation, hunger, and poverty around the world and the increasing threat of a nuclear war offer us many reasons to be fearful, even despairing. When we hear the voices of death all around us and see so many signs of the superiority of the powers of death, it becomes hard to believe that life is indeed stronger than death. Long before anyone knew about nuclear war, Peter warned his people: "Your opponent the devil is prowling like a roaring lion looking for someone to devour" (1 Pt 5:8). These words have a new and concrete relevance for us. They summarize well our fear.

What is Peter's response to this lion? "Resist him," he says, "solid in faith" (1 Pt 5:9). And that indeed is the summary of the spiritual resistance based not on our experience, skills, intelligence, or will power, but on our faith in Christ who has already overcome the powers of evil and death that rule the world. Through Christ's victory over all death, individual as well as collective, death has no final power over us any longer. We are no longer locked in the dark world of despair but have already found our home in God where death has no place and life is everlasting. Though we are still in this world, we no longer belong to it. Our faith allows us even now to be members of God's household, and taste even now the inexhaustible love of God. It is this knowledge of where we truly belong that sets us free to be fierce resisters against death while humbly, compassionately, and joyfully proclaiming life wherever we go.

Let it be clear that resistance does not stand in contrast to prayer, but is in fact a form of prayer itself. It is hard to overcome our tendency to consider resistance the active part of peacemaking and prayer its contemplative part. But I am increasingly convinced that we will fully grasp the meaning of peacemaking only when we recognize not only that prayer is a form of resistance but also that resistance is a form of prayer.

It has taken me many years to understand this fully. The reason for my new understanding is probably that I have stayed away from most public forms of resistance and for a long time even had a deep resistance to resistance. Every time I saw people demonstrating against nuclear war I experienced some inner irritation. I often rationalized this irritation by thinking about the demonstrators as angry people who had nothing else to do. I was also convinced that these small bands of poorly dressed sign carriers were totally ineffectual, not only unable to change anything but also making things worse for those who want to work for peace through normal means.

But when friends invited me to come closer and watch more attentively, I gradually came to realize that I might have been turned off as much by Jesus and his disciples as by these small groups of resisters. What they did, said, and enacted referred to a reality with which we have lost contact. It is the reality of God's forgiveness and love by which divisions among people are removed and unity is restored.

Then, one year, during Holy Week, a small group of theology students invited me to join them in a prayer vigil at Electric Boat, the nuclear submarine shipyard in Groton, Connecticut. I knew them as hard working, intelligent, and deeply believing men and women. Their invitation was sincere, personal, and based on their knowledge of my own convictions. I realized that I was being asked for little more than to proclaim the Word of God at a place where it would clearly be heard as confronting the powers of death and calling for conversion. Although I felt a certain fear of making a fool of myself, I knew that there was only one answer: "Yes."

On Holy Thursday we all gathered in preparation for this Good Friday peace action. The first thing I discovered was that this action group was indeed a prayer group. For many months these women and men had come together at least once a week to pray. During these times they had gradually grown into a community of people able to listen to God's guidance. Together they had read and studied the scriptures, spoken about their fears and apprehensions, and tried to find words to express their deepest convictions. Together they had come to the decision that they should be willing to bring their prayers right to the place where their deepest fear found its cause: the place where the Trident submarine was being built.

It had been a hard and slow spiritual journey for most of these theology students. Many of them had come from traditional American families, in which respect for the authority of church and government go hand in hand. Public protest against what the government considers necessary for the protection of the people would create deep indignation. And yet, quiet listening day after day and week after week to the Word of God while reading more and more about the final destruction that the Trident submarine can bring about had brought these men and women to a new clarity: "We have to say 'No' to what our government is doing in Groton." Some felt that they had to break the law and let themselves be arrested. Others were less clear about that. But everyone was united by the inner call to say "No" to death and "Yes" to the God of life in a way that was exceptional and visible enough for the world to respond.

What most impressed me was that these friends did not want to go to Groton to shake their fists at the warmakers and confront them with threats. If anything had emerged from their prayers it was that they themselves were the first who needed to be converted and that there was no basis whatsoever for self-righteousness. It was not "We," the good people against "Them," the bad people. On the contrary, there was a deep awareness that those who work long days at Electric Boat are people caught in the same trap of warmaking as we are. They want to earn enough

money to care for their families and educate their children. They
work for their own dignity and self-respect. They work because
they love their fellow human beings, their country, and their
God. The unspeakable tragedy is that if the products of their hard
work are ever used, there will likely be no one left to care for.

The more I listened to the students who had invited me to
join them in their Good Friday peace action, the more it sounded
like a pilgrimage of repentance, a witness to themselves as well
as others, a call for conversion that includes first of all the one
who makes the call. They reminded me of the prophet who responded to those who criticized his effectiveness with the words:
"I do not preach against the evils of the world just to change the
world, but to prevent the world from changing me."

On Good Friday we went to Groton to witness for peace in
front of the administration building of Electric Boat. The leaders
of the group asked me to lead the community in the Stations of
the Cross. I couldn't resist a smile when I heard that we, people
from very different denominations (Baptist, Presbyterian, Luth-
eran, United Church of Christ, and Catholic) would make the
Stations of the Cross. As a child I had often made these fourteen
stations in church. They commemorate fourteen events between
Jesus' being condemned to death by Pontius Pilate and his burial.
These events have been vividly portrayed in paintings and sculp-
ture, and I remember well how my Dutch teen-age friends and I
walked from station to station in the chapel of our high school,
not once in a while, but many times a week during our lunch
breaks.

But as I grew older, the Stations of the Cross soon became a
pious childhood memory. The Second Vatican Council had so al-
tered my religious consciousness that, along with most of my fellow Catholics, I dropped this devotional practice and focused on
official liturgical celebration. Who could have dreamt that twenty years after the Council I would lead an ecumenical group of
theology students in the Stations of the Cross on the streets of
Groton, Connecticut, in prayerful resistance against an impending nuclear holocaust?

We prayed fervently with words and songs as well as in silence. We heard the story of Jesus' suffering in a way that we could not have heard it in any church. It was hard for me to know fully how I felt, but something new was happening to me that I had never experienced before. It was the deep awareness that prayer was no longer a neutral event without danger. Moreover, the words I had so often spoken from pulpits about death and resurrection, about suffering and new life, suddenly received a new power, a power to condemn death unambiguously and call forth life.

If I have created the impression that the ideal form of peace work is a liturgy on the street, that would be the wrong impression. I simply wanted to explain through a concrete example that resistance is indeed a form of prayer and devotion. This for me is of crucial importance, since so many resisters experience burnout when they realize that no significant change in the political situation has been achieved. Many people who have worked very hard for years in the hope of bringing about change have finally given up in despair. When they realized that things had not gotten better, but worse, that political parties, corporations, and elected officers had not changed their ways, they withdrew into passive resignation, no longer believing it worthwhile to keep struggling.

But Christian resistance cannot be dependent on signs of success. It is first and foremost a spiritual resistance, based not on results but on its own inherent integrity. Once we have let go of the compulsions of our success-driven world and have entered into God's house of prayer and praise, our resistance can be free from the need to be "useful." Then our resistance can be a clear witness to the living God in the midst of a world obsessed with death. Whatever we do to resist the powers of death, it must first and foremost be an expression of our worship of the living God.

When we see the behavior of Christians in peace demonstrations, we may be tempted to laugh at their "useless" activities. But when we come to see that these people are doing what they are doing first of all to be faithful to their God and to offer God praise at all times and at all places, we may come to see them as we see the three young men who refused to worship the golden statue King Nebuchadnezzar had made, and instead worshiped God in the fiery furnace.

Indeed, more important than our effect on people is our own spiritual authenticity. If we want to be faithful to our new self, which we have received from our Lord Jesus Christ, then we cannot remain silent and passive in the presence of the mounting forces of death. We owe it to God to say "No." Here we are touching the core of all resistance. It is an act flowing forth from our own deepest understanding of who we are. It is an act of spiritual integrity. It is a way of proclaiming the peace we have found in God's house. It is an expression of what we have become through the transforming power of Jesus. In this sense, it is a true act of prayer. And true prayer does not calculate its consequences.

So far I have not yet felt called to be arrested and go to jail for the sake of peace. I have always wondered if my going to jail would not alienate people from the cause of peace rather than attract them to it. But maybe I am concerned too much about influencing others and not enough about faithfulness to my own spiritual commitment. Frankly, I am not sure whether it is prudence or cowardice, conviction or practicality, faithfulness or fear that holds me back. I only know that what seemed so alien and unacceptable to me a few years ago now presents itself as at least an invitation to rethink my previous attitudes.

What should be clear in all this is that our differences of opinion about demonstrations and nonviolent civil disobedience should not be an argument for not working for peace. It is not important that all Christians act in the same way for peace or that everyone agree on every style of peacemaking. It is important that their varied actions are all done and experienced as a form of personal or communal prayer. Because only then can we be lifelong resisters. This resistance may mean participation in peace education programs, prayer services, public demonstrations, peaceful vigils, and civil disobedience. It may involve public speaking or writing. It may be a gentle response to a militaristic friend. It may even include visiting the sick, helping the hungry, or protecting the weak. But as long as such actions come forth from an angry, hostile heart they may do more harm than good. On the other hand, when they express gratitude for belonging to the house of God, we will no longer have to worry about whether they are fruitful, since what comes from God never returns to God empty.

It is hard for me to see how resistance can be fruitful unless it deepens and strengthens our relationship with God. Prayer and resistance, the twin pillars of Christian peacemaking, are two interlocking ways of giving expression to our life in the dwelling place of God. They come from the same source and lead to the same goal.

4

Living in the House of Love

Once there was a people that surveyed the resources of the world, and they said to each other, "How can we be sure that we will have enough in hard times? We want to survive whatever happens. Let us start collecting food, materials, and knowledge so that we are safe and secure when a crisis occurs." So they started hoarding and hoarding, so much that other people protested and said, "Hey, you have much more than you need, while we don't have enough to survive. Give us part of your wealth."

But the fearful hoarders said, "No, no no, we need to keep this in case of emergencies, in case things go bad for us too, in case our lives are threatened."

Time passed, and then the others said, "We are dying now. Please give us food and materials and knowledge to survive. We can't wait. We need it now."

And then the fearful hoarders became even more fearful, beause they were afraid that the poor and hungry would attack them. So they said to one another, "Let us build walls around our wealth so that no stranger can take it away from us." And thus they started erecting walls so high that they could not see any more whether

An address to the Presbyterian Peace Fellowship Breakfast during the 197th General Assembly of the Presbyterian Church (USA), Indianapolis, Indiana, June 1985.

there were enemies outside or not. And as their fear increased they told each other, "Our enemies have become so numerous that they may be able to tear down our walls. Our walls are not strong enough to keep them away. We need to put bombs on top of the walls so that nobody will dare to even come close to us."

But instead of feeling safe and secure behind their armed walls, they found themselves trapped in the prison they had built with their own fear. They even became afraid of their own bombs, wondering if they might harm themselves more than their enemy. And gradually they realized that their fear of death had brought them closer to it.

I wrote this short parable to say to you that we are always tempted and tempted again to become fearful hoarders. If there is anything that has struck me while traveling in this country, speaking and talking to people and teaching, it is how afraid we are. Somehow we people of the First World are fearful people. We are afraid of the unknown, the unknown in our deepest heart. We want to stay away from the feelings and passions that scare us. We are afraid of the unknown stranger who comes to us and who threatens our safety and our jobs. We are afraid of the unknown god; even though our theology might be correct, we fear that one day he is going to get us anyway. Our sense of fear seems to be so deeply rooted in us that we really do not know any more what it is not to be afraid. Our fear has taken away our true freedom. We have indeed become prisoners of our fear.

One of the most astounding observations that we can make is that those who make us afraid have power over us. Those who can make us buy into the agenda of fear are those who have control over us. Those who say, "Better do what I tell you because, if you are not doing what I tell you, you will lose your job. Do you want to lose your job? You don't, do you?" And we say, "Oh, no! So I will do what you say." Those who say, "If you do not follow my directions and support my policies you might get a war. And you don't want a war, do you?" And we say, "No, no, we don't want a war, so we will do whatever you say." Those who say, "If you are not obedient to me you might get an illness, you might get a war, you might lose your job, you might find yourself unhappy, and you don't want any of that, do you?" And we say, "Oh, no, no, so please tell me what to do." Those who can make us buy into the agenda of fear are those with power over us. Those who can make us live in that house of fear and keep us there are those who can take our freedom away.

When I was in Latin America and lived among the poor and oppressed people, I suddenly started to realize that they were not fearful people. Where I noticed hunger and oppression, torture and agony, I found more gratitude, more joy, more peace, and less fear than among those who have so many more of the world's goods. Suddenly I realized that the other side of oppression, the other side of the poverty in the South, is the fear and the guilt and the loneliness and the anguish in the North. Somehow those two can never be separated. Our suffering, which is often fear and loneliness and anguish and lack of freedom, is not separated from the oppression and from the poverty and from the anguish of those who live in what we call Third World countries.

But Jesus speaks to us in the Gospel with very strong words. Throughout the Gospel, we hear, "Do not be afraid." That is what Gabriel says to Zachariah. That is what Gabriel says to Mary. That is what the angels say to the women at the tomb: "Do not be afraid." And that is what the Lord himself says when he appears to his disciples: "Do not be afraid, it is I. *Do not be afraid, it is I.* Fear is not of God. I am the God of love, a God who invites you to receive—to receive the gifts of joy and peace and gratitude of the poor, and to let go of your fears so that you can start sharing what you are so afraid to let go of."

The invitation of Christ is the invitation to move out of the house of fear and into the house of love: to move away out of that place of imprisonment into a place of freedom. "Come to me, come to my house which is the house of love," Jesus says. Throughout the Old and the New Testaments we see that invitation: "Oh, how much I desire to dwell in the house of the Lord.

The Lord is my refuge, the Lord is my dwelling place, the Lord is my tent, the Lord is my safety." "Where do you live?" the disciples ask. "Come and see," the Lord says. And they stayed with him. The word became flesh and pitched its tent among us so that God could dwell among us in the house of love. "And I am going to the Father to prepare a house for you, a space for you, because in the dwelling place of my Father there are many places for you. Make your home in me as I have made my home in you. Live in the name of the Lord—the name of the place where you should dwell. Where are you? Are you in the name? Are you in the place of love?"

So, brothers and sisters, peacemaking starts every time we move out of the house of fear toward the house of love. You and I will always be scared somehow, somewhere. But if we keep our eyes fixed on the One who says "Do not be afraid, it is I," we might slowly be able to let go of that fear and become free enough to live in a world without borders, to see the suffering of others, and to bring good news and receive good news.

I would like to mention three qualities of living in the house of love. The first is prayer, the second is resistance, and the third is community. I want to discuss those three qualities as qualities of a spirituality of peacemaking, as ways in which we very concretely can move from fear to love, to that perfect love of God that casts out all fear, as John says.

Prayer is the way out of the idolatry of the interpersonal. Prayer helps us to overcome the fear that is related to building our life just on the interpersonal, in the sense of "What does he or she think of me? Whom do I like? Whom do I dislike? Who rewards me? Who punishes me? Who says good things about me, and who doesn't?" So much of us is concerned with questions like these, and so much of our identity gets wrapped up in them. "How many like me, and how many don't? Who are my friends, and who are my enemies?" As long as our sense of who we are depends upon what people think about us or say about us, how they respond to us, we become prisoners of the interpersonal, of that interlocking of people, of clinging to each other in a search for identity, and we are no longer free people.

Prayer is the way to a love that transcends the interpersonal, to that love that is called the first love. Love one another because God has loved us first! You and I have to keep believing that we can be free only if we are in touch with that original love, that total, unconditional, unlimited love. It's that love that will set you free. It's that love that will allow you to say "no" when you have to say no and "yes" when you have to say yes. It's that love that allows you to travel this world, breaks down your borders and boundaries, and lets you feel free and connected. It's that love that will release you from alienation and separation and give you a sense of who you really are: a person who is loved.

If we really want to be peacemakers, you and I have to have a solid discipline of prayer... of silence... of quiet time... of solitude to hear that voice that says, "I love you, whoever else likes you or not. You are mine. Build your home in me as I have built my home in you." And we won't always be running around wondering if we have a home. The sadness for us is that we have an address, but we are so seldom there. So we cannot be addressed and we cannot hear.

What I would like you to see is that if you come in touch with that first love you will discover not only that you are loved unconditionally, but that the one who loves you unconditionally loves all of humanity unconditionally, with that same all-embracing love. And the fact that God loves you so intimately and personally does not mean that God loves anyone else less or differently. Uniquely, yes. But whether they are Nicaraguans or Russians, people from Afghanistan or Iran or Africa, they all belong to the house of God. And therefore, when you enter into intimate communion with the God of the first love, you will find yourself in intimate communion with all the people of God, because the heart of God is the heart that embraces the whole of humanity. That's why intimacy with God always means solidarity with the people of God. To put it more precisely: God pitched his tent among us and took on our flesh so that there is no human flesh that has not been accepted by God. Therefore, prayer is not just communion with God in the privacy of your own place. It is communion with the people of God over the centuries and around the world that gives you a sense of belonging, a sense of overcoming the fear that separates you; it is that communion that sets you free.

In the house of love, we resist. Resistance helps us to overcome the fear that is the result of our ongoing fascination with death. It is unbelievable how fascinated with death we have become in our culture. It's in the entertainment world, in our own personal world, in the military world—it's all over. Instruments of death are being created, millions and millions and millions of dollars are spent to keep people fascinated with the possibility of death. Death has great power in this world. But in the house of love, a love that's stronger than death, we have to resist all the forces of death. Obviously, that means saying "no" to the death of the nuclear threat. Obviously, that means saying "no" to death in the form of capital punishment. Obviously, for me, it involves also saying "no" to death that involves the unborn.

But what I want to say to you right now is something that is a little closer to home, something that we have to deal with every day, and that is the little death games we play. We have to dare to say "no" to them, too. We have to begin to start saying "no" much earlier than we usually do. The first little death game that we play I would call prejudice: giving people names; putting people in little boxes and saying, "You don't have to talk to me about him or her. I know who she is, where he belongs, what she is about." So many times we make assumptions and decide that another person or group of persons does not belong to us. What I would like to make a plea for is that we in our churches continue to struggle against this labeling, this speaking in judgment.

I've seen so many situations in which people were killed first with the word before they were killed with the gun. The real violence usually starts with words. The real violence starts in the way we speak about people, make assumptions about them, and decide that they are not like us. Right now the great fear is not just that we might enter into Central America with weapons that kill, but that we have already created a language that kills. While I was in Guatemala a priest was murdered. His successor said to the people who did it, "You killed him first with your mouth, years before killing him with your shotgun." I keep seeing that happening right now. The words that are being used are so devastating. As long as people keep buying into these words, it will not take much more for them to buy into the action that has to follow. It starts right here at home, with words like "communism," or "totalitarianism," or euphemisms like "peacekeeping" for "bombs." Those words are terribly dangerous. The word of God is the word of love. But when the word "hate" becomes flesh, it leads to violence, and we have to start right there. And we have to say "no."

We also have to say "no" to something else—to our own self-rejection, to our own feeling of guilt. We have to fight that guilt in us, because guilt can never be a source of peacemaking. Guilt always creates more guilt. As people of God, we have to learn that we must live as people who have heard the words of forgiveness, so that we can finally not just blame ourselves, or tear ourselves down and say that we'd better do something for the poor because we have too much. As long as we act out of guilt we are not fully free people. We have to move from guilt to gratitude. We have to realize that, although we are sinners, God has forgiven us. And we have to act from that place. But this "no" requires a "yes," because life requires a "yes" every time.

The forces of death are heavy. The forces of death are stiff, shiny, bombastic. The forces of life are very gentle, very vulnerable, very small, sometimes even unnoticeable. Where there is life, something is growing. And, strangely enough, we seldom see it grow. We only recognize that it has grown. Much more important than saying "no" to the forces of death is saying "yes," again and again and again, to those vulnerable sources of life. That's why we should love the poor, the handicapped, the lonely, those separated, those locked in their apartments, the little people around us. If we only say "no" to the demon, we might get too fascinated with the demon. We might be lured into him—he always wants our attention anyhow. Talking too much with the demon might make us his partners. We have to be focused on the Lord of life, and have eyes to see life. Real peacemaking means an eye for small people, the little ones, the broken ones, those with whom one cannot have success, those with whom one cannot accomplish great things.

I'm convinced that this world will be saved by the little ones, by the hidden ones. Ask yourself where these little ones are. There might be some in your neighborhood, even just one person, but that person can bring you into contact with life: that lonely woman, that dying person, that little, lonely child, that poor person who comes over the border and says, "Do we have a place?" That's how sanctuary started. I remember talking to a priest in Nogales who said to me, "I really never thought about sanctuary, but when somebody came to my house I never really asked questions. I said, 'Do you have something to eat? Do you have a place to stay?' And when he said, 'No,' I said, 'Well, come in.'" And before the priest knew it, he was part of the sanctuary movement. But it started with his response to a little one. That's very simple.

Peacemaking should never be abstract. It should have a human face. Where is that human face in front of you, the person to whom you can say, "Come stay with me?" You will discover that those little people are the ones who give you the peace and the joy and the harmony of heart, who blow out your fear and give you some real freedom. If you want to be a real peacemaker, always look for the little ones, and your fear will slowly go, because it is through the little ones that God reveals to us God's perfect love. So resistance is saying "no" to death and "yes" to life—especially where it is most vulnerable.

Prayer and resistance need to be lived together. It is community that gets us away from the fear that is related to the search for individual heroism. Community breaks down the idol of individual heroism like resistance breaks down the idol of death and prayer breaks down the idol of the interpersonal. Community is that place where we can come together and forgive each other continually, recognizing that we are not God and that we cannot fulfill each other's needs totally. Every time we expect another person or group of people to take away our fear and anxiety, we will find ourselves so frustrated that, instead of becoming gentle, we will become violent.

"Please take my loneliness away." And our hands no longer caress but grab... our lips no longer kiss, but bite... our eyes no longer gaze lovingly, but look suspiciously... our ears no longer hear, but overhear. Suddenly we realize that, in wanting from other people a divine solution, we make them into gods and ourselves into demons. We become violent precisely because we expect more from each other than we can give.

Community is the place where people give to one another. We are not God, but we can be mediators (in a limited way) of the unlimited love of God. Community is the place of joy and celebration where we can say to one another, "Be of good cheer: the Lord has overcome the world, the Lord has overcome the evil one. Do not be afraid." In that sense the victory has already come. It is the victory of the cross, it is the victory of the naked one on the cross, a victory over death. Love is stronger than death, and community is the place where you and I continue to let the world know that there is something to celebrate, something to be joyful about, something to be ecstatic about—ecstasy, *exstasis,* in the sense of moving out of the static place of death. Community is the place from which we speak the Good News to the world: "Don't be afraid. Look, it has already happened. Christ is risen." We have to be people of celebration in order to be peacemaking people. Sour, somber, utterly serious peacemakers are not real peacemakers. We have to be people who have seen a vision and celebrate that vision together.

Prayer, resistance, and *community.* Let me conclude with a little story. It's God's story.

> There was a man and his name was Jesus. One day, after he had spoken to the people for many hours, he noticed that they were tired, and he said to his friends, "Look, all those people. They haven't had anything to eat for such a long time. Give them something to eat." And his heart was so full of love, so connected with the God of love, that he wanted to give food to all the people. And

his friends said, "Can't you count? We can't feed all these people. Why don't we eat the little we have so at least *we* will survive?"

There was a little kid with five loaves and five fishes, and he came walking up through the crowd. And they said, "Ha! Little kid, get away. Five loaves, five fishes. Ha, ha, ha. What do you say, little kid? Don't you see all these people? Your little loaves and fishes aren't worth anything. The statistics have proven it: it could never work."

And the man said, "Let him come here, the poor one, the little one, the hungry one, come." And he took those five loaves and five fishes. He blessed them, "bene dicce," saying good things about them ("bene," "good," "dicce," "to speak." Benediction). He said good things about them because they were not just the property of the little kid; they were God's gift to the people. And the man broke them and he gave them away. And they multiplied.

And suddenly they realized that this man had said "no" to the pessimism and the so-called realism of his friends and "yes" to life. And he had broken the bread and he had given it. And all the people could eat and celebrate. All the people could form community. And they had such a big celebration that it was even visible in the leftovers.

The Lord is so good. Brothers and sisters, when you hold on to what you have, it always gets less. When you give away what little you have, it always multiplies, whether it is food or knowledge or affection or love. Peacemakers are those who give away, not only from their abundance but from the little that they have. And they discover that all people are God's people and all people belong to the house of love.

Let us pray. Give us peace, Lord, the peace that the world cannot make, the peace that is your gift to us. Help us not to be so fearful, but to dare to take the risk of life. Teach us how to pray. Teach us how and when to say "no" and how and when to say "yes." Bring us together as people who know that love is stronger than death. You have overcome the world. Help us begin our celebration now. Give us peace and make us peace-makers now in the very concrete moments of our daily lives. We ask this in the name of Jesus, the One who is our peace. AMEN.

5

"No" to the Vietnam War

We are trying to do a very difficult thing. We are trying to say
NO to war, *NO* to the indiscriminate killing of men, women, and
children, *NO* to the horrendous destruction of villages, cities, and
fertile lands, in short, *NO* to all the evil powers that sow death
instead of life. Why is this such a difficult task? Because we
want to say *NO* in such a way that the possibility of peace becomes visible in our words, hands, and eyes. When our words
are only angry curses, our hands only clenched fists, and our
eyes filled with hostile gazes, then we are trying to end a war
with a war, and we add narrow-mindedness to narrow-mindedness, hostility to hostility, fear to fear, and violence to violence.

When we walk downtown with empty hands and return with
candles instead of guns, we want to express not only our deep
sadness, but also our expectation that sadness will lead to repentance, that repentance will lead to compassion, and that compassion will lead to peace.

If we want to respond to the incredible violence in our world
with a credible nonviolence, we have to be willing to realize that
nonviolence is not a technique to conquer peace, but a deep personal attitude which makes it possible to receive peace as a gift.
Therefore we are called today to confess that the evil we are
protesting against is alive in our own selves, to repent with contrite hearts for the sins of the world, to witness to the possibility

---

A speech given at a moratorium rally against the Vietnam War on May 4,
1972 at Yale University, New Haven, Connecticut.

and desirability of peace in the midst of a war-ridden society, to show a deep compassion not only for our friends but also for those we have called our enemies, and to work with hope for the liberation that frees both the oppressor and the oppressed from the tyrannical automation of violence.

Let us therefore go forth in the peace which the world cannot give, a peace we want to share with each other and with everyone we meet on our way.

6

A Cry for Peace

Out of the depths I cry
    to You, O Lord!
Lord, hear my voice!
      Let your ears be attentive
      to the voice of my supplication!

If You, O Lord, should mark our iniquities,
    Lord, who could stand?
But there is forgiveness with You,
    that You may be feared.

I wait for the Lord, my soul waits,
    and in God's word I hope;
my soul waits for the Lord
      more than watchmen for the morning,
      more than watchmen for the morning.

O Israel, hope in the Lord!
For with the Lord there is steadfast love,
    and with God is plenteous redemption.
And God will redeem Israel
    from all its iniquities.

                  (Psalm 130)

A reflection offered at a memorial service for the dead of Southeast Asia, victims of U.S. warmaking; Yale University, New Haven, Connecticut, April 21, 1972.

Out of the depths. Not from the top of our lungs. Not out of the immediacy of our emotions. Not out of the need just to do something. Not out of pure frustration, anger, desire for revenge. Not out of the superficiality of our restlessness.

Out of the depths of our being, we cry to God for peace. Out of that fearful place where we have to confess that we too are part of the destruction against which we are protesting. Out of that center where we discover that we too are so high up in the air that we have become numb and no longer see, feel, and hear the agony of the thousands who are struck by the seeds of destruction, which are mercilessly sown in Asian ground. Out of that empty spot of silence where we feel helpless, embarrassed, and powerless, where we suffer from our own impotence to stop the reign of death in our world. Out of those depths we cry to the Lord and say: "Lord have mercy."

If we do not enter into those depths, we can only say to each other: "We have seen this before"; we can only be caught in the uncanny and paralyzing feeling of déja vu. If we do not enter into those depths, we can only be cynical, skeptical, and sarcastic as we naively attempt to say "no" again, an attempt that has already been made so often without visible results. If we do not enter into those depths we will become strangled in our own pre-occupation with strategies and plans and prevent ourselves from seeing the horrendous power of evil at work in our midst. If we do not enter into those depths we will never be able to fashion a contrite heart and confess that we are not standing over against the evil but are co-conspirators and participants in the works of the leaders against whom we are protesting, but who are the leaders we deserve.

Our hearts are broken, our minds confused, our souls tired after years of words, plans, and attempts to end the war and heal our guilty conscience. And here we stand, poor in mind and spirit, with a deep sense of futility and inability to carry through our good intentions and live up to our commitment to joy, peace, and justice.

But maybe it is this sense of helplessness which will make us one with the thousands of men, women, and children who are running away from their homes, their lands, and their villages to escape the merciless rain of bombs. Maybe our helplessness will bring us to a deep sense of solidarity and our contrite hearts will make us slowly die to all the illusions of righteousness and generosity and the pretension of being saviors and redeemers in this world. Maybe we will finally come to a real confession of our brokenness and our need to be forgiven, not just as individuals but as a community, a city, a nation. Maybe we will finally let go of the need to make the results of our protest the condition for its value, and the temptation to use our cries as an expression of hate instead of as an invitation to love. Maybe we will finally reach the depths out of which we can cry to the Lord and say: "Let their ears be attentive to the voice of my supplications. I wait for you O Lord more than they that watch for the morning. Yes, more than they that watch for the morning, my soul waits and in your word I do hope."

We are not alone. We have each other. Together we can carry each other's burdens and help each other break through our paralysis by sharing our helplessness and by leading each other to purity of heart on the road to peace.

II

THE JOURNEY
TO RACIAL EQUALITY

7

We Shall Overcome

A Pilgrimage to Selma, 1965

It all began with a feeling of restlessness, an inner compulsion, a fierce gnawing, a painful question: Why aren't you in Selma? You talk about integration, you say that it's more than a national problem, you believe in the right of men and women to be free, but you're not in Selma. No time, no money, or no courage?

Seldom have I felt this inner restlessness so strongly than after Martin Luther King made his appeal to his people to help in the struggle for freedom. And seldom have there been so many people coming up with excuses for not going. "It's a local affair and it's not up to you to interfere, especially since you are a foreigner." "You're looking for thrills and excitement; better to do your duty where you are instead of running off to a problem for which you can't possibly bear any lasting responsibility." But the restlessness wouldn't go away; it even increased as the days passed.

On March 7, 1965, an historic civil rights march from Selma to Montgomery, Alabama, was blocked at the Edmund Pettis Bridge outside Selma. Police used tear gas and beat the unarmed marchers with clubs, injuring 140 people. In response, Martin Luther King, Jr., called upon church leaders and people of faith from around the country to come immediately to Selma for a second march to Montgomery, which began on March 21, 1965. Henri Nouwen was studying at the Menninger Clinic in Topeka, Kansas, at the time and decided to join the civil rights march.

I'm not one for demonstrations. I've never had much sympathy for the people who march down the streets of London or Amsterdam. But this seemed different. It became difficult to sleep, to eat, and to work. That question kept hounding me: Why aren't you in Selma?

I knew that they had already left. On Sunday, March 21, they had once again crossed the bridge over the Alabama River. Two weeks after being cruelly beaten by the state troopers they were back, but this time there were thousands of them, determined to complete the fifty miles to Montgomery. I knew that the song had been sung ten, a hundred, a thousand times:

> *Which side are you on, boy? Which side are you on?*
> With billy clubs they slew us down,
> they hit us with a cane.
> But we came back with thousands more
> and walked our way again.
> *Which side are you on, boy? Which side are you on?*

On Sunday, March 28, at eleven o'clock at night, tossing and turning in my bed, I suddenly knew that I had made a mistake. With alarming certainty I realized that I still had four days to undo the damage. That was when I made my decision. By midnight I was in my Volkswagen, driving out of Topeka, Kansas, and heading for the South, the deep, deep South. A remarkable change took place. The restlessness disappeared, and there was a deep, palpable certainty and sense of determination. No fatigue, no sleep. I trained my eyes on the endless roads of Kansas, flooring it, fast and sure.

From Kansas to Oklahoma, from Oklahoma to Arkansas, from Arkansas to Louisiana, from Louisiana to Mississippi, from Mississippi to Alabama. Every now and then I'd get a few hours' sleep in a highway motel and then head another thousand miles farther, down to Selma.

In Vicksburg, Mississippi, there was a black man standing by the roadside, keeping a safe and rather timid distance from the roadway. Charles, age twenty, my first friend. After climbing into the car he said, "God has heard my prayer. He sent you as an angel from heaven. I've been standing here for hours and nobody would pick me up. The white man only wants to run at me and push me off the road. When you hitchhike you take your life in your hands, but I want to go to Selma. I made a cross in the sand with my stick, and I prayed to God that he would bring me to Selma to help my people. He heard my prayer." As we drove through the night Charles told me about the dark days of Mississippi.

He'd been imprisoned five times in his fight for freedom. He'd demonstrated with thousands of others, for the integration of schools, courts, restaurants, and shops. "Never go alone. Go with thousands. The more there are in jail the sooner you'll get out. They have to feed you, and that's expensive; they have to have room for you, and that's scarce; they need guards and there aren't enough. Go with thousands. That'll cost them money and they'll just have to release you."

He told me about the murder of his friend and leader, Medgar Evers, the civil rights champion, the man with courage. The Klan had sent a thug who shot him when he was coming home one evening. The perpetrator was walking around free, but the movement lay dead with its leader.

And the whites? "Aren't there any white people who are helping you?"

"Oh, some high school kids, but it's dangerous for them. Their father loses his job and the boy gets teased at school. A 'white nigger' is more hated than we are."

Slowly but surely it dawned on me that Charles was turning me into a black man. Gradually I felt my innocence and unquestioned sense of freedom disappear. This country is your enemy. You're riding in a car with a black man, your license plate betrays you as a Freedom Rider on your way to Selma. "They hate the guts out of you." And the fear began to take shape deep in my heart. At first I dismissed it with "It won't get that bad," but it anchored itself deeper and deeper within me. The fear gave me new eyes, new ears, and a new mouth.

"Look, a state trooper, slow down your car.... Did you hear what that guy said? He called you a nigger.... You belong with us and that's all there is to it.... You've made a decision and you've got to suffer the consequences."

After riding through the night for eight hours you get thirsty. There were restaurants along the way where coffee was being served, but not for us. Charles knew it. "We can't stop anywhere. Otherwise we'll end up in jail before we get to Selma." But I was thirsty, and I told him he was exaggerating. One look through the window was enough for me to realize that he was right. A woman saw us coming and quickly shoved a sign into her shop window: "Whites only."

"Do you have enough gas? I hope we can make it to Selma." It's too dangerous to stop at a gas station. They hate us.

On Tuesday morning at six o'clock, tired, dirty, and unshaven, we drove into Selma.

"Let's just keep driving," Charles suggested. "The marchers are probably about twenty miles from Selma." We drove over the notorious bridge. "Here's where it started. This is where the state troopers were." After we had driven about fifteen miles we noticed that we were approaching the camp where the marchers had spent the night. Soldiers stood along the roadside with their rifles poised. These were the members of the National Guard who were there under federal order. It was clear that we could feel protected here, but the military trucks, the hundreds of jeeps, and the police cars reminded me of occupied Holland during the war.

It began to rain, first a little drizzle, then a downpour. Charles took out his diary and wrote, "With a total lack of freedom on my face I slowly watch the pouring rain, and it seems like an instrument of destruction. It's like living under a waterfall. But somehow I wish that I were outside, walking with the others. I only hope that this rain doesn't drown their spirit. But deep in my heart I do believe that we shall overcome some day. And no matter what we do, we won't forget our Creator, our guide and savior, our Lord of all. And as long as we don't forget to pray, everything will be all right. God and my freedom is my goal."

As the rain fell harder than ever and the land grew gray and forbidding, we reached the camp.

We couldn't join in the walk. The local road was only two lanes wide and a court order had been issued restricting the number of marchers to three hundred. They were scrupulously counted. One too many might cause an argument and lead to difficulties. Obedience and subservience to the whites: that was the only way out. But tomorrow everyone could march, tomorrow the road was a four-lane highway and the thousands of marchers could all walk together again on the long road to Montgomery.

We watched the three hundred leave with pain in our hearts. Leading them were the American flag and the flag of the United Nations, wrapped in plastic sleeves, and behind the flags were the men, women, and children of Selma and Montgomery who had the privilege of belonging to the three hundred. They were dirty and still tired after the damp night in tents, but they sang with irrepressible repetition:

We're gonna march when the Spirit says, "March."
We're gonna march when the Spirit says, "March."
And when the Spirit says, "March," we're gonna march,
    O Lord.
We're gonna march when the Spirit says, "March."

Clapping hands reinforced the rhythm; stamping feet increased the rage; swaying hips accelerated the movement. I watched them leave wrapped in pieces of plastic that had been applied in great haste, a group of paupers, but prouder than kings.

We returned to Selma. Those who had not been allowed to walk that day had gathered at Brown Chapel. They sat on the steps of the church, lay in the pews of the choir, and stood in groups around the pulpit. There was laughing and talking and weeping. A crew was hard at work in the kitchen below the church, working to prepare food for everyone. There was always plenty of food. It was one of the mysteries of Selma. Countless people ate bread, soup, eggs, and meat; and they drank coffee and juice. Trucks pulled up, one after another, carrying food, free and unlimited. Thousands were fed during those five days in Selma, in Montgomery, along the road, and in the tents; there was always enough.

It seemed as if nothing had been organized and everything was always threatening to collapse in confusion, but somehow it always turned out all right. I realized what it's like to live with people who know the necessity of improvising and reacting with immediate spontaneity. Many Freedom Riders walked into humble homes, and everywhere you looked there was food on the table. No matter what the setting, people ate, laughed, talked, and prayed.

In a small room there were two twelve-year-old black boys sitting behind a table. They took care of the registration: "What's your name? Where do you live? Who should we contact if anything happens to you?" Those were the questions.

What kind of people had gathered here? God's fools, I suddenly realized. Young people from the Northeast and the West. They had come from Chicago, New York, San Francisco, and Los Angeles. People whom we're quick to label anti-social. The young artist with his little red beard and sparkling eyes who kept on saying, "I don't give a damn." The good-natured, melancholy drifters from the big cities. The indifferent beatniks with their tight pants and painted sweatshirts. Strange people, crazy people, odd characters, and sinners. Not a cent to their names, but always restless and wandering around. Not knowing where they're going to be from one week to the next, where they're going to eat or where they're going to sleep. "I don't care." "We'll see." They all came to accompany the oppressed blacks in Selma. They were prepared to march to Montgomery, to sing to the God who delivers people from slavery, and to help people in need.

There were also the idealists. The pacifists, the conscientious objectors, God's witnesses. Young students who spoke about God with a prophetic look in their eyes, romantics who silently stared into space and wrote pages and pages of poetry, and surrealists who spoke in an abstract language.

These were the people who had come to Selma. They had no obligations to fulfill, they had no appointments for the coming week, they had no boss to stand in their way. They went where the Spirit sent them.

This was the refuse, the remnant of Israel, the people of God. Blacks and whites came from the North to Selma where the blacks lived in fear, and joined them in a nonviolent war. And it was a war. Up until now I had thought this was an exaggeration. But it wasn't.

A black boy from Chicago had gone to a Baptist church that was located near a white neighborhood. Evening was approaching. Children and grown-ups were in the church. Then came the report that the Ku Klux Klan was roaming around. One of the black church leaders refused to allow his people to leave. The church doors were bolted shut. Not another word was spoken, and everyone knew that to leave the church was suicide. Anxious mothers called the church to ask if their children were there. But no one answered the phone because they were afraid the Klan would pull one of their tricks. They slept in the church pews, and only when it was full daylight and the "all clear" signal had been given did the group leave the church and return to the black neighborhood where their friends were.

Fear. It lasted all day long. I felt it more and more. I no longer saw people. I saw blacks and whites, friends and enemies. I felt my skin turn black and I slowly began to realize what it means to be black.

As noon approached, Charles and I drove back to the camp where the marchers were to spend the night. An English student from Cambridge, who was studying as a provisional student at Yale, rode with us. His name was Nicholas, and he knew more about the problems in the South than most Southerners do. He told us the history of the movement and many of the stories behind what was taking place between Selma and Montgomery. He had worked as a Freedom Rider in Mississippi during the summer and he knew the dangers. His vast knowledge of history combined with his laconic British humor—and an improbably tall body that barely fit in my VW—made him an unusually striking figure that quickly attracted the attention of many journalists. He himself wrote for the *Manchester Guardian*. He read his newspaper at the most impossible moments and sang out of tune with a grating voice that seemed incongruous for such a well controlled gentleman. But he was ashamed of nothing: *"I'm gonna die when the Spirit says die."*

The camp was in chaos. The downpour had turned the pasture into a big mud puddle. We rode in a truck to a nearby farm where a black farmer was giving all his straw to the marchers. "I thank God that I saved this straw till now. At first I wanted to sell it, but I didn't. Now I know that God had me save it till today to help the poor people who are tired from the march." And with a proud smile he watched as all the bales were hauled out of his barn and spread out on the wet ground.

When the three hundred singing marchers finally arrived and had stretched themselves out on the straw floors of the big tents, the feast began. It seemed as if nobody could party better than these oppressed people. The flush of victory seemed to have them in its grasp, combined with the certainty that they would lose. No one expected that the march would make any difference. Everyone knew that when it was over the fear would only grow more intense. George Wallace cannot be converted. The doors of the Capitol cannot be opened. We won't get any farther than the steps.

Nevertheless we celebrate. It's the celebration of those who have nothing to win, but who also have nothing to lose. Guitars appeared, and groups formed around the tent. Spirituals were sung. All my worries faded when I heard the songs. "Who's singing? Who's rhyming? Who's calling? And who's crying? Come on boy, sing! Clap your hands!"

The sounds of the guitar pressed forward with their insistent rhythm, and every time the refrain was heard another voice piped up with a newly created verse. Every phrase was new, sung for the first time. What were the words about? About the Selma bridge, about George Wallace and the Capitol. About pain in the feet, sweat on the back, mud in the shoes, sunburn on the face. About the people of God walking to Montgomery. About the city that will be taken like Jericho, about the whites who came from the North to help the Lord in his work, about Martin Luther King, the new Moses. About the rain and the sun, the hard road and the soft shoulder. About the state troopers and the cops, about the sticks that were used to beat the marchers, the tear gas used to blind them, the horses that ran them down. And so it went. Up and down, high and low. And when the singers became over-heated from anger and malice, another voice arose from the crowd:

> *I'm gonna cool it when the Spirit says, "Cool it."*
> *When the Spirit says, "Cool it," I'm gonna cool it,*
>   *O Lord.*
> *And I'm gonna bow when the Spirit says bow.*

And the dancers bowed deeply and lowered their voices to a soft whisper, until the cry rose up:

> *But I'm gonna shout when the Spirit says, "Shout."*
> *And I'm gonna fight when the Spirit says, "Fight."*

The hours passed, but no one grew tired. We all wanted more. The rhythmic singing formed a safe bed for all our feelings of joy and pain, gratitude and hate, courage and despair. If God had not given the gift of song, this march could never have been nonviolent. "We are on the move," and no one is going to hold us back. A new song was born:

> *Ain't gonna let nobody turn me round,*
> *Turn me round, turn me round.*
> *Ain't gonna let nobody turn me round.*
> *I'm gonna keep on walkin', keep on talkin',*
> *Marchin' up to freedom land.*

I couldn't grasp the melody very well. But Ronald, a big black man from Chicago, said, "You're not angry enough. Say it again, 'Ain't gonna let nobody, ain't gonna let nobody.'" And, growing angry in the endless repetition of the song, I automatically slid into the melody, which swept me along with irresistible power through the deep levels of love and hate. There was hardly a moment's silence amidst all the singing. When, after half an hour, one of the melodies died out, there was always a new voice, a new melody, a new spirit. And when a star broke through the clouds overhead, a voice began to sing, and everyone followed the voice with a soft, melancholy humor:

> *This little light of mine, I'm gonna let it shine.*
> *All over Montgomery, I'm gonna let it shine.*

Then a sense of satisfaction seemed to descend on everyone. The tent grew quiet. The fatigue was a joyous fatigue, and the silence was deep. Beside me lay Nick. His heart had been deeply moved. He had to talk. While silence reigned everywhere else, he whispered to me about himself—about his dreams and disappointments, his passionate longings and his weaknesses.

"Yale is a very nice name, but it sounds like 'jail,' and I feel trapped by my insecurities. I try to find out what it is that's worth living for, but I haven't found it. I thought that I would find the answer by traveling, but traveling has given me nothing. I thought that resisting it would be the answer, but it's not. I searched for friends, but they don't stick with you. I searched for love, but I couldn't find any. I'm going back to work with the poor of India. Only the poor can help me."

The next day was the day of the big march. The road was a four-lane highway, and everyone was welcome. More than a thousand of us had left the camp that morning, and eight thousand had arrived in Montgomery the night before. Buses with new participants stopped along the way, cars brought people from every corner of the United States, and the procession stretched itself out like a miraculous rubber band.

It was a nonviolent group, but helicopters hovered over our heads; jeeps were parked on the shoulders, with military police giving orders on their walkie-talkies; in the bushes stood the National Guard, barely hidden, with their weapons at the ready; and the state troopers patrolled the route.

Defenders and enemies at the same time. Everyone knew it. The entire National Guard consisted of white men from Alabama who permitted no blacks within their ranks and who wore the flag of the Confederacy on their uniforms with defiant pride. The state troopers, who had broken up the demonstration a week earlier with rubber bullets and tear gas canisters, had become defenders by order of Washington. With growing fear the marchers watched the police officers film the whole column with movie cameras. Everyone knew what that meant. This film would become evidence that would later be used to prove charges of inciting to riot, and countless people realized that if they were identified they would lose their jobs. Protected by the enemy, that was the paradox of this march.

It wasn't really a march. It was an irregular walk, sometimes a limp. Everyone tried to keep up, and every now and then a few would have to run to close ranks. Then the march leader would grin and sing, *"When the Spirit says run, we're gonna run."*

I kept thinking about the people of Israel wandering through the wilderness, a disorderly group that was always in danger of breaking up but was unified by the constant threats from without. And there was the thirst and hunger to contend with. But a big army tank with water followed the marchers, and women stood along the roadside with big baskets filled with sandwiches to keep the people fed. It was all there, water from the rock and manna from heaven, everyday things, and you forgot that it was a miracle.

The songs became louder and louder as the column lengthened, and the drone of the helicopters was drowned out by the ceaseless singing and the tireless hand-clapping. Deep in my heart. And there was the Montgomery bridge. There was the city that would be taken tomorrow. Deeply stirred, the marchers looked out over the city from the height of the bridge. What would happen? A mixture of anxiety and longing could be felt, of courage and fear, hope and despair, tears and laughter. "We're hated by every white in the city, but God is with us." And while the people surveyed the city they sang the song, the civil rights anthem, that was able to turn their deepest fear into courage:

> *We are not afraid.*
> *We are not afraid.*
> *We are not afraid today.*
> *Oh, oh deep in my heart I do believe*
> *We shall overcome some day.*

As the song swelled the clouds burst open and the rain poured down in buckets. Never during the whole march had the rain been as cruel as it was that hour at the city limits. It was a cloudburst that in two minutes succeeded in clearing the road and soaking the unprepared marchers right through to the skin. But it was a challenge that only stimulated more fire and enthusiasm. The songs became stronger and the singers kept repeating:

> *Deep in my heart*
> *I do believe*
> *We shall overcome some day.*

At 6 o'clock on Wednesday evening we entered the City of St. Jude, a Catholic institution for blacks that included a hospital and a school. The rector had put the grounds at the disposal of Martin Luther King for one night. It was a generous and courageous gesture. He was acting in defiance of his bishop—who had forbidden every priest in Alabama to participate in this march—and all the whites, who would hate him and his "City" even more because of this decision. But he had made up his mind and took a risk, like so many others who had hazarded their future and their jobs on this march.

One priest said, "If I join in this march I'll lose the sympathy of my parishioners and my bishop may kick me out of the diocese; if I don't join in this march I'll regret it for the rest of my life. What should I do?"

In the meantime many ministers, priests, and nuns had arrived. The Sisters of St. Jude received them with great hospitality but also with great pain, because they themselves had been forbidden to join in the march for their own fellow Montgomerians under threat of excommunication. Archbishop T. J. Toolen had publicly requested that all priests and religious leave the city immediately and not get involved in the internal affairs of his diocese. He had declared his solidarity with the governor and condemned all participation in the demonstration. That was the tragedy of this march. The church was there: hundreds of ministers and priests had come from every direction to give voice to their convictions. And the church wasn't there: the bishop and priests of Alabama kept silent and bitterly looked on as the priests from the North reproachfully entered their diocese.

Leroy, a black boy, said, "The greatest thing about this march is the preachers, the ministers, and the priests. Now we know that the church is behind us and we feel strong." But he didn't know that in a certain sense it was the beatniks of the church, the angry ones, the offended, who had come. Here, as well as elsewhere, the church was divided and the witness weakened.

The City of St. Jude became like an army camp outside the ramparts of a city that had to be taken. Spirits were tense and the urge to get on with it created wild restlessness. Cutting straight through the camp came a group of young men, clapping their hands, stamping their feet, performing together in an ecstatic choir. They sang, they shrieked, they cried.

Martin Luther King stood up, and with his deep, heavy voice he cried, "What do you want?" And the people's answer thundered back, "FREEEEEDOM!" And he cried out again, "When do you want it?" And the people answered, "NOOOOW!" And he asked, "How much of it do you want?" And the furious response, "ALL OF IT!" "Then let's go to the Capitol, everyone. Don't be afraid. God is with us. Come back tomorrow and gather behind the flags. No one can hold us back." And the people sang:

Nobody can turn us around.
We're gonna keep on a-walkin',
keep on a-talkin',
Marchin' up to freedom land.

The night was restless. I slept among hundreds of teenagers who just couldn't wait. Sleeping was impossible. They called to each other through the dark tent. They cursed and joked. The hours that remained until morning passed too slowly for them. They were ready to go. Now.

By six o'clock in the morning the camp was in full swing. Countless people who had arrived in the early morning from the North, the East, and the West joined with the nervous marchers. The procession was to begin at 9:30, but the leader was missing. Martin Luther King was in trouble. A last attempt had been made to prevent the march on the Capitol from taking place. Charges had been brought against King and a fine of a thousand dollars had been imposed to compensate for the damages he had inflicted on the city.

At eleven o'clock he finally returned. One man said, "We've waited all our lives, a few more hours won't hurt." And slowly the procession began to move. It began like the victory march of a triumphant army. The procession passed through the small streets of the black neighborhood. All along the road, blacks stood in tightly packed rows, clapping and cheering, waving little flags and handkerchiefs. The men sang their hearts out, the women stood on chairs and waved their arms, the children ran alongside the procession. The joyous shouts warmed our hearts. Men and women cried, children laughed or looked at the strange spectacle with bewilderment.

Rather nervously, the hundreds of soldiers with arms at the ready walked along the procession to prevent mishaps. But nothing happened. It was a party, a victory, a triumphal entry. A sixty-year-old woman grabbed my arm and leaned against me, wanting to walk with me. She had already walked four days and she didn't want to miss this last part. She wanted to tell George

Wallace how much he had made her suffer, and she was determined to get to the Capitol.

In the meantime, the procession had grown longer and wider. "Join us, join us," was the call to all the blacks along the road. There was hesitation written across their faces. Participation could mean certain loss, marching could bring about trouble for their families. Here and there children jumped among the marchers, but the enthusiasm was so strong and the songs had such a compelling force that the column became like an irresistible magnet, attracting thousands with its enormous power and sucking the whole neighborhood dry. We left St. Jude with ten thousand people; we approached downtown Montgomery with fifty thousand.

Suddenly everything changed. The border between the black neighborhood and the white city was as sharp as a knife. The cheering stopped, the feeling of victory disappeared. All along the road stood white men and women with their lips pressed together. Some of them turned their backs on the procession to demonstrate their aversion. Young men with cigarettes in their mouths leaned nonchalantly against front doors.

The cold hatred was palpable, and again it occurred to me: this is no victory march, this is a lost battle. Who were we, anyway? The white racists along the way had an answer: a group of agitators, meddlesome Northerners, the impertinent foreign invaders. We knew it. We were hated and despised. And they didn't just stand there silently. The exasperated people on the sidewalk shouted at us with anger: "Hey, father, is your mother a nigger?" A priest walking with two black students was spit at in the face. He became so angry that he wanted to leave the march. But the blacks held on to him and cried, "No, no, don't do that, do like we do and stay cool. You're a white nigger and you're the underdog. Father, you've got a lot to learn."

Then we descended on the city. The road widened into a spacious avenue and led into the downtown area, past large bank buildings, hotels, and shops. As I stood at the top of the hill and watched the people descend into the city, my heart was filled with joy and pain. The hot mass of people flowed between the houses like an unstoppable lava stream. They sang louder and louder to suppress the fear that was growing in their hearts. No more clapping women along the side of the road, no more cheering children. Only the chilly gaze of the many whites who had paused in their work, standing on the sidewalk or hanging out of the window to observe the invasion.

This is where the question began to gnaw at me: "When will this hate manifest itself?" What would happen if the troops were to pull back and the whites were allowed to show their true feelings? Up until now it was safe. Every street corner was manned by military police who had surrounded the entire center of the city and had made it perfectly clear that any hostile movement could be deadly.

What I saw next I will never forget for the rest of my life. When the procession turned the corner, there opened before our eyes a beautiful broad avenue stretching from the center of the city to the Capitol, set like a white palace atop a hill. The government building, glittering bright white in the sunlight, blinded me, and I was overwhelmed by the unbelievable sight of a huge dome supported by many white columns and encircled by two white arms.

My eyes began to focus in, and on the proud steps of the Capitol I could see the legislators of the State of Alabama dressed in their dark suits and standing like a gloomy platoon. In front of them, ten steps below, a protective cordon of yellow helmeted soldiers stood rigidly at attention. The sight of the white Capitol, illuminated by the sun, and the black-suited gentlemen on the steps was enough to communicate hatred to all the thousands of paupers who had marched to this cradle of the Confederacy. Atop the dome waved the flag of the State of Alabama and the flag of the Confederacy. No Stars and Stripes. They were all in the army that had marched with such powerful strength to the steps of this bulwark of segregation. A phalanx of hundreds of American flags advanced like a defiant symbol to the palace of those who still didn't believe that they'd lost the Civil War.

Feelings overwhelmed our hearts. The songs were war songs, and the civil rights anthem was a mighty battle hymn.

We are not afraid.
We are not afraid.
We are not afraid today.
Oh, oh deep in my heart
O Lord I do believe
we shall overcome some day.

It took more than one hour for all the people to gather in front of the Capitol steps. Harry Bellafonte sang and led the waiting marchers with his melancholy voice. It was a melancholy that knew that we would never get any farther than those steps, that George Wallace would not appear, and that nonviolence signified the acceptance of a loss before the battle had begun.

Then everyone sat down on the street. Fifty thousand people sat on the Capitol's stately avenue. Black against white. This is a civil war, a holy war, a crusade, and it's only the beginning of a long struggle. "When God's people are in trouble, he sends them a leader," cried Ralph Abernathy through the loudspeaker. "Martin Luther King, the greatest leader of this century, the Moses who is leading us through the wilderness to the land of freedom."

Then King spoke. He spoke differently than the others, who could no longer control their seething rage. He spoke slowly, with conviction, and with enormous, penetrating power. His phrases were like explanations that went beyond the realm of doubt. He spoke about the history of his people, about the days of slavery, about the struggle for human freedom, and about the many martyrs: Jimmy Lee Jackson, murdered in Marion; Medgar Evers, killed in Jackson; the four children who died in the bombing of the church in Birmingham; Rev. Reeb, beaten to death in Selma. "They did not die in vain, because we are on the move."

King's voice rose to a level of holy wrath, and with accelerated rhythm he repeated the words, "We are on the move." "We won't get any further than these steps today, but let it be known: we are on the move. We will go back and we will continue to suffer, but now we know: we are on the move. Others will be killed, tears will flow, the people will bow down, but we are on the move. We can't vote, we can't govern, we can't determine our own fate, but we are on the move."

And then the people took over. The repeated cry sounded like the blast of trumpets at the walls of Jericho: "We are on the move." What began as their leader's cry quickly became the cry of thousands, striking the Capitol walls like sledgehammer blows.

"The walls will go tumbling down," shouted King, "and no one can hold us back. Today there are fifty thousand of us here, tomorrow there will be a hundred thousand, the day after tomorrow millions. We're going away, but we're coming back. God is with us and He will lead his children to the land of freedom. Glory hallelujah, Glory hallelujah, Glory hallelujah."

King had spoken. For half an hour his voice had resounded and the world had listened. These fifty thousand people represented millions who were with them in spirit and who participated in this march of freedom by means of radio and TV. King knew that, and the people felt it profoundly, surrounded as they were by countless cameras and TV vans.

Then a prayer was offered, the American national anthem sung, the blessing given. And we turned our backs on the Capitol, toward home, convinced that this was only the beginning.

Was this the end? Actually my story only begins here. Because now fear began to do its work. At four o'clock that Thursday afternoon the jurisdiction of the troops came to an end, and we knew that we were outlaws. We walked back feeling hungry and thirsty after the day's long hours, but all the shops were closed. "Closed, closed," we read everywhere, and we knew that it was the first act of vengeance.

"Walk close together." "Walk as fast as you can to the black neighborhood, you can eat there." "Don't stay in the city, it's suicide." Somewhere on a side street a man was beaten. A minister who walked into a bar was hit on the head with a chair. White boys cursed at the retreating army and hoped for a reaction that might become the occasion for a fight.

I still can't believe it, but I felt rage when a man who saw that I wanted to park my car angrily came up to me and roared,

"Get out of here, get out." We quickly realized that there was absolutely no reason to feel any relief.

Five hours after Martin Luther King's speech, Viola Liuzzo, a mother of five children from Detroit, was shot dead on the same road that we had walked the day before. She was run off the road and peppered with bullets by the Ku Klux Klan. Indignation, anger, fear, and hatred took control of our hearts.

"We're like defenseless foreigners in enemy territory," said a boy from Chicago. "The National Guard is the Ku Klux Klan in uniform, and now they have their chance. Let's get out of here, out of this den of fear and hatred."

"Are you going north?" asked three blacks from Illinois. "Can you take us out of this damn country? We don't have any money and we're scared."

I had lost Charles and hoped that he had found his way back. Nick was busy telephoning his article to Manchester, but he was constantly interrupted by the "operator." The mood was tense, the situation was disorderly and confused. We had to go and we wanted to go. Nick decided to fly back to Yale. He had no more patience for the long drive. Another new friend, Kerley, was worried about his young brother Carlos. "I'll come back to Selma and help, but first I want to take that boy back to Chicago. I don't want anything to happen to him."

In a safe house in Montgomery, where the Freedom poet John Beecher was staying, we studied the map. "This is the shortest route," said Roland, "but let's go back another way . . . not through Mississippi. I won't feel safe until we're out of this blackbelt. Let's drive due north. We can be in Tennessee in six hours, and it's safe there."

I still wasn't convinced, but they were adamant. "Take the main road. The back roads are real dangerous, that's where the three Freedom Riders from Mississippi were killed. I'm not interested in becoming a martyr. I'd rather be a coward than a martyr." "And don't drive in the dark. Please—not in the dark."

That afternoon we drove to Birmingham. The flush of victory had completely dissipated, the exuberance had turned into nervousness and the loud cries into timid murmurs. The songs of "Freedom now" and "We shall overcome" were hidden away, and whenever we sang we first closed the car windows. I don't know if I am exaggerating, I only remember that we were scared, scared to death, and that we shook all over whenever we rode through a city and were wary of every state trooper we saw.

"Watch out, you're driving too fast." Many Freedom Riders who had broken the speed limit had been jailed with fines of $100 to $150, so we had every reason to be careful. "Watch out, you're driving too slow. Pull up along the side of the road and let the whites pass you. They're the only ones who can break the speed limit, and when you go slow it makes them mad."

No matter what I did, there was always danger. "You're not a free man here, and that's all there is to it," said Ronald. I couldn't avoid it. Suddenly I saw a flashing red light that ordered me to stop. I was terrified. "Do you have a driver's license?" asked the state trooper. I showed him my international driver's license with Dutch, English, French, German, and Chinese text. He'd never seen anything like it before. His curiosity weakened him.

"Where do you come from?" From Holland. "My grandmother comes from Holland, too." I realized that I'd never get a ticket now, and I said, "Maybe we're related!" He laughed and said, "Maybe, but drive within the speed limit from now on. You're driving too fast." "I'm sorry," I said. "I'll be careful. There are so many signs here, it's easy to miss one." That was all. With a sigh of relief we drove on to Birmingham.

Ronald's relatives received us like princes, like the liberators of the oppressed. I didn't feel that way, but they did. "You can't keep driving tonight. Sleep here and set out in the morning. That's safer."

The next morning at seven o'clock we found the table laden with riches. We ate well, and then Ronald's old grandmother said, "Let's pray together, that the Lord will protect you on this dangerous road and bring you safely home." And we prayed.

As we were finally approaching the state line, Ronald said, "You know what my philosophy of life is? An old man on the march told me: 'Risk in faith, decide in hope, and suffer the consequences in love.' That's my life. God is with me and now I know it." And when we finally arrived in safe country, he suddenly said, "You know, I think I'll go back next week to help my people. Now they're going to suffer more than ever before."

Nighttime brought Saturday to a close. We said goodbye in St. Louis, Missouri, and I drove on alone through the darkness to Kansas City and Topeka. I knew that that week had touched my soul far more than one year of study. And as my car sped through the night, I felt a newfound joy.

Deep in my heart, I do believe, we shall overcome some day.

8

Were You There?

The Death of Martin Luther King, Jr., 1968

"Did you hear the news? They shot Martin Luther King."

It was 7:15 P.M. Thursday night, April 4, 1968. We were driving over the Kennedy Expressway leading into Chicago's Loop.

"You mean someone killed him?"

"They didn't say. All they said on the radio was that he was shot." The traffic was dense. More cars were leaving the city than entering it. It was getting dark. The high-rise buildings celebrated the approaching night like huge Christmas trees covered with millions of flickering lights and as we turned onto Lake Shore Drive, the city revealed itself as a splendid stage on which the great show could start any moment. The conversation drifted aimlessly from one topic to the other, afraid for a fatal certainty. We didn't know each other. He had picked me up at O'Hare Airport to bring me to a place where I was supposed to give a lecture on religious development. The car now zoomed faster and faster on the six-lane highway, diving under many overpasses and catching the green lights at the last minute. "We are lucky," he said, "We will be home in a minute."

His wife opened the door. "Did you hear anything more?" he asked. "Yes—he is dead." There were candles on the table tastefully arranged for a special dinner. As I took off my coat I saw a black woman sitting in the small kitchen listening to the radio. I said, "Hello." She smiled, glowed a little and said, "Hello Sir."

She didn't cry. She just listened as if the reporter had told her what she had already known for centuries. Should I say something to her? "He was killed by a white man, that is all they know," someone said. The woman in the kitchen sitting on the small wooden stool with her hands folded in her lap seemed the only one who understood. She was calm. She didn't ask for a word of consolation. She had to prepare a meal and to finish her work. Her silence said, "Why are you so upset? Are you strangers in this world?" She didn't accuse. She served the meal, received her money, and left saying: "Good night everybody, goodnight."

At the lecture everybody was friendly. There were many kinds of drinks and many kinds of food. Young charming people, a community of friends, vital, vibrant, and curious. We talked and talked. Many questions, many answers. What does faith really mean? What makes a Christian different from others? How should you educate children in religion? Words, concepts, and ideas were tossed around, thrown in different directions and played back and forth with intelligence and humor.

Martin Luther King was dead. Everybody knew it but nobody wanted to know it. Not yet at least. It was a cruel but unavoidable delay of grief which concealed under its cover all the possibilities of destruction, despair, and undirected anger. And while the rain of words and arguments provided a poor curtain to shield the raw sorrow, there was a cloud over the evening and a false tone in the laughter. But there was hardly an alternative. How often can we allow ourselves to be shocked, thrown off balance, and immersed in misery? We are surrounded by a war burning thousands of people alive, by prisons pervaded by unknown hatred and cruelties, by houses filled with poverty and misery. How much can a person allow himself to know? So the party went on and the subject was religion. We drank a lot of beer, talked about God and God's ways, and sipped coffee for a safe trip home.

The next morning I flew to Kansas City, surrounded by a horrifying world of artificiality. The Braniff airplane was painted orange. The stewardesses, dressed like exotic clowns in blue, purple, and gold, handed out to the few people, hardly awake in the early morning, superfluous pamphlets, superfluous food, and superfluous compliments. "We all hope you have a pleasant flight with Braniff and should we displease you by an unfortunate delay we will give you a dollar with which you can buy a drink on one of our other flights." The passengers didn't pay attention. They kept staring at their *Chicago Sun Times* with the fat words printed across the front page, "KING SLAIN IN MEMPHIS, TENNESSEE," trying to understand what was going on in this circus of confusing madness.

As I drove from Kansas City to Topeka, the reality slowly mastered my awareness. We were killing our prophets and confronted with the bottomless wickedness of our own sins. Between the hollow voices of those who tried to advertise their latest product, it became clear that violence was cutting through the thresholds of restraint. Chicago and Washington were burning cities and the leaders were concerned with only one thing: law and order. The repeated reassurance that the police were close to finding the murderer helped to minimize this human tragedy to the single act of a foolish man. "A senseless and useless act," the governor of Alabama declared. But the old spiritual raised again its loaded question: "Were you there when they crucified my Lord?"

The people who kill their leaders are deaf and blind and terribly afraid to bow their heads and look in the poisoned corners of their hearts. The many discussions triggered by this tragic murder kept us away from the only response: penance and reconciliation. In the early Friday morning of April 5th, one Topekan said to the other, "Finally they got him, the troublemaker, and I hope that Stokely [Carmichael] will be the next." "He always wanted to be a martyr, at least he got what he asked for," someone else said. Topeka seemed a cool and indifferent city, shrugging its shoulders and going back to work as if nothing had happened. While the radio, TV, and newspapers fed the growing feeling that we had brought ourselves to the edge of a ravine, nobody offered a way of directing that feeling into creative channels. Two hundred people came to the Capitol for a memorial service and only the rabbi seemed to be sensitive to the powerless grief of his audience. The priest and minister showed fear.

"Let us follow his example and refrain from violence. Let us keep order and go back to work and fulfill our daily duty." The white Jew understood. The white Christians remained closed to the new warning. Except for a short formal letter of condolence by the bishop, to be read from the pulpit on Sunday, there was no sign of grief or penance. I said to a priest, "I guess you had a special service for Dr. King this morning at your high school." His eyes were dull. "Sure, we had Mass this morning," he replied, "which is what we have every morning."

On Monday I drove back to Kansas City, feeling like a man who refrains from crying only because there is nobody to receive his tears. Someone had blown a horn and called for peace but few had moved and followed the call. Lent had come. The dogwoods showed their white blossoms as signs of a new life. The Kansas fields were green again and the hills covered with many colors, but the heart of humanity was hardened, grimacing with the sour joy that the restless voice pounding on the doors of conscience had finally been silenced and everybody was the same again. Just another spring.

A side road led to Fort Leavenworth where I talked with a nineteen-year-old boy who did not believe in war. For the past ten months he had lived behind bars and this had only strengthened his conviction that he could never go to war. His small and sharp face, his smiling eyes and thick hands contrasted with his green prisoner's uniform, the heavy walls and militant atmosphere in which he found himself. All he could talk about was Dr. King. "When they heard that he was dead, they doubled the guards," he said, "They did not understand that we were just crying, my Afro-American friends and me.

"Violence and revolt were not in our hearts," he continued. "We were paralyzed, shocked, disarmed, hopeless and sad. But we felt more together than we ever did. This is not a community, but when he died we came together. How different we might be. He brought us together, at least for a while. They doubled the number of guards. They were scared. They did not understand. I was wondering lately if nonviolence is a real possibility for me. I started to doubt. My friends had been trying to convince me that

I was wrong. Revolution seemed the only way. But now I've found my faith again. His death made me believe again. I know I have to be here and stay here as long as they want me to go to war. We all started seeing what he meant with nonviolence. He knew that he had to give his life for it. But he also knew that it was the only way."

As I listened to the words of this young man, I smiled. Pilate sent extra guards to the tomb, but he didn't know that he was making a fool of himself. We still don't understand. "Few of us go to church or belong to any religion," my young friend continued, "but yesterday we all went for Dr. King. We all wanted to pay our respects and pray. But the priest didn't mention his name. One of us stood up in the middle of the service and said, 'Ain't you going to tell us about him? That is why we are here!' The priest gazed at him somewhat amazed and said, 'I was not planning on it. This is just a regular Sunday Mass.' Then one prisoner left the chapel and many followed him and when the Mass was over the priest said: 'It was better they left. They are not Christians anyhow.'"

After these hours which seemed more like time spent with a Trappist monk than with a prisoner, I was swallowed up again by the raging traffic on the many highways crossing over the Kansas and Missouri Rivers and plunging into the heart of Kansas City. Surrounded by the hundreds of nervous people trying to catch planes and the carefully rehearsed friendliness of the airline personnel, I forgot for a moment that Dr. King was really dead until the empty halls of O'Hare Airport at the midnight hour hit me like a macabre mausoleum.

There was an empty seat left on the night plane to Atlanta and I knew that I had to go. During the last four days, the sorrow and sadness, the anger and madness, the pains and frustrations had crawled out of the many hidden corners of my body and spread all over like a growing disease of restlessness, tension, and bitterness. I had been fighting it all the way, but now it was clear that only his own people could cure me. Only in the anonymity of their crying, shouting, marching, and singing would I be able to meet the man of Selma again and find some rest.

It was two o'clock in the morning now. The inhospitable splendor of the huge airport overwhelmed me. The total lack of intimacy made it impossible to keep the mind at rest and think about anything other than the time of departure. Meanwhile, many people were gathering around the same gate, mainly black people, a few whites, all restlessly pacing the marble floors waiting for the same flight through the night.

On the airplane, I talked softly with a young white man, hardly realizing the great distance we were covering. Chicago, Cincinnati, Atlanta. I noticed that his two books were about existentialism and theology. But he didn't talk about them. He talked about Dr. King. "I believed in what he had to say," he said, "and I just wanted to go to his funeral." Then his thought wandered away to the prisons in which he had lived, the cruelties he had seen, the violent madness of men living together behind bars. He spoke about the tears of grown men, the moments of tenderness in a society of hatred. "I believe in nonviolence," he said. "That is why I am here now. But sometimes I wonder if I can keep this faith. Dr. King just tried to take Christ's words seriously. He realized that he had to follow Jesus all the way. All the way. What would happen if we would really just do that? It is a dangerous thing to do. It means not being afraid to die. Death then becomes a small thing. Perhaps unavoidable but not unbearable. Just a narrow gate."

He did not speak dramatically. "What's your profession?" I asked with some hesitation. "Oh, I am just an ordinary cab driver. But from the point of view of a cab driver, there is little hope for this world. What I hear from the back seat of my cab is pitiful. Sex and violence, that seems to be about all people believe in. You must be a little crazy to believe in Martin Luther King, Jr. That is why I'm going to the funeral—to stay that way."

In Atlanta everything was different. A strange lightness contrasted with all my heavy feelings and expectations. No crying or sobbing, but smiles and laughter. No dark suits, but white dresses and colorful hats as if people were on the move to a great festival. Perhaps my doubt at being welcome at the funeral of the black man had made me apprehensive. But there were only friendly questions: "Do you need any help? Transportation, breakfast, a place to stay?" I was puzzled by these open faces. "Here is a pamphlet which tells you about things. Go to that man, he will give you a ride to the church." An old school bus took us into the city. At the Ebenezer church there was a long line of people waiting to pass by the body. In a small old building a lady took my luggage and said, "Just put it here in the closet, so it won't bother you today." Then she added, "Why don't you come in and have some breakfast?" There was some hesitation but the problem, as always, was on my side. I entered a large room where many people were sitting talking with each other, pouring coffee, eating cake, and smiling at me. "Sit down, have some coffee with us." I was the only white man. They asked about me. I asked about them. They had come from many faraway places, traveling in buses and cars for long hours over long miles. They were tired but they didn't show it, dressed in their Sunday best. It was a special occasion in which joy and happiness merged with sadness and distress. Perhaps it had never been different for them. Few days with pure sorrow, few days with pure joy. It was a celebration of life and death at the same time.

Meanwhile, the line grew. We were still four hours away from the funeral service but thousands and thousands started to congregate around the small red-brick church. A black Baptist minister standing beside me in the long line which slowly moved to the entrance of the church spoke about the early days in Atlanta. "I was still in the seminary," he said, "when we started our sit-ins in the restaurants here and I spent a few days with Dr. King in the city jail. We were together, a whole bunch of us, and if it hadn't been for him, it would have been quite different. He was always calm and composed. We prayed together, sang together, and talked together. Thanks to Jack Kennedy, we suddenly got out of jail. He was running for President and he set us free."

I listened to him and did not understand why he was standing with me in this long line. Why wasn't he in the front row of the church as a special guest of honor? But then I knew that thousands in these lines were like him. "He knew that he was going to die soon," the minister said. "Death didn't mean so much for him. He knew it from the beginning. When I was sitting at the counter with him and the man came in with his revolver I knew that anything could happen. I was afraid, sure, but then, it didn't matter that much." He talked easily and freely but suddenly stretched out his arms in amazement, looked at me and said, "Think of it, think of it! Is there a better way than to die for garbage collectors? He died for the poorest, the lowest of this earth. Think of it! That is what the Lord did." His eyes were wide open and his face shone with happiness and joy.

We had come close to the church entrance, but it was too late. The thousands had multiplied themselves in the last hour and it was hardly possible to move. The doors of the church were closed. I squeezed myself through the crowd and found a place on the small dike opposite the entrance. The sun grew stronger and I was sure that this was going to be a hot day. People stood in the street as far as I could see. There was little order or organization. It seemed that those invited to attend the service would have a hard time reaching the door. "Move back, move back," someone shouted from the roof of a black car stuck in the crowd. "Everybody just move back one step." Then Ralph Abernathy took the microphone and said: "We are here to honor Dr. King. Let us have respect for one another, respect for him. Just move back, move back a step, out of respect for him." The crowd said: "Yes, yes," but there was nowhere to move. Everybody hoped to see the dignitaries who would soon be arriving. "Let us have respect for Dr. King," shouted a heavyset woman, leaning on my shoulders so that she wouldn't slide on the dike. Many agreed with her, but didn't move. "We shall have respect," two men started to sing, to the melody of "We shall overcome." There was much laughter and, within seconds, the new song was taken up by the crowd. "We shall now move back." Everybody joined in and sang, loud and convinced, but nobody moved.

The hours went by slowly. "Did you hear what Wallace said?" someone asked. "He said it was a tragic and senseless act. Yes, that is what he said, whether he meant it or not." People laughed. An older woman said: "Perhaps deep down there is something good in him." "Yes, yes," they said and their attention drifted to the front of the church. Suddenly, people were applauding. "It is Mahalia," someone cried. "Yes, Mahalia," and they applauded. "Look! there is Jackie!" "Where? Where? I can't see her!" Mrs. Kennedy was caught in the crowd and could hardly reach the door, but the people on the dike caught a glimpse of her when she came to the steps of the church. Meanwhile, Eugene McCarthy, Richard Nixon, and Nelson Rockefeller tried to find their way to the church. When Bobby Kennedy tried to enter, the thousands could not restrain their emotions. They shouted, clapped, and applauded him as he moved slowly through the crowd.

Then there was silence. A moment of quiet silence. "The family," my neighbor whispered. Mrs. King and her children together with other members of the family came to the church. The crowd watched curiously but silently. "The family," many said to themselves with a certain awe. "The family." Everybody knew that now the service would begin.

The helicopters roaring above the church made it impossible to follow much of what came to us through the loudspeakers. It was long and hot and tiresome. I thought about those sitting in front of the TVs able to see every moment of this historical service but then I felt it was better to be on this dike, sweating and listening and waiting for the march to start.

His last march. Everybody knew it. This was what they had come for, to march with him once more. They had marched in Birmingham, Selma, Montgomery, Chicago, Memphis and many other places. He was their leader. Marching through cities, marching through fields, marching over highways and sideroads. Marching through the desert to Jerusalem, to the top of the mountain, to the promised land. "We're going to march, when the Spirit says 'March,'" we sang. "When the Spirit says 'March' we're going to march. Yes, Yes." That was the new song in Alabama and King had been their leader. But there was something strange about his last march, something new. There was no fear. There were no angry people on the sidewalks ready to throw stones. This was a victory march, a march for him who had reached the mountain top.

The two mules slowly pulled the old wooden wagon with the casket. One of King's aides, dressed in blue jeans, guided the mules through the city. Mrs. King and the children followed. I could see the little daughter dressed like a bridesmaid holding her mother's hand, walking the long hot tiring miles through the awesome city. And behind them the long river of people, hand in hand, arm in arm, coming like endless curling waves through the wide avenues of the city.

When I looked back over the mile of people behind me, I had the feeling that there was no end to this victory march, no end to the stream of people singing the same song again and again. "We shall overcome.... We are not afraid.... Black and white together...." A black preacher gave me his arm and asked me to join him in song, and we pulled each other forward over the long road out of the city into the quiet gardens of Morehouse Seminary.

There I sat in the grass, too tired to watch what went on at the rostrum. Many words, many songs, many exclamations. Too much to absorb and understand. I wanted to be alone. Sitting on the ground surrounded by the countless people standing around me, I felt safe and protected. A black man smiled at me when I woke up from a deep sleep. I felt exhausted, hungry, and heavy. The long hot day had burned me and the final march had broken me. But a strange satisfaction went through my body. This was where I wanted to be: hidden, anonymous, surrounded by black people. It had been a long restless trip since that Thursday night. Nervous, frantic, yearning, filled with anger, grief and frustration. It had led me to Morehouse. And here I rested, carried by people who kept on singing and praying, and I knew that out of my exhaustion, a new faith could grow, a faith in the possibility of nonviolent love. And while they carried away his body and started to move away from me, I felt a new joy, reassured that tomorrow was a new day with a new promise.

III

The Cry of the Poor
in Central
and South America

9

Christ of the Americas

When I came to the United States in 1971, not for a visit, a course, or a sabbatical, but to make my home here, I had an intuition that would grow stronger as the years went by. The intuition was that the spiritual destiny of North America is intimately linked to the spiritual destiny of South America. Somehow I sensed that in order to come to know the living Christ among the people in the northern part of the Americas I had to be willing to expose myself to the way the living Christ reveals himself in the southern part of the Americas. This intuition at first was very vague and even seemed somewhat far-fetched, but it was strong enough to make me spend summers in Bolivia and Paraguay and familiarize myself increasingly with the language and the life of the Latin American people. During the 1970s I started to explore more and more the ways in which North and South were interconnected, not just in socioeconomic and political ways but also—and even more so—in spiritual ways.

Could it be possible that the pain and struggles of the North American people are an intimate part of the pains and struggles of the people of South America? Could it be said that the experience of loneliness, guilt, shame, and disconnectedness that I had shared so fully with the students I taught at universities in the United States cannot be fully understood without the experience of poverty, oppression, and exploitation that I came to know in Latin American cities? Could it even be true that underneath all the political and socioeconomic dependencies that have been so powerfully described by contemporary historians there is a deeper spiritual dependency the nature of which we have hardly explored?

These questions have been with me during the last ten years, though I have hardly had words for them. When, however, I went to Central America and witnessed the immense agony of people there, these questions suddenly became burning questions asking for an immediate response. In Central America, that inflamed cord binding the two continents together, my hesitant intuition became an undeniable vision, the vision of the living Christ stretched out on the cross of the American continents from five centuries of human unfaithfulness. I came to realize that the word of Jesus had come to Central America during the end of the fifteenth and the beginning of the sixteenth century and had spread north and south over the continents. I came to see that the word was a word of reconciliation, unity and peace, a word that wanted to become flesh in human history. I came to understand that this living word of Jesus wanted to form one body of people bound together by a love stronger and deeper than the fear that divides races, cultures, and nations. And I came to the painful insight that the word has not been received but is being tortured and broken by the same people who are called to witness to its reconciling power. Christians are imprisoning Christians, Christians are torturing Christians, Christians are murdering Christians, and an immense darkness covers the world in which the incarnate Word is dying again.

When I saw that divine event taking place, I knew that indeed the suffering Christ of North America and the suffering Christ of South America are one. They cannot be separated or divided without reenacting the crucifixion over and over again. Jesus Christ is not just a historical person who died long ago outside the walls of Jerusalem and whose life we remember as a source of inspiration for us. Jesus Christ is the Lord of history whose death, resurrection and coming in judgment is the deepest and most revealing event of our own daily history. As Christians, we are challenged to recognize that the tragic political, economic, and military events that we are living today are the symptoms of a spiritual event of which we are part. We are challenged to manifest to the world that Christ is dying among us, that Christ is being raised up among us, that Christ is coming again and again in judgment among us. It is this divine knowledge that allows us to see what is really happening, to continue to have hope even when we see death and destruction, and to recognize the concrete task that this vision reveals to us. Thus we may slowly grow in the understanding of the mysterious spiritual connection between the continents and find new ways to live as people of light in the midst of an ever-deepening darkness.

Let me therefore try, though with much trepidation, to speak about Central America with the words that summarize the mystery of our human pilgrimage: Christ has died, Christ is risen, Christ will come again.

CHRIST HAS DIED

The Word of the living God, in and through whom all have been created, became flesh in Jesus Christ who died for us humans so that we may have life everlasting. This central affirmation of the Christian faith has profound implications for the way we understand and relate to the agonies of the Americas. When we say "Christ has died," we express the truth that all human suffering in all times and places has been suffered by the Son of God who also is the Son of all humanity and thus has been lifted up into the inner life of God. There is no suffering—no guilt, shame, loneliness, hunger, oppression, or exploitation, no torture, imprisonment or murder, no violence or nuclear threat—that has not been suffered by God. There can be no human beings who are completely alone in their sufferings since God, in and through Jesus, has become Emmanuel, God with us. It belongs to the center of our faith that God is a faithful God, a God who did not want us to ever be alone but who wanted to understand— to stand under—all that is human. The Good News of the Gospel, therefore, is not that God came to take our suffering away, but that God wanted to become part of it.

All of this has been said often before, but maybe not in a way that makes a direct connection with the agony of the world that we witness today. We have to come to the inner knowledge that the agony of the world is God's agony. The agony of women, men, and children across the ages reveals to us the inexhaustible depth of God's agony that we glimpsed in the garden of Gethsemane. The deepest meaning of human history is the gradual unfolding of the suffering of Christ. As long as there is human history, the story of Christ's suffering has not yet been fully told. Every time we hear more about the way human beings are in pain, we come to know more about the immensity of the love of God, who did not want to exclude anything human from his experience of being God. God indeed is Yahweh Rachamin, the God who carries suffering people in her womb with the intimacy and care of a mother. This is what Blaise Pascal alluded to when he wrote that Christ is in agony until the end of time.

The more we try to enter into this mystery, the more we will come to see the suffering world as a world hidden in God. Outside of God human suffering is not only unbearable but cannot even be faced. Understandably, many people say, "I have enough problems of my own; do not bother me with the problems of the world. Just making it from day to day in my family, my town, my work is enough of a burden. Please do not plague me with the burdens of people in Central America or other places. They only make me feel more angry, more guilty, and more powerless." Outside of God even small burdens can pull us down and destroy our physical, emotional, and spiritual health. Outside of God burdens are to be avoided at all cost. Seeing people's misery and pain outside of God becomes a burden too heavy to carry and makes us feel darkness inside.

But when we come to know the inner connectedness between the world's pain and God's pain, everything becomes radically different. Then we see that in and through Jesus Christ God has lifted up all human burdens into his own interiority and made them the way to recognize his immense love. Jesus says, "My yoke is easy and my burden light," but Jesus' burden is the burden of all humankind. When we are invited to carry this burden of Jesus, we are invited to carry the burden of the world. The great mystery is that this very burden is a light burden since it is the burden that makes known to us the unlimited love of God.

Here we touch the spiritual dimension of all social concern. The hunger of the poor, the torture of prisoners, the threat of war in many countries, and the immense human suffering we hear about from all directions can only call us to a deeply human response if we are willing to see in the brokenness of our fellow human beings the brokenness of God, because God's brokenness does not repulse. It attracts by revealing the loving face of the One who came to carry our burden and to set us free. Seeing the agony of the people then becomes the way of coming to know the love of God, a love that reconciles, heals, and unites.

One of the most remarkable—and disturbing—aspects of our relationship with the people of South and Central America is that we know so little about them. It seems that we feel closer to the people of Europe than to those who live below our southern border. Few North Americans know where Honduras, El Salvador, Guatemala, Nicaragua, and Costa Rica are located. It might even be easier for us to draw a map of Europe than a map of Central or South America. And who knows much about the long and often torturous history of its peoples? It seems that we are afraid to pay attention to their struggles, vaguely realizing that when we start connecting our lives with their lives, our lives cannot remain the same.

And still the peoples of Central and South America are our brothers and sisters who belong to the same body of Christ we do. That bond can help us overcome our fears and face each other as members of the same family who need each other. It is the bond of word and baptism by which we are united in the same Lord who allows us to let down our defenses and reach out to each other. We have to come to know each other, not just in general terms but in the concrete context of our daily lives. We have to come to know each other's names, each other's families, each other's work, and—most of all—each other's hopes. So much violence comes from fear, and so much fear is the tragic result of the artificial distance we have kept between us. "Do not fear; it is I," Jesus said. That means that we will meet the Lord of love when we let go of our fears and look each other in the eye, take each other's hands, and carry each other's burdens.

Once we know that we can come together without fear, we can enter into each other's pain and grow together—even where many problems remain unsolved and many questions unanswered. The complexity of the situation in Central America is often a reason for us not to become involved and to withdraw behind the misleading slogans of Communism, Marxism, imperialism, democracy, and free enterprise. These words mostly hide the concrete reality of the human struggle and offer us an easy way out. But as a people of God we are called to stay close to one another and to travel together, even though we might be unable fully to grasp or comprehend the situation in which we find ourselves.

THE NICARAGUAN CHURCH

For me personally, one of the most difficult challenges in Central America was to face the divisions within the church. When I went to Nicaragua, I had hoped to find a Christian community that could speak clearly and unambiguously the Word of God and thus be a true sign of hope in the midst of the struggle of the Nicaraguan people to find a new national identity. To come to the awareness that the words "Christ has died" refer not only to the physical and emotional pains of the people, but also to the divisions among the Christian communities was extremely painful for me. The Word of God was clearly torn and the body of Christ tortured by dissent and conflict among its members. But I knew that I had to dare to face this even though it might shake the foundations of my own faith and hope.

One Sunday I attended three different Catholic services. The same Gospel was being proclaimed and the same Eucharist was being celebrated, but there was no unity among them. It seems that the Word of God meant totally different things at each place.

At 8 A.M. I went to a church where I found some poor people, mostly elderly, gathered around the altar. After reading the Gospel the priest said, "Dear brothers and sisters in Christ, four years ago you had no voice. Four years ago nobody paid any attention to you. Four years ago you couldn't write or read. Four years ago you were afraid that the national guard of Somoza would suddenly appear to kill and destroy. Four years ago you felt like slaves without any freedom of word or action. But now you have a voice. Since the triumph of the revolution you have become people whose experience and opinion count in the making of a new future. Now you can read and write, now you can walk without fear on the streets of Managua, now you have a new-found freedom. You no longer are like the Israelites in Egypt. You have been led out of Egypt and are on the way to the promised land. And I'd like you to realize that as Christians we have a new opportunity to come to know more fully what it means to live a Christian life. There is no contradiction between the revolution and Christianity. The revolution makes it possible to become better Christians who can claim their human dignity and fully express the gifts God has given them. Let us therefore work together with all those who want to make our land a free land, a land that can determine its own destiny and its own course. We do not have to hesitate because God is with us in this new and exciting journey."

At 10 A.M. I went to another church very close to the one I had just attended. This church was beautifully decorated. There were many people, young and old, mostly families who looked as if they belonged to the middle and upper classes of Nicaraguan society. After the priest had read the Gospel he said, "If you think that you can truly love God without obeying your bishop, you fool yourselves. Those people of the so-called popular church or the so-called base communities who think they can be Christians of the revolution do not understand that the Sandinista regime is not at all interested in their religion, but only uses it for its own political interests. Anyone who has read Karl Marx knows that during the first phase of a leftist revolution there is always a certain tolerance toward Christianity. But when the second phase starts it aims at the establishment of an atheistic society. As a priest who has fought Communism all his life, I am willing to protest loudly and clearly together with our bishops against the atheistic and totalitarian regime that wants to destroy our church and persecute its leaders and its members. I am willing to give my life in the struggle against the Communist regime that increasingly robs us of our freedom. Because I know that when those Christians of the revolution appear before the throne of God on the day of judgment, the Lord will say to them, 'I don't know you,' and he will send them to eternal fire."

After the Mass I asked the priest if I could talk with him. He welcomed me into his house and spoke to me openly and freely. There was little doubt in my mind that he was as sincere in his convictions as the priest I had heard at the earlier Mass.

Finally, at 5 P.M., I attended a Eucharistic celebration held by a group of small Christian base communities. During the dialogue homily one of the women stood up and said, "Do you remember how four years ago we all thought that now the good time had come? Do you remember that we expected enough food for all, a good job, a decent house, and our own plot of land? Do you remember how we all had fantasies about an ideal country with an ideal government? But today, four years later, there are long lines of people waiting for bread, there are many unemployed people, there are only a few of us who have a good house to live in or a good piece of land to work on. Things did not work out as smoothly as we had hoped. Our government made more mistakes and our people became more divided than we had expected. But, brothers and sisters, let us not fall into the temptation of wanting to return to the time of slavery and oppression. Let us not be seduced by the fleshpots of Egypt, saying 'Under Somoza we at least had enough to eat!' Although we have not yet reached the promised land, we are no longer in Egypt. We have left the land of oppression and exploitation and are now together in the desert, tempted to become morose and even resentful. But let us realize that we are moving toward something new and that we need patience and perseverance to let it become true. Let us not look back, but forward, trusting that what we have begun will come to its fulfillment one day."

When I went home that night after having heard these three sermons, I felt confused and very sad. Three times I had heard the word of God, but it sounded like words from three different gods. Whom to believe, whom to trust, whom to learn from? In the following days I listened to many more people—not only priests but also Protestant ministers, leaders in the government, leaders in the church, people in the marketplace and working on the tobacco farms. And when I returned to the United States, I spoke there to three senators, to representatives, lobbyists, and many American citizens belonging to different churches, living in different states, and coming from different backgrounds. But the same questions kept returning: Whom to believe, whom to trust, whom to learn from? Some say, "What is happening in Nicaragua is nationalism: it is a country trying to determine its own future." Others say, "No, it's internationalism: it is a country becoming the victim of Cuban-Soviet domination." Some say "What you see in Nicaragua is the best example of a revolution in which Christian values are truly integrated." Others say, "No, it is a revolution based on atheistic principles and bent on the eradication of all religious beliefs." Some say, "What Nicaragua is trying to accomplish is a socialistic society in which all the people can equally enjoy the fruits of the land and the products of human labor." Others say, "No, Nicaragua is gradually becoming the subject of a totalitarian regime in which the state will control every part of life and in which even the little bit of freedom that existed under Somoza will be taken away."

And so we see words being used in many different ways, whether in the government, the church, or the marketplace. My first inclination was to make up my mind quickly and choose sides. But who am I to take sides, I who am a stranger in a land whose history I have not lived and whose people I hardly know? There is a great attraction to solving ambiguities by quickly taking one side or the other. But this type of solution, while giving a sense of security, might become the fertile ground for more conflict and violence. In order to prevent myself from moving in that direction, I had to remind myself constantly that underneath those conflicting political and socioeconomic evaluations it was being made clear to me that Christ was dying among his people. I had to hold on to the truth that the tearing apart of the Word outside as well as inside the church was the bitter fruit of five centuries of unfaithfulness. The poverty and oppression that gave rise to the revolution in Nicaragua, as well as the way the powerful nation of the North responded to that revolution, show in a dramatic way that "He came to his own domain and his own people did not accept him" (Jn 1:11).

The increasing tensions and the rapid escalation of war and violence in Central America have to be understood in terms that range far beyond the discussion that takes place in the circles of psychologists, sociologists, historians, economists, and politicians. Their arguments are valuable and important, but for those who have eyes to see and ears to hear, something is taking place the dimensions of which can be perceived only by people of faith. And for them there is a call, not first of all to solve all ambiguities but rather to stand in the midst of them and become part of the suffering of the living Christ, a suffering that leads to salvation. Maybe after all is said the real question for us is not what to do about it all but how to repent for the sins that led to the crucifixion of the Lord who came to bring life.

CHRIST IS RISEN

Can we face the death of Christ without knowing about his resurrection? The Good News of the Gospel is that the death of Christ was the gateway to new life. I think that the story of Christ's death can be told as a story of hope only by those whose faith is deeply anchored in his resurrection. Just as sin can be truly known to us only in the light of forgiving grace, so death can be faced squarely only in the light of the new life to which it leads. This is important to realize when we want to see not only the death but also the resurrection of Christ as part of the historical reality in which we live. Maybe we have to say that only in the context of the new life that we see being born out of human agonies are we able to face these very agonies. I say this to suggest that all that I wrote in the previous section somehow presupposes what I will write in this section. Just as the story of Christ's death was written after the knowledge of his resurrection, so too were the previous thoughts only possible in the light of the following.

"Christ is risen" means that guilt, loneliness, hunger, poverty, war, and devastation no longer have the last word. Death and all its symptoms in our individual and communal lives are not the final reality any more. This has been stated many times in many ways, but one of our greatest challenges is to affirm it in our concrete life situation. The constant temptation is to experience a concrete appearance of the power of death as too much to resist and look beyond. Depression, resentment, revenge, and hatred are all forms of surrender to the power of death and signs of our inability to see that, in and through Christ, death has lost its final power.

When it comes to the nitty-gritty of daily life, it is very, very hard to believe that the "sting" has been taken out of death. When your child dies from a sudden illness, when you lose a dear friend in an accident, when your job and your source of income are taken away from you, when you feel you have no support from anyone, when your son is kidnapped or your husband tortured or your friends killed, when an earthquake destroys all you had carefully built, when you are surrounded by constant threats on your life, when everyone around you wonders if this world will still be here when the year 2000 comes—when any of these or other death situations arise, it is very hard not to be seduced by their darkness and not to surrender to the despair they bring. From a certain distance it sometimes seems easy to speak about hope when we hear or read about death and destruction, but when we ourselves experience the power of death right where we are, it seems close to impossible to call death powerless and to perceive it as a gateway to new life. The feeling of doom that haunts so many people today reminds us of how hard it is to say: "Death no longer has the final word."

And still, that is precisely what the Christ event is all about. Our Lord who died on the cross has overcome death, has conquered the evil one, and has triumphed over the powers of this world. There is no power of death, not even a nuclear holocaust, that has not been conquered in the resurrection of Christ. Just as there is no human suffering that has not been lifted up into the intimate life of God through the death of Christ, so there is no human suffering that has not been overcome in his resurrection. "Jesus Christ overcame death when he rose from the grave" is not just a statement about a past event. It is also a statement about the life of the Christian community as the living body of Christ saying: "Jesus is being raised up among us." When we recognize that Christ is dying among us on the cross of the continents, we have seen at least a glimpse of the new life his death brings among us. The great mystery of the presence of Christ among the people is that it is a life-giving presence that continues to become visible in the most horrendous death situations. Something totally new is being born among the suffering and dying people in Central and South America, and it is that new life that is being given to us for our conversion.

I would never have been able to say this with such confidence if I had not witnessed the presence of the risen Lord among the suffering people of Nicaragua. It was, in fact, a very concrete event on the border between Nicaragua and Honduras that made it possible for me to say: "Christ is risen. He is risen indeed." I even dare to say that what I saw and heard there was the most revealing experience of my visit to Central America, an experience so deep and powerful that it gave me the strength and courage to return to the United States and call Christians here to a new task of peacemaking.

With 150 North Americans I went to Jalapa, a small Nicaraguan town very close to the Honduran border. Jalapa had been the victim of many attacks by the U.S.-backed counter-revolutionaries (the contras) who have their camps in the southern part of Honduras and regularly enter Nicaragua with the purpose of establishing a bridgehead there and gradually undermining the Sandinista regime. During the month prior to our visit, many people in the Jalapa area had suffered severely from these hostilities. This was the reason we wanted to go there. We wanted to have some first-hand experience of the war going on at the border between Honduras and Nicaragua and pray for peace with the people who suffered because of the war.

I vividly remember how during the prayer vigil five Nic-araguan women joined us. They stood very close to one another and quietly spoke to a group of about twenty North Americans. It was an intimate gathering of the people huddling together and trying to understand one another. One of the women raised her voice and said, "A few months ago the counter-revolutionaries kidnapped my seventeen-year-old son and took him to Honduras. I have never heard from him since, and lie awake during the night wondering if I will ever see him again."

Then another woman spoke: "I had two boys and they both have been killed during the last year. When I grieve and mourn, I grieve and mourn not only because they have been killed but also because those who killed them dismembered their bodies and threw the parts over the fields so that I could not even give them a decent burial."

Then the third woman spoke: "I had just been married and my husband was working in the fields. Suddenly the contras ap-peared. They burned the harvest, killed my husband, and took his body away. I have never found his body."

There was a long and painful silence. Out of that silence a voice was heard. One of the Nicaraguan women said, "Do you know that we found U.S.-made weapons in our fields? Do you realize that your government paid for the violence that is taking place here? Are you aware that our children and husbands are being killed because your people make it possible by their sup-port? Directly or indirectly, willingly or unwillingly, you are causing our agony. Why? What have we done to deserve this? What did we do to you, your people, or your country to be sub-jected to so much hostility, anger, and revenge?"

For a long time no one said a word. What could be said? But then a question came from us that sounded like a prayer. Some-one quietly asked, "Do you think you can forgive us? Do you think it is possible for you to speak a word of forgiveness?" I saw how one of the women turned to the others and softly said, "We should forgive them." She then turned to us, looking us in the eye, and said clearly: "Yes, we forgive you." But it seemed that we could not yet fully hear it.

Someone else said, "Do you really forgive us for all the sorrow and the pain we have brought to your village and your people?" And the women said, "Yes, we forgive you." Another voice spoke: "Do you truly forgive us for killing your husbands and children?" And the women said, "Yes, we forgive you." And there was another voice, "Do you also forgive us for all the fear and agony we have brought to your homes?" And the women said, "Yes, we forgive you." And, as if we still were not hearing it fully, another begging question was heard, "But do you forgive us too for the many times we have invaded your country in the past and for the fact that we have made you subject to our decisions and rules for most of this century?" And again the women said, "Yes, we forgive you."

Suddenly I realized that I was being lifted up in this litany of forgiveness: "Do you forgive us?" "Yes, we forgive you." "Do you forgive us?" "Yes, we forgive you." As this prayer was going on, it was as if I could see for a moment that the broken heart of the dying Christ, stretched out on the cross of the Americas, was being healed. The five women appeared as representatives of all the men, women, and children of Central and South America. Their voices were like the voices of millions of people who had suffered during the last five centuries, bringing all the agonies of poverty and oppression together and lifting them up to us. They opened our eyes to the immense suffering that is being experienced by the poor of our countries and said, "Do not be afraid to look at it. We show it to you, not to make you feel guilty or ashamed, but to let you see the immensity of God's forgiveness." The five women of Jalapa are the women standing under the cross. They speak for us that divine prayer: "Father, forgive them; they do not know what they are doing" (Lk 23:34). They are the voices of the dying Christ speaking of new life being born in suffering.

No hatred, no revenge, no lashing out in anger, but repeated words of forgiveness that create unity and community. As these words were spoken, the women of Nicaragua and the men and women of North America became one people. They embraced one another, cried together, and said over and over again, "Peace,

peace, peace be with you." As this was taking place, I and many of us had a glimpse of the resurrection. The risen Christ, the Christ who came to take our sins away by his death, rose to make us into a new body, a new community, a new fellowship, a church. When the North Americans and Nicaraguans became one, they revealed that the power of divine love is stronger than death and reaches far beyond ethnic, national, or cultural boundaries. The forgiveness of the women of Jalapa, offered to us as the fruit of their suffering, gave us a vision of the unity that God's Word came to bring us.

At that moment we saw again that the sting has been taken out of death and that Christ indeed is victorious over the power of evil. It is the vision of the risen Christ emerging in the midst of human suffering. Precisely at the moment that we saw human agony as we had never seen it before, the light of God's forgiveness was revealed to us. Precisely when we touched the deepest human sorrow, a moment of gladness became visible. Precisely when we were most tempted to despair, words of hope were being spoken. That is the mystery of the resurrection. "I tell you most solemnly you will be weeping and wailing while the world will rejoice; you will be sorrowful but your sorrow will turn to joy....I have told you this so that you may find peace in me. In the world you will have trouble, but be brave: I have conquered the world" (Jn 16:20, 33).

Here all the ambiguities vanish. While I felt called to life in the midst of the diverse opinions, convictions, and evaluations concerning the political events in Central America and suffered the ambiguities as part of the dying of Christ, I realized in Jalapa that there is an undeniable clarity arising out of the ambiguities. It is the clarity of the risen Christ who is the Lord of life and who reaffirms in his resurrection that God is a God, not of the dead, but of the living. I might not be able to have a final word about the meaning and direction of the revolution in Nicaragua. But I do have a final word about the U.S. intervention in that country, because the forgiveness of the Nicaraguan women who had been victims of U.S.-supported violence and murder made our sins undeniably manifest.

What the U.S. government and, indirectly, the U.S. people are doing is unjust, illegal, and immoral. It is unjust because we intervene in a country that in no way threatens us; it is illegal because we break every existing international law against intervention in an autonomous country; and it is immoral because we inflict destruction, torture, and death on innocent people. As Christians we should have no doubts or hesitations in protesting clearly and loudly against any form, covert or overt, of U.S. intervention in Nicaragua. "Christ is risen" means that Christians are a people of reconciliation, not of division; people who heal, not hurt; people of forgiveness, not of revenge; people of love, not of hate; in short, people of life, not of death.

When I heard the words of forgiveness spoken by the five Nicaraguan women in Jalapa, my paralysis about how to speak about Central America was gone. I knew that these women had empowered me to return to my people and to call them in the name of the risen Christ to their task of peacemaking. I could do this now, not because I feel guilt-ridden and want to clear my conscience, but because I had heard the words of God's reconciling forgiveness that are words for all the people of North America.

Now I can announce: "Have hope! We have been forgiven. We no longer have to be afraid! We no longer have to hide behind walls stacked with bombs. We no longer have to speak words of suspicion and hatred. We no longer have to prepare ourselves for war. Now the time has come to accept the forgiveness offered to us and realize that we belong to one body. Now the time has come to reach out to our suffering sisters and brothers and to offer food, shelter, and health care. Now the time has come to heal the wounds of centuries and make visible to the whole world that Christ is risen indeed. Let us be peacemakers as we are called to be and thus come to realize that we and all the people of Central and South America belong to the household of God and can indeed be called God's children."

It seems essential that we start realizing that our first task is not to do something for the Central and South American people, not to help them with their problems or assist them in their needs. All of that is very important, but all forms of help become forms of violence when giving does not presuppose receiving. Our first task is to receive from the suffering people the fruits of their suffering. Only then can we truly give.

We need the people of Central and South America as much as they need us. We need one another as much as members of the same body need one another. In the midst of the present international crisis, we are becoming aware in a new way that not just our physical and emotional well-being but also our spiritual destiny—our salvation—cannot be realized without the people of Central and South America. We need them for our salvation. They offer us forgiveness, gratitude, joy, and a profound understanding of life as mature fruits of their struggle for freedom and human dignity. They offer us these fruits for our conversion, so that we too may be saved. By their suffering they have indeed been ordained to be our evangelizers. It may be hard for us to recognize this divine irony by which the oppressed become the healers of the oppressor, but it is this recognition that might be the beginning of our conversion. While it is true that the resurrection of Christ has become manifest in a totally unexpected and new way among our suffering and dying fellow Christians in Central and South America, we will be able to become real witnesses of the resurrection only when we allow these Christians to become our spiritual guides. Then and only then will we be free to help them, not out of obligation, guilt or fear, but out of gratitude for the gifts we already have received. Thus we can become together again one people, the people that manifest the risen Christ to our despairing world.

CHRIST WILL COME AGAIN

The Christ event embraces more than his death and resurrection. It will be complete only when it includes his coming again to judge the living and the dead. Just as Christ's dying and rising refer not only back to past events, so his coming again refers not only to a future event. As Christians, we are called to recognize in the concrete events of our daily lives not only the dying and rising of Christ, but also his coming again.

The coming again of Christ is his coming in judgment. The question that will sound through the heavens and the earth will be the question that we always tend to remain deaf to. Our lives as we live them seem lives that anticipate questions that never will be asked. It seems as if we are getting ourselves ready for the question. "How much did you earn during your lifetime?" or, "How many friends did you make?" or, "How much progress did you make in your career?" or, "How much influence did you have on people?" or, "How many books did you write?" or, "How many conversions did you make?" Were any of these to be the questions Christ will ask when he comes again in glory, many of us in North America could approach the judgment day with great confidence.

But nobody is going to hear any of these questions. The question we all are going to face is the question we are least prepared for. It is the question: "What have you done for the least of mine?"

It is the question of the just judge who in that question reveals to us that making peace and working for justice can never be separated. As long as there are people who are less than we, in whatever way or form, the question of the last judgment will be with us. As long as there are strangers; hungry, naked, and sick people; prisoners, refugees, and slaves; people who are handicapped physically, mentally, or emotionally; people without work, a home, or a piece of land, there will be that haunting question from the throne of judgment: "What have you done for the least of mine?"

The question makes the coming of Christ an ever present event. It challenges us to look at our world agonized by wars and rumors of war and to wonder if we have not fallen into the temptation to think that peace can be separated from justice. But why would there be wars if all people had enough food, enough work, enough land? Why would there be so many guns, tanks, nuclear warheads, submarines, and other instruments of destruction if the world were not divided according to those who have the most, those who have more than enough, those who have just enough, those who have less than enough, and those who have the least?

When we look at the painful struggles of the people in Central and South America, it is not hard to realize who the least are. In most of the countries below our southern border, a very few have the most, and most have the least, and there is little in between. This state of flagrant injustice that causes the oppression and exploitation of many by a few is artificially maintained by the nations in which most people have the most, and a few have the least. "Protecting our vital interest" has become the standard euphemism for maintaining the inequality among people and nations. It also is the main rationale for an international, interlocking military network built on the illusion that an ever-increasing power is the only thing that keeps this world from disintegrating into chaos. Thus the world becomes an absurd world in which every year thousands of people die from hunger and violence, and in which those who cause these deaths are convinced that they do this to defend the great spiritual values of the free world. As Jesus predicted, many will commit crimes thinking that they are doing something virtuous and in the name of God. And as death and destruction increase, there are fewer people who can explain what is happening. Thus the world plunges itself deeper and deeper into absurdity—which literally means "deep deafness"—becoming less and less able to hear the question of the coming Christ, "What have you done for the least of mine?"

It is my impression that most people understand the question of the coming Christ as a question directed to individual people. All through Christian history there have been men and women who have listened with great attentiveness to this question and radically changed their lives in response to it. Many have dedicated their entire lives to working with the poor, the sick, and the dying. Thus we can say that the question of the day of judgment has already borne fruit.

But when we read the twenty-fifth chapter of Matthew's Gospel carefully, it becomes clear that the question of the coming of Christ is not directed to individuals alone but to nations as well. The story of the last judgment opens with the words, "When the Son of Humanity comes in his glory, escorted by all the angels, then he will take his seat on his throne of glory. All nations will be assembled before him" (Mt 25:31-32). These words open a new perspective on the final question: "What have you done for the least of mine?" They make us wonder what it means that we not only will be judged as individuals but as nations as well.

Often it seems that we have heard the invitation of Jesus to be humble, compassionate, and forgiving, to take the last place, to carry our cross and lose our life as an invitation relating to our individual lives, our family lives, or our lives within communities of prayer and service. We even "encourage each other to follow this gentle way of the Lord and praise those who follow the advice always to consider the other person as better than ourselves." (See Philippians 2:3, 4.) But when it comes to the relationships among nations, when we are dealing with decisions that have implications for our nation's role in the world, when we are thinking about our national security and its political ramifications, then we suddenly reverse our attitude completely and consider the Gospel demands as utterly naive. When it comes to politics, power is the issue, and those who suggest that the powerless way of Christ is also the way to which the nations are called find themselves quickly accused as betrayers of their country. As nations—so we hear—we cannot seriously listen to the question, "What have you done for the least of mine?" Looking at small nations struggling to overcome their hunger, thirst, estrangement, nakedness, and imprisonment as the least of our brothers and sisters would require a radical change in the use of power; a change from using power to dominate to using power to serve. Many would consider such a change political suicide.

When Nicaragua, a country of 2.8 million people, threw off the yoke of decades of oppression and tried to determine its own destiny, the powerful nation of the North did not respond by encouraging her sister nation with food, clothes, words of welcome, and friendly visits, but by arrogant rejection, isolation and hostile threats. The United States did not reach out to help one of the least of the nations but soon considered it a potential Soviet missile base that needed to be brought back under absolute control as soon as possible.

The response of the United States toward Nicaragua is the response of a fearful power. Words such as "Marxist-Leninist regime," "Cuban-Soviet domination," and "atheist-totalitarian development" are used to insinuate that a direct danger exists for the safety, security, and well-being of the people of the North. A boycott is organized to prevent Nicaragua from receiving necessary aid and loans, thus paralyzing its economic life. Honduras is turned into a huge military base. The counter-revolutionary forces in Honduras and Costa Rica receive increasing support for their attacks on Nicaragua. Meanwhile, naval forces are sent to the Pacific and Caribbean waters off the Nicaraguan coasts.

Thus a small country of mostly hungry, poor, and oppressed people is being regarded by the most powerful nation of the world as a serious menace to its "vital interest," treated with suspicion, isolated and hated and pushed in a direction that its Northern "masters" feared it would go. Thus the cry of a people asking for the recognition of their human and national dignity is misinterpreted as part of the seduction of a faraway Communist totalitarian state trying to subvert the free democratic state close by. Thus the East-West dimension of the Nicaraguan problem is so stressed and manipulated that the obvious North-South dimension is pushed into the background. Thus the less powerful Southern countries, desiring only to live their own lives, make their own mistakes, and celebrate their own successes, are being cut off by their sister country from the sources that could provide help. Thus the wounds of five centuries of unfaithfulness are torn open and deepened.

The Apostle Paul writes, "In your minds you must be as Christ Jesus. His state was divine, yet he did not cling to his equality with God but emptied himself to assume the condition of a slave and become as we are" (Phil 2:5, 7). Are these words also words for the nations? Is it possible that a nation can become one among the nations as Christ became one among us? If it is true that the question of the returning Christ is also a question for the nations, then that question requires not only an individual but also a national conversion. As long as the overarching goal of the United States is to be at all costs the most powerful nation on earth, we may become the reluctant participants in the hastening of the Judgment Day, since in this nuclear age the cost for remaining the most powerful nation on earth quite likely is the end of all human life on this planet.

Thus we are faced with the greatest spiritual challenge ever presented: to be converted as a nation and follow the humble way of Christ. Is that a possibility? It has become a necessity for our survival. It has become our most urgent task to find our true identity among the nations and to let go of the illusory identities that continue to breed one war after another. The tragedy is that the political discussion among our people and their representatives has been narrowed down so much that no truly political concern can be brought to the foreground without threatening the nation's political survival. When the main question has become, "Should the Sandinista regime be overthrown overtly or covertly?" politics has already become the victim of the totalitarianism it is trying to stop from coming close to its borders.

The real issue that faces us today is, "What does it mean to be a nation in a world that is able to destroy itself at any moment?" That is the issue that has to be brought to the center of the attention of our people. If ever, it is today that politicians are called to be wise people, that is, women and men who can raise the issue of national identity and offer a vision of how to be a nation living in harmony among nations, freely using its power to serve rather than dominate. I sense that many personal sacrifices in the political arena will be necessary to reach the point of national discussion aiming at national conversion. Many who possess political power today will need to risk their own political futures and will have to be willing to let go of oppressive power in order to empower other nations and thus further justice and peace in the world. Without such sacrifices there will no longer be a true dialogue in the world of politics, but only a tyrannical monologue leading to the absurd silence not only of politicians but of all human beings. Then we will have created our own day of judgment and will have become our own judges.

This is precisely what the last judgment is all about. The Lord who becomes one of us in humility does not really judge us. He reveals to us what we have become to one another. The day of judgment is in fact the day of recognition, the day on which we see for ourselves what we have done to our brothers and sisters, and how we have treated the divine body of which we are part.

Thus the question, "What have you done to the least of mine?" is not only a question about injustice, a question about war, it also is the question by which we judge ourselves. The answer to that question will determine the existence or nonexistence of our human family.

"Christ has died, Christ is risen, Christ will come again." That is the divine event taking place on the continents of the Americas, the event which we as Christians are called to recognize. Without this recognition we cannot truly be peacemakers. Jesus himself makes this clear when he says, "May you find peace in me. In the world you will have trouble, but be brave: I have conquered the world" (Jn 16:33). Peacemaking means to find peace in Christ, the dying, rising and coming Christ who reveals himself among the peoples of the Americas. Recognizing the dying Christ among his people allows us to live in the midst of confusion, ambiguity, and agony; recognizing the risen Christ among his people allows us to receive the fruits of suffering as gifts offered to us for our conversion; recognizing the coming of Christ among his people allows us to search for a new identity, not only as individuals, but also as a nation. Thus we can find peace in Christ, a peace that does not make us stay aloof from the bitter reality of our history, but a peace that makes us stand in the midst of our world without being destroyed by its seductive powers.

There is one question left. It might prove to be the most important one. "Can we see Christ in the world?" The answer is, "No, we cannot see Christ in the world, but only through the Christ in us can we see Christ in the world." This answer reveals that the Christ within us opens our eyes to the Christ among us. That is what is meant by the expression "Spirit speaks to Spirit." It is the Spirit of the living Christ dwelling in our innermost being who gives us eyes to contemplate the living Christ as he becomes visible in the concrete events of our history. Christians who become interested in Central America, therefore, do not move from prayer to politics: they move from prayer to prayer.

All that I have been trying to say about the Christ of the Americas was meant to broaden the spectrum of our life of prayer. The Christ whom we encounter in the center of our hearts is the same Christ we see stretched out on the cross of the American continents. Without interior prayer we will remain blind to the spiritual nature of what is happening in Central America. But without the prayerful recognition of the living Christ among our sisters and brothers below our southern borders, we can easily slip into a world-denying piety that does not lead to the transformation Christ calls for. This explains why prayer continues to be our first and—in a sense—our only task. Describing the end times, Jesus says, "When you hear of wars and revolutions, do not be frightened, for this is something that must happen.... Nation will fight against nation and kingdom against kingdom...people dying of fear as they await what menaces the world.... Watch yourselves... stay awake, praying at all times for the strength to survive all that is going to happen, and to stand with confidence before the Son of Humanity" (Lk 21:9, 36.). Praying at all times means keeping our eyes always fixed on Jesus the Christ. As Peter began to sink as soon as he moved his eyes from Jesus to the restless waters on which he walked, so too will we lose heart as soon as we stop praying. But as long as we keep the eyes of our hearts and minds focused on Jesus we can walk confidently in this world, bringing peace wherever we go.

10

The Message of Oscar Romero

I just finished reading the collection of quotations from El Salvador's martyred Archbishop Oscar Romero, *The Church Is All of You* (Winston Press, 1984), that James Brockman, S.J., has so ably brought together. As I was reading I felt as if Oscar Romero's spirit was drawing me closer and closer to the truth, that is, the true relationship with God. When I finally reached his last words, a deep silence came over me and I realized that something new had happened to me.

It is not easy to describe this spiritual event that took place during my reading of Oscar Romero's unpretentious, unadorned, and unambiguous words. Maybe the best way to summarize what happened to me is to say that I had encountered a man of God marked by humility and confidence calling me to conversion and action. I want to express more fully the meaning of this encounter. Thus I hope to offer a spiritual place in which a similar encounter can take place for others.

Oscar Romero is a humble man of God. His humility pervades all he says. That probably is the main reason why it was possible for me to read these very challenging and demanding words. They are spoken by someone who is very close to me. Oscar Romero does not speak from a distance. He does not hide his fears, his brokenness, his hesitations. There is a warmth in his words that opens my heart to listen. It is as if he puts his arm around my shoulder and slowly walks with me. He shares with me his struggles: "God knows how hard it was for me to become archbishop. How timid I have felt before you...." He explains to

me who he wants to be for his people: "The attitude to be taken
...is not 'I am in charge here!'...You are only a human being.
...You must...serve the people according to God's will and not
according to your whim." He does not want to be different: "The
shepherd does not want security while they give no security to
his flock." He is aware that he receives as much as he gives:
"Precisely in those charisms that the Holy Spirit gives to his people the bishop finds the touchstone of his authenticity....With
this people it is not hard to be a good shepherd. They are a people that impel me to their service...." He asks for forgiveness
and prayer: "I beg pardon for not having shown all the fortitude
the gospel asks....I ask your prayers to be faithful—that I will
not abandon my people but that together with them I will run all
the risks that my ministry demands." As I hear him speak to me
in this way, I know that he is indeed the good shepherd who lays
down his life for his friends. He lays down for me his own broken humanity, his fears, his sins, his hopes, and thus opens my
heart to listen to his words of faith.

Oscar Romero's humility is the fruitful ground of his confidence. He is a man "con fide," with trust, an unlimited trust in
Jesus Christ. As I listen to him I realize that I am listening to
someone who has fixed his eyes on Jesus and thus can walk safely amidst the pain and suffering of his people. In the midst of despair he calls for hope: "The more full of troubles and problems
we are, the more bewildering life's ways, the more we must look
up to the skies and hear the good news: 'A savior is born to
you.'" In the midst of powerlessness he offers courage: "Let us
not be disheartened as though human realities made impossible
the accomplishment of God's plans." In the midst of agony he
announces the resurrection: "Those who have disappeared will
reappear....Affliction...will become Easter joy if we join ourselves to Christ...." In the midst of violence he preaches the
beatitudes: "There are people who opt for guerrilla war, for revolution....The church's option is for the beatitudes....Christ was
sowing a moral revolution in which we human beings come to
change ourselves from worldly thinking." In the midst of hatred
he proclaims love: "I wish to show that the nucleus of my life is

to witness the love of God to humans and the love of humans among themselves....I have tried to follow the supreme shepherd, Jesus Christ, who directed his love to all." His confidence is so strong that he can say without any ambiguity: "I simply want to be the builder of a great affirmation, the affirmation of God, who loves us and who wants to save us." As I let the words of Archbishop Romero enter more deeply into my heart, I gradually come to experience that this humble but confident man becomes also for me the great affirmation of God's inexhaustible love.

Let me now speak about the other side of this encounter. It is my side! How can I respond when a voice, so humble but so strong, touches me deeply? Oscar Romero's words are a clear call to conversion and action. When Archbishop Oscar Romero first spoke, he directed himself to all the people in El Salvador, people from the left as well as people from the right, people supportive of the guerrillas as well as people in the government and the army, people who were being killed as well as their killers, the oppressed as well as the oppressors. But now, after these words have been sanctified by his martyrdom, they have become words for all people, and especially for the people of the United States. Now they have become words asking for a response not only from the people of El Salvador but also from us, who participate, willingly or unwillingly, knowingly or unknowingly, in the violence and destruction suffered by the Salvadorans. And who are we? Whether we want to hear it or not, we are the rich, the powerful, the oppressors who pay the bills for the weapons that kill and torture in El Salvador.

Thus Oscar Romero's words are a call to conversion. He says it loudly: "I call to everyone: Let us be converted so that Christ may look upon our faith and have mercy on us." To me, a Christian of the first world, he says without hesitation: "When one knows that financial capital, political influence, and power are worthless...that is when one begins to experience faith and conversion." To me, the rich Christian, he says: "When we speak of the church of the poor, we are simply telling the rich also: Turn your eyes to this church and concern yourselves for the poor as for yourselves." It is painful to hear these words as directed to myself, but since they come from a man as faithful as Oscar Romero, I may be able to let them come close and lead me to repentance and conversion. I am not an outsider to El Salvador's agony. I participate in it by continuing to adore the idols of "money, political interest, and national security" and by not letting the God of Jesus Christ, who became poor for my sake, guide all of my life and all of my actions. Thus I am called to confess my role in the violence that Oscar Romero condemns, to ask for forgiveness for my sins against the people who are exploited and oppressed, and to be converted.

But Oscar Romero asks for more. He asks for action that leads to justice and peace. One of the dominant themes of his sermons is the incarnation: Christ is the Word that became flesh in history. Conversion leads to engagement: "Some want to keep a Gospel so disembodied that it doesn't get involved at all in the world it must save. Christ is now in history. Christ is in the womb of the people. Christ is now bringing about the new heavens and the new earth." He leaves little doubt that a true Christian must participate in the work of liberation: "Christ appeared . . . with the signs of liberation: shaking off oppressive yokes, bringing joy to hearts, sowing hope. And this is what God is doing now in history." Again and again Oscar Romero stresses the active nature of God's word. "We cannot separate God's word from the historical reality in which it is proclaimed. . . .It is God's word because it enlightens, contrasts, repudiates, praises what is going on today in this society."

A commitment to the Word requires a commitment to history. Such a commitment challenges us to recognize, criticize, and change the unjust structures of a society that causes suffering. Such a commitment leads to conflicts and persecutions. Such a commitment can even ask of us that we give everything, even our life, for the cause of justice and peace. Archbishop Romero calls us to the hard service of the Word. "What marks the genuine church is when the word, burning like the word of the prophets, proclaims and denounces: proclaims God's wonders to be believed and venerated, and denounces the sins of those who oppose God's reign, so that they may tear those sins out of their hearts, out of their societies, out of their laws—out of the structures that oppress, that imprison, that violate the rights of God and of humanity. This is the hard service of the word." To this active service I feel called by Oscar Romero, the martyr of El Salvador. It is indeed a very great demand, but it is the demand of Jesus himself, re-spoken in the concrete historical context in which we live.

As a Christian I am invited—yes, required—to work with all my energy for the salvation of the world. Oscar Romero makes it clear that such a work cannot be spiritualized: "All practices that disagree with the gospel must be removed if we are to save people. We must save not the soul at the hour of death but the person living in history." Thus conversion opens me to action, action for justice and peace in the concreteness of our contemporary society.

The words of Oscar Romero, the humble but confident man of God calling me to conversion and action for peace and justice, lead to an encounter with Oscar Romero. I never met Archbishop Romero during his life. But I met him in a very special way in his words, which truly became flesh not only through the way he lived but also through the way he died. His life and death have given these words a unique authority. It is the authority of the compassionate shepherd, the shepherd who suffers with his people and gives his life for them. One day Oscar Romero said to his people: "I sense that there is something new in the archdiocese. I am a man, frail and limited, and I do not know what is happening, but I do know that God knows." This spiritual intuition proved to be true. Something very new is happening in the church of Central America. Out of the anguish and agony of God's people, the Spirit of God is fashioning a new creation. I pray that those who will read the words of Oscar Romero will allow them to enter into their innermost being and sense that something new is happening in them.

11

"We Drink from Our Own Wells"

A significant event in the development of liberation theology was the publication of *We Drink from Our Own Wells: The Spiritual Journey of a People* (Orbis Books, 1984) by Gustavo Gutiérrez, a 55-year-old priest of the archdiocese of Lima. Father Gutiérrez's new book fulfills the promise that was implicit in his *A Theology of Liberation* which appeared in 1971 (Orbis, 1973) and soon became a charter for many Latin American theologians and pastoral workers.

In that earlier work, Father Gutiérrez was already speaking of the need for and the importance of a spirituality of liberation. He realized from the beginning that a theology that does not come out of an authentic encounter with the Lord can never be fruitful. In 1971, he wrote: "Where oppression and the liberation of humanity seem to make God irrelevant—a God filtered by our longtime indifference to these problems—there must blossom faith and hope in him who comes to root out injustice and to offer, in an unforeseen way, total liberation."

More than ten years were to pass before Gustavo Gutiérrez had the opportunity to develop this spirituality fully, but it was worth waiting for. *We Drink from Our Own Wells* is the nuanced articulation of the Christ-encounter as experienced by the poor of Latin America in their struggle to affirm their human dignity and claim their true identity as sons and daughters of God. As in all true spiritualities, this spirituality of liberation is deeply rooted in the lived experience of God's presence in history, an experience that is as unique and new for the poor in Latin America as it was for St. Benedict, St. Francis of Assisi, St. Ignatius Loyola, and their followers.

The title of this new book expresses the core idea it describes. St. Bernard of Clairvaux's observation, "Everyone has to drink from his own well," raises the question: "From what well can the poor of Latin America drink?" It is obviously that unique and renewing encounter with the living Christ in the struggle for freedom. "Spirituality," Father Gutiérrez writes, "is like living water coming up from the ground of faith experience." To drink from your own well is to live your own life in the Spirit of Jesus as you have encountered him in your concrete historical reality. This has nothing to do with abstract opinions, convictions, or ideas, but it has everything to do with the tangible, audible, and visible experience of God, an experience so real that it can become the foundation of a life project. As the first epistle of John puts it: "What we have heard, what we have seen with our eyes, what we have looked upon and our hands have touched—we speak of the word of life."

I must confess that my conviction about the importance of Gustavo Gutiérrez's new book is older than the book itself. In Lima, during 1982, I attended the course in which Father Gutiérrez first presented the main themes of a spirituality of liberation. I remember this course as one of the most significant experiences of my six-month stay in Latin America—not simply because of what was said but also, and even more, because of how it was received. I was part of an unusual learning event in which approximately two thousand "pastoral agents" participated. These people had come not only from all the districts of Peru but also from Chile, Brazil, Colombia, Paraguay, Uruguay, Argentina, Panama, and Nicaragua. This youthful, vital, enthusiastic student body recognized in Gustavo Gutiérrez's words its own deepest soul. The spirituality that was described for these Latin American Christians was not perceived as an alien or imported way of thinking but as an expression of what they had already come to know in their daily living of the Gospel.

My own sense of the importance of *We Drink from Our Own Wells* comes from having been with these young men and women who had lived the Latin American reality and there encountered the Lord and drunk from the fountains of living water flowing from within him. Most of these students had been born and raised in poor barrios and were active pastoral agents in the process of liberation. They knew their own people and had learned to think with one eye on the Gospel and one eye on the painful reality they shared with these people. They worked in their various districts and countries as catechists, social workers, or project coordinators. They were all deeply immersed in the Bible and had come to think of themselves as the people of God called to the promised land. They knew it would be a long, arduous, and often painful journey, but the encounter with their Lord had given them the strength to be faithful in the struggle even when immediate results were not visible.

When Gustavo Gutiérrez explained that the spiritual journey would not be a journey from nothing to something but a journey in which they had already met the One for whom they were searching, it was clear that his audience understood what he was talking about. The way in which these young Christians spoke about their Lord was so direct and fearless that it became clear that their pastoral work among the poor was not based on any mere idea or theory but on a deep, personal experience of the presence of a loving God in the midst of the struggle for justice and peace. There was joy and gratitude; there was warm friendship and generosity; there was humility and mutual care, and these gifts were received from the Lord who had called them to be his witnesses among a suffering people.

In this course, given during the Peruvian summertime, Gustavo Gutiérrez's spirituality came alive for me precisely through those who were receiving it with open minds and eager hearts. I would now like to explore in more detail some aspects of this spirituality of liberation. To do this, I shall not only make use of the ideas expressed in *We Drink from Our Own Wells*, but also recall the way in which these ideas were received by men and women who have committed themselves to pastoral ministry in Latin America.

The spirituality of liberation touches every dimension of life. It is a truly biblical spirituality that allows God's saving act in history to penetrate all levels of human existence. God is seen here as the God of the living who enters into humanity's history to dispel the forces of death, wherever they are at work, and to call forth the healing and reconciling forces of life. It is precisely in the context of the struggle of the Latin American poor that the powers of death have become visible. "Poverty means death," Gutiérrez writes. This death, however, is not only physical but mental and cultural as well. It involves the destruction of individual persons, peoples, cultures, and traditions. In Latin America, the poor and marginalized have become more and more aware that these forces of death have made them strangers in their own land. They recognize more clearly the ways in which they are bound by hostility, fear, and manipulation, and they have gradually come to understand the evil structures that victimize them. With this new self-consciousness, the poor have broken into history and have rediscovered that the God whom they have worshiped for centuries is not a God who wants their poverty but a God who wants to liberate them from the forces of death and offer them life in all its dimensions.

This spirituality, as Gustavo Gutiérrez articulates it, makes it impossible to reduce liberation theology to a political movement. The struggle to which the God of the Bible calls people is much larger than a struggle for political or economic rights. It is a struggle against all the forces of death wherever they become manifest and a struggle for life in the fullest sense.

But as I reflect on the impact of this spirituality on my own way of living and thinking, I realize that a reductionism has taken place on my side. Talking with the pastoral workers during that summer course, I became aware of how individualistic and elitist my own spirituality had been. It was hard to confess, but true, that in many respects my thinking about the spiritual life had been deeply influenced by my North American milieu with its emphasis upon the "interior life" and the methods and techniques for developing that life. Only when I confronted what Father Gutiérrez calls the "irruption of the poor into history" did I become aware of how "spiritualized" my spirituality had become. It had been, in fact, a spirituality for introspective persons who have the luxury of the time and space needed to develop inner harmony and quietude. I had even read the Gospels in a rather romantic way. I had come to pray the Magnificat as a sweet song of Mary. I had come to look at the children in the New Testament as innocent, harmless beings, and I had come to think of humility, faithfulness, obedience, and purity primarily as forms of personal piety.

But the spirituality of *We Drink from Our Own Wells* does not allow such reductionism. The poor in Latin America have made us realize that living as Christians in our contemporary world, with an open eye and an open heart for the real problems of people, challenges us to break out of our individualism and elitism and start listening to the Bible with new ears. The poor help us recognize the power of the words of Mary's song: "God has deposed the mighty from their thrones and raised the lowly to high places." They help us see that the children who were touched by Jesus were the forgotten ones, and they help us rediscover the social dimensions of humility, faithfulness, obedience, and purity.

A second crucial aspect of the spirituality of liberation is its Christ-centeredness. Gutiérrez begins his book with the words, "Following Jesus defines the Christian," and he dedicates the core chapter of this work to an exploration of those opening words. Those who do not grasp the centrality of Jesus in the struggle for full human freedom will always misinterpret liberation theology as well as liberation spirituality. Gutiérrez pays careful attention to the intimate encounters with Jesus that are recorded in the New Testament. All discipleship, he emphasizes, is rooted in these most personal encounters, and the messianic community is formed from them. The disciples recognize Jesus as the Messiah and thus become part of a community destined to give testimony to God's Kingdom in the midst of the concreteness of human history.

It is here that the profound importance of a liberation spirituality as the undergirding of a liberation theology becomes clear.

Those who see in liberation theology a theological rationale for a class struggle in which the poor claim their rights and try to break the power of their oppressors have ignored the center of the struggle for freedom. Jesus is the center. Jesus the Lord loves the oppressor as well as the oppressed and entered into history to set all men and women free. Knowing Jesus in the way the disciples knew him does not allow for a cool and calculated strategy aimed at the overthrow of the oppressor and the acquisition of power by the poor. The good news that Jesus announces is the news that love is stronger than death and that the evils of hatred, destruction, exploitation, and oppression can be overcome only by the power of God.

In his lectures, even more than in his book, Gutiérrez stressed the importance of warm, affectionate, and caring relationships among those who struggle for and with the poor. Those who can say "We have encountered the Messiah" are not fighting for a far-off cause, nor are they forming groups because of a common fear of an enemy or a common desire for power. On the contrary, their struggle is already won. By encountering the Lord they already possess that for which they strive, already taste that for which they hunger. By their struggle they aim to make fully visible a victory over death that has already been accomplished. This makes possible a community life that is one of joy, peace, and true love.

Father Gutiérrez points out that the initiative for the encounter with Christ comes from the Lord himself. To those who ask, "Where do you live?" Jesus answers, "Come and see," and later he directly invites them to become his followers. Discipleship is first and foremost the response to an invitation. This insight is essential for an understanding of the spirituality of liberation. Some have accused liberation theology of Pelagianism as though it called upon people to redeem the world themselves. Nothing is further from the truth. In *We Drink from Our Own Wells*, Gutiérrez avoids any suggestion that the world's salvation depends on our efforts. It is precisely the gratuitous quality of God's love revealed in Jesus that sets us free to work in the service of God's Kingdom.

As one who has been exposed to many styles of theological liberalism, I am struck by the orthodoxy of this Christ-centered spirituality. It is solidly rooted in the teachings of the ecumenical councils. The Christians of Latin America, as Gutiérrez himself once pointed out to me, came to a realization of the social dimensions of their faith without going through a modernistic phase. He used Archbishop Romero as a striking example. Through his direct contact with the suffering people, that traditional churchman became a social critic without ever rejecting, or even criticizing, his traditional past. In fact, Archbishop Romero's traditional understanding of God's presence in history was the basis and source of his courageous protest against the exploitation and oppression of the people of El Salvador. A similar quality is characteristic of Gutiérrez's spirituality which is fed by the age-old Trinitarian faith of the church and by the religious experience of the great saints who incorporated that faith in their lives.

A third aspect of the spirituality developed in *We Drink from Our Own Wells* is its inductive character. By that I mean that this spirituality is drawn from the concrete daily experience of the Christian communities in Latin America. "The truth is," Gutiérrez writes, "that the daily contact with the life experiences of some, the reading of texts written by many, as well as the testimony of others, convince us of the depth of the spiritual experiences that are being lived among us."

The third and final section of *We Drink from Our Own Wells* is filled with deeply moving texts written by Christian men and women who have experienced persecution and suffering but have been witnesses to the living and hope-giving God in the midst of their sufferings. From these testimonies we can indeed see that "something new is being born...in Latin America."

Gustavo Gutiérrez has not simply written another book about the spiritual life. For many years he participated with his whole being in the painful struggle of his people. Out of this intimate solidarity he was able to identify the traits of a new spirituality, traits that he could read in the faces of the people with whom he lived. The words he chose for these traits belong to the treasury of the Christian spiritual tradition: conversion, gratuity, joy, spiritual childhood, and community.

But these old words sound fresh and new when they have been distilled from the life experience of the suffering Latin American church. Conversion then emerges as part of a process of solidarity with the poor and the oppressed; gratuity as a climate of fruitful work for liberation; joy as victory over suffering; spiritual childhood as a condition of commitment to the poor, and community as a gift born out of the common experience of the dark night of injustice.

This is a very dynamic spirituality that asks for constant, careful listening to the people of God and especially to the poor. It does not allow for a fixed and definitive theory that can be applied at all times and in all places. It requires great attentiveness to the continually new movements of the Spirit among the children of God. That in turn requires an ear that has been well trained by the scriptures and the church's understanding of those scriptures. A constant dialogue is necessary between the "old knowing" of scripture and tradition and the "new knowing" of the concrete, daily life experiences of the people of God. Since in Latin America that daily life includes the experience of flagrant injustice, political manipulation, and paralyzing corruption, this dialogue often has more the character of a confrontation than of any easy conversation. But only through faithfulness to that dialogue can an authentic, vital, and fruitful spirituality develop.

It is hard to fully grasp the depth of this spirituality. Gutiérrez summarizes it in St. Paul's words as a teaching that sets us "free to love"—words that describe not only a spirituality of liberation but all Christian spirituality from the Desert Fathers to such men and women of our own time as Charles de Foucauld, Dorothy Day, and Thomas Merton. When Gutiérrez points to this freedom as the goal of a spirituality of liberation, he connects the struggle of the people of Latin America with the spiritual struggle of all the great Christians throughout the centuries. More clearly than before, we can now see that this is the struggle not just of heroic individuals but of the people as a community of faith. It is precisely the new understanding of the church as the people of God that has made this perspective possible and fruitful.

This freedom to love is the freedom to which many Latin Americans dedicate their lives. The great paradox is that we North Americans, who have the word "freedom" written all over our history books, are now being challenged to learn from our oppressed brothers and sisters in the South the full meaning of freedom. In the "free" world of the United States, where most of the world's wealth is concentrated, spiritual freedom is often hard to find. Many Christians in the North are imprisoned by their fears and guilt. They have more than they need but less freedom than their fellow Christians in Latin America who are struggling hard to survive.

I had direct experience of this paradox during three months in Peru last year. Although I had gone there hoping to be able to give, I found myself first of all the receiver. The poor with whom I lived revealed to me the treasures of a Christian spirituality that had been hidden from me in my own affluent world. While having little or nothing, they taught me true gratitude. While struggling with unemployment, malnutrition, and many diseases, they taught me joy. While oppressed and exploited, they taught me community. During my short stay among the poor of Peru, I had just a glimpse of that spirituality which Gustavo Gutiérrez articulates in such a masterly way. *We Drink from Our Own Wells* is an important book, not just because it is an intelligent and insightful presentation of a Latin American spirituality, but more so because it is a gift from the poor that through Gustavo Gutiérrez's ministry of solidarity has now become available for the conversion of us who always thought of ourselves as self-sufficient.

The spiritual destiny of the people of North America is intimately connected with the spiritual destiny of the people of South America. What is happening in the Christian communities of Latin America is part of God's way of calling us in the North to conversion. I even feel that knowing God in North America can no longer be separated from the way God is making himself known in South America.

As we see the increasing violence in Central America, we must humbly confess that something more than political conflict is happening there. It is a deeply spiritual crisis that involves both Americas, North and South. It is a crisis that reveals the failure of five centuries of Christianity to bring unity to the Americas. The oppression, violence, and mass murder that ravage El Salvador and Guatemala remind us that we are crucifying Christ again. But his death among us is also a *kairos,* an opportunity for conversion. In the name of millions of the nameless poor, Gustavo Gutiérrez reaches out a hand to us and calls us to open our hearts again to the life-giving Spirit of Christ so that healing and reconciliation may be realized among Christians and the Risen Lord be victorious over the power of death.

IV

LIFE AT L'ARCHE

12

L'Arche and the Heart of God

Considering all the books you've written and all the places you've been, did you ever wonder if you were being obedient to God's will?

When I was asked to come to Yale, my bishop said I could go for a few years; I stayed ten. Meanwhile, I became an associate professor, then a tenured, full professor. I was doing well on the level of my ambitions, and I am ambitious in a certain sense. But I began to question whether I was really doing God's will. Was I being obedient? Was I the priest I wanted to be? Was I really looking for God, and not for my own success and career? After all, you can become successful talking about God—but that can be a trap. You can be praised for your sermons on humility! I felt I needed to get back to basics.

How did you respond to the questions?

I prayed: "God, you know what I should do. Let me know, and I will follow you. I will go anywhere you want. But you have to be very clear about it." I liked being at Yale. I liked teaching, but I knew it wasn't for life. During my time at Yale, my spiritual life wasn't deep. I wasn't praying much. I was lonely and needy. I needed to be liked by people, and I needed to be successful. I didn't have much inner peace.

In 1981 I suddenly had this feeling that I wanted to go to Latin America and work with the poor. I'd been there many

---

An interview by Arthur Boers, published in *The Other Side,* 1988.

summers and felt that I should go. I resigned from Yale, and people questioned if I was doing the wise thing. I didn't have much support.

So you tried to find a vocation in Latin America?

But I quickly realized that wasn't my vocation at all. God had not called me there. I was driven there. At some level I wanted to prove to myself that I could do something for the poor. I felt guilty for having been in academic settings.

While in Latin America, I spent a lot of time with liberation theologians—especially Gustavo Gutiérrez. He didn't encourage me to stay there. He said, "Maybe they need you more at the university to talk about Latin America. Do reverse mission to the First World from the Third World. You have the gift of the word, and you can write. Perhaps that's what you should do instead of being busy in a parish."

More deeply, I felt it hard to be there. People were good to me, welcoming. But being in Latin America didn't seem to be my vocation. It wasn't God's call. Meanwhile, Harvard had asked me to join its faculty. So though I left Latin America, I was unclear about where I was headed.

When you returned to North America, you were active on behalf of Central American issues.

Right before I joined the Harvard faculty, I visited Nicaragua. I was so impressed by what I saw, and I was so convinced of the dangers of military intervention that I felt I had to go back to the U.S. and speak about the situation. So a tour all over the country was set up for me. I spoke about the spiritual struggles of the people in Central America and called churches to think about that. It was spiritual work—not political. Though my message had political implications, I was calling Christians to consciousness.

When I finished this tour, I was exhausted. Not just tired. My soul was somewhat broken. It was as if someone was saying to me, "Are you trying to save the world? Where is your heart in all this? Who holds you safe?" I felt I was losing my soul and that God was not supporting me.

What did you do?

I was so exhausted that I asked Jean Vanier if I could visit his community. I went to L'Arche in France and collapsed for six or seven weeks. Then I realized that this community felt like home. The people were radically different. They said, "Henri, why don't you come and waste some time? Why don't you just pray? You don't have to do anything. We are so glad to see you not doing things." Finally, people were caring for me.

I also realized that handicapped people didn't love or care for me because I write books or take trips. They don't know that. If they express love, it comes from God. When I came to L'Arche, my whole life was tired. But God said, "I love you. I want to hold you." Finally God had the chance to really hug me and lay divine hands onto my heart through this community.

Did you then decide to join L'Arche?

Though I felt a lot better, that's as far as I went at that time. I returned to Harvard. I tried to talk about Latin America, but discovered that everyone had an enormous need to talk about prayer and contemplation. They asked me about the inner life, the spiritual life, ministry. Even though I was integrating a lot of the Latin American dimension, I was focusing on the life of the spirit. I loved it.

But at the same time, I had the feeling that Harvard was not where God wanted me. It's too much podium, too much publicity, too public. Too many people came to listen. Plus Harvard is intensely competitive. It's not an intimate place. It's a place of intellectual battle. On the one hand, I loved being there. I made some beautiful friends. But, at the same time, I didn't feel it was a safe place where I could deepen my spiritual life.

I had to pray more. I had to be more quiet. I had to be in community. So I resigned from Harvard, not knowing where to go. Except that I had a connection with Vanier and his community. So I went to L'Arche for a year; I wasn't saying I would stay.

During that year, I did a lot of thinking. I prayed, "God, what do you want me to do?" But I wasn't doing much. I was just being there—listening and feeling what the world was doing. Then I got a beautiful letter from the Daybreak community in Canada calling me to be their priest. They said, "We have something to offer you, and we have something to receive from you." It was the first time in my whole life I felt called to anything. All the other times, I had made a lot of initiatives. But this time I felt God was calling me. I wondered if this letter was the answer to my prayer.

In your book ¡Gracias! *you mention your niece being born with Down's Syndrome. Did this influence your decision to come to L'Arche?*

Her condition was a very real experience for me, but it didn't make me interested in working with mentally handicapped people. My desire to go to L'Arche was much more part of a spiritual journey. In fact, I discovered mentally handicapped people only in the context of my spiritual search. I just wanted to find a place where I could live the spiritual life more radically and with more integrity.

Isn't that Jean Vanier's story as well?

Yes, Vanier was never interested in mentally handicapped people per se. He was interested in the poor for the sake of his own salvation. He wanted to bind himself to the poor. He happened to be in France where his spiritual director Thomas Philippe lived. Thomas, a Dominican priest, was a chaplain for mentally handicapped people. He said to Jean, "Maybe it would be good if you could take some people out of the institution and live with them." For Jean, the fact that they were mentally handicapped people was secondary. They could have been prisoners or drug addicts.

In being here I have discovered what a gift mentally handicapped people are and how wonderful relationships with them are. But only now am I coming to see that. It wasn't what brought me here.

Why is L'Arche so special?

L'Arche has its own unique tone. It's not an institution. It's not a group home. It's a spiritual community where handicapped people are in the center. L'Arche exists not to help the mentally handicapped get "normal," but to help them share their spiritual gifts with the world. The poor of spirit are given to us for our conversion. In their poverty, the mentally handicapped reveal God to us and hold us close to the Gospel. That's a vision we have to nurture and deepen. I'm just beginning to discover it. I'm no expert on it. Nobody really is. But we live it very tenderly.

What is your role here?

I try to live my vocation as a priest in this community. I am not a chaplain. A prison has a chaplain. The army has a chaplain. I am not the director. I am a member of the community, first of all. Then I am the priest here, ministering to an ecumenical group. I'm responsible for the spiritual life here. My particular vocation is to call people to prayer, to be sensitive to needs, and to do some spiritual formation.

Do you feel like you fit in?

I feel God sent me here. What's so amazing is that I don't know anything about mentally handicapped people. Second, I have never lived in a community before. Third, I was called here to that which I was least prepared for. No lecturing—nobody wants to hear lectures. Writing is practically impossible here. This is a hard place, because it asks a lot of a person's soul. Yet I have never felt so clearly called, and I never felt so clearly the paradox of being called where they don't need all that I have. I feel God wanted me to just come and discover what mentally handicapped people, the broken people, the poor in spirit—poor is a better word than *handicapped*—were going to teach me.

But why do you think God wanted you here?

To teach me what the seminary and theology didn't: how to love God and how to discover the presence of God in my own heart. This was a gift to me. The poor also taught me to be willing to receive from others. People are not looking at me as somebody who does things by himself. I still get invitations to speak all over the world, but I have to say no. My community says it's more important to stay here instead of flying all over. It's more important to spend an evening with someone who can't speak or do anything than speak to thousands of people. God wants me here to be obedient to a more hidden way.

What are you learning?

One of the beautiful lessons this community has taught me is that if I do go and lecture, I take one of the handicapped people with me. I can stay close that way.

With our new house of prayer here, we have more time to pray than usual. The community suggests that I stay in touch with the "first love." Those words, "first love," are important to me. God loves us with a first love. John says, "Love one another, because I first loved you." The love of people is beautiful, but it's a reflection—a refraction, actually—of God's first love.

The second love—whether it's friends, men, women, or community—cannot fulfill my heart. But I can be grateful for that love if I am deeply rooted in the first love. It means an enormous loneliness at times, a recognition that no human being is going to fulfill your heart, and you're really alone. But that is a good aloneness. Because that's where God speaks to you. That's a loneliness you have to nurture, instead of trying to get over it.

Have you experienced any "dark nights of the soul" here?

Last summer, my inner struggle became intense. I realized I needed to deepen my spiritual life. Also, being among handicapped people, I discovered my own handicaps—particularly with regard to issues of affection and friendship. I didn't know what God wanted me to do in terms of my need for more intimacy than the community was able to give.

All of this was too deep to consider while living here. So I had to leave for a bit. The community supported my decision. I lived basically as a hermit. I did a lot of writing and had some good spiritual direction. I was able to work on important questions: Do I really give my whole heart to God or do I still want all these goodies? Can I really let go? Can I really die to a lot of stuff that seems to be so important?

In all those earlier years of my career, I had tried hard to prove to myself and the world that I'm OK. But now God was saying, "I love you even when none of that takes place." I didn't know how to believe that God loves me with a first love.

God wants my heart to be totally given to the first love, so that I will really trust God and give everything away. I'm still not able to do that. I say, "Leave your father, leave your mother, leave your brother, leave your sister, leave your possessions, leave your success. Don't cling to friends. Trust that God will give all you need." But do I really believe it? Jesus said, "Are you able to drink the cup? Are you able to be baptized with the baptism I'm baptized with?" I say I can—sometimes. But when I realize what it means, I start balking.

I'm still in the middle of a journey. It's not like I have figured it all out and now everything is wonderful. In fact, coming to L'Arche has opened up so much I'm just beginning to discover. There's so much more to go through. I have an incredible feeling that I'm called to be here, but it's also the hardest place for me to be.

How long do you think you'll stay at L'Arche?

The bishop in Utrecht gave me formal permission to be here three years. I obviously hope to stay longer. The church can continue to call me any place, and I have to be obedient. But I have a deep feeling my bishop will be sympathetic to my staying. I personally feel I'm just discovering not only L'Arche but also the world that it represents. And I would probably be more faithful to my vocation and to the church if I could continue living here. But that has to be affirmed by my bishop.

If God has something else in mind, I am convinced it will become clear. I did feel when I came to L'Arche that it was a different thing from going to Harvard or Yale. I *never* thought about remaining there for life. That was merely a professional identity. Here it's much more like belonging to a family.

How do you live out your commitment to the world and the issues of your day in this "hidden" calling?

By coming I made a choice, a choice that I had to interiorize. After two years, I'm just getting a glimpse of the real spiritual life. I have to learn every day—not about mentally handicapped people; they're my friends and they're part of my life. It's more learning about God, humility, community, prayer, and being one of God's broken people. I'm learning to trust that God wants me to be here.

The issues of the world are very important. But I have to learn to approach them from the heart of God. I have to be deeply rooted in God's heart before I can know how to respond faithfully to these issues.

I know that this community, although very small, has something to say to the world. I don't feel I have left the world and hidden myself. I have to be careful not to dissipate myself with all sorts of burning issues. I have to trust that by staying home and staying more focused, new connections with the larger world will grow and I will discover how God wants me to respond to them. Maybe by speaking once in a while. Or maybe by inviting people into this community. But my whole way of looking at the world is shifting radically. Not away from it, but more to the heart of it.

So in staying close at home, you see the truths of liberation spirituality?

Yes. I've seen that God speaks to us through the poor. And the people I live with here are really poor. Not in an economic way, but they are empty. They don't have much capacity to analyze things. They're poor in terms of even their emotions at times. But their heart is open to God. They may be stripped of a lot of human skills, but in their poverty they are open to God. Their heart—and by heart, I mean the center of their being—is so poor in a way that God can dwell there.

I'm more and more convinced, in the deepest sense, that God's preferential option for the poor—a liberation theology concept—is true. But I never expected to see it here. I now realize how much I'm learning and receiving from the poor. The church really needs to hear more and more of that.

One of the most mysterious things is that the poor hold us together. The poor here make us a community; they make us a church. We have people from the Philippines, the United States, Canada. I'm from Holland. We're from different religious backgrounds. What holds us together as a community is not an idea or a vision. It's the poor.

In that sense, liberation theology is still very important for me. Maybe not in the way it's thought of in Latin America. I am with people who are poor in spirit. They teach me that being is more important than doing, the heart is more important than the mind, and doing things together is more important than doing things alone.

What would you say to those of us who are trying to live out the interconnectedness of justice and faith?

You must make the connection between prayer and life. The closer you are to the heart of God, the closer you come to the heart of the world, the closer you come to others. God is a demanding God, but when you give your heart to God, you find your heart's desires. You will also find your brother and sister right there. We're called always to action, but that action must not be driven, obsessive, or guilt-ridden. Basically, it's action that comes out of knowing God's love. You want to be with the poor because with them you're not trying to please the world and be accepted.

That's my big inner struggle: to be so convinced of God's love that I don't need all these human affirmations. I want to enjoy being with people and not be anxious over whether they like me or not. I believe if I'm drawn into the heart of God, then I'm free to really care for people without wanting anything in return. Our spirituality should come from living deeply with the poor. A spirituality of being with vulnerable people and of being vulnerable with them—that's the great journey!

13

L'Arche and the World

There is an expression that I have often heard since I came to L'Arche. The expression is: L'Arche is given to the world. Frankly, that expression irritated me because it sounded so pretentious. What is L'Arche? It is an international network of seventy-eight communities in which people with a mental handicap and their assistants try to live in the spirit of the beatitudes. Less than three thousand men, women, and children are part of this small network. What is the world? It is the context in which the whole of humanity struggles to find its destiny. This struggle is marked by deep divisions among peoples, immense suffering, and the threat of total destruction of the planet. To say that L'Arche is given to the world has an insane ring to it, because L'Arche is like a flashlight in a dark universe, like a leaking rowboat on the ocean of the human race, like a newspaper stand among the skyscrapers of New York City, or like one letter in the trains filled with undelivered mail standing somewhere on the tracks outside of Naples. The only way to save the expression, "L'Arche is given to the world," from being a clear symptom of insanity is to realize that L'Arche's main concern is not sanity but sanctity.

Anthony's solitude was given to the world. Benedict's silence was given to the world. Francis' poverty was given to the world. Ignatius' apostolic zeal was given to the world. Marthe

---

Previously unpublished notes for a talk to a gathering of the International L'Arche Federation meeting.

Robin's agony was given to the world. They were not insane, but saints, saints who have their witnesses. Behind Anthony stands Athanasius; behind Benedict, Gregory the Great; behind Francis, Innocent III; behind Ignatius, a Borgia Pope, and behind Marthe Robin, a simple priest, Pere Finet, and a complicated philosopher, Jean Guitton. They all testify that small people were given to the world to manifest the power of God's Spirit, a Spirit that abolishes the distinction between small and large, irrelevant and relevant, useless and useful, unnoticeable and famous. They all declare in different ways that what comes from the Spirit of God comes not from the world, but from above, and that all that comes from above is given for those who are below in the world.

Let me be very honest with you. I do not know much about L'Arche. So far I have only lived for eight months in a foyer. And what can I know about L'Arche after eight months among handicapped people who keep reminding me that they were there long, long, long before I appeared on the scene? When Raymond, one of the handicapped men I live with, announces at each dinner, "Those who cook don't do the dishes," I realize the futility of trying to break with this old venerable tradition. And what do I know about the world after fifty-five years among the windmills of Holland, the skyscrapers of New York and Boston, and the Wendy's and McDonald's and Pizza Barrels of Richmond Hill?

The question is: How is our small, daily, routine life at L'Arche connected with our immense world, groaning in labor pains, eagerly waiting to be set free?

I propose to look for a response to this question in the resurrection stories as we find them in the four gospels. There we may get a glimpse of the inner connection between L'Arche and the world.

It belongs to the core of my faith that the resurrection of Jesus is the event around which the history of the world turns. If the world is the context in which humanity engages in a constant battle against the powers of death, and if indeed the resurrection of Jesus is the decisive moment in which God disarms these powers, all good news culminates in those few pages which describe the empty tomb and the appearances of Jesus after his resurrection. I, therefore, think that there is no better way to explore the question of how L'Arche relates to the big struggles of the world than by looking carefully at the stories about the resurrection of Jesus. By choosing such an explicit Christian perspective I do not want to exclude people from non-Christian religions. I hope that by speaking from the depth of my own particular religious experience I may touch places of the human heart which have a universal resonance.

Let us first look at how Jesus appears as the stranger. Then we can see how he reveals himself as the intimate friend. Finally we need to listen to Jesus as our teacher who teaches us a new way of living our pain.

THE STRANGER

What is most striking about the resurrection stories is that the resurrection of Jesus is described as a hidden event. When we speak about the hidden life of Jesus we have to go far beyond his years at Nazareth. The great mystery of Jesus' life is that all of it has a hidden quality. First of all his conception and birth, then his many years lived in obedience to his parents, then his so-called public life in which he kept asking those he cured not to speak about their healing, then his death outside the walls of Jerusalem between two criminals, and finally also his resurrection. Indeed, the resurrection of Jesus is not a glorious victory over his enemy. It is not a proof of his powers. It is not an argument against those who condemned him to death. Jesus did not appear to Annas, Caiaphas, Herod or Pilate, not even to his doubtful followers Nicodemus and Joseph of Arimathea. There is no gesture of "being right after all." There is no "I always told you so." There isn't even a smile of satisfaction.

No, the most decisive event in the history of creation is a deeply hidden event. Jesus appears as a stranger. Mary of Magdala sees a stranger in the garden. Cleopas and his friend find themselves walking with a stranger to Emmaus. The disciples see a stranger coming and think it is a ghost, and Peter, Thomas, Nathanael, John, James, and two other disciples hear a stranger calling out to them from the shore of the lake. How much of a stranger Jesus remains is succinctly expressed in that mysterious moment around the charcoal fire when Jesus offers bread and fish to his friends. John the Evangelist writes: "None of the disciples was bold enough to ask, 'Who are you?' They knew quite well it was the Lord" (Jn 21:12). Nowhere better than in this sentence is expressed the hiddenness of Jesus' resurrection. They knew who was giving them bread and fish, but didn't dare to ask who he was. The difference between knowing and not knowing, presence and absence, revealing and hiding, have been transcended in the presence of the risen Lord.

Here we touch the heart of L'Arche: revelation in hiddenness. I live at Daybreak with a profoundly handicapped twenty-five-year-old man called Adam. Adam does not speak; he cannot dress or undress himself; he cannot crawl, stand, or walk alone. He cannot eat without help, and suffers from seizures every day. But after living with him for eight months, carrying him to his bath, washing him, brushing his teeth, shaving his beard, combing his hair, and just sitting with him when he eats his breakfast, I am gradually discovering that he reveals his greatest gift to me in hiddenness.

People who visit us always ask: "Can Adam recognize you? Does he see you? Does he feel pain? Does he know the difference between good food and bad food?" These are the questions I myself asked when I first met Adam. But these are the curious questions about how normal he is, how much he is like me, how much he can be understood, how familiar he is. But now I am coming to sense that he reveals himself to me as a stranger, in hiddenness, and that there, in that unknown, unfamiliar, empty place, he holds the mystery of life for me.

It is hard to express myself well here. But what I want you to hear is that the hope that Adam offers is not bound to the places where he is like me, but held in a sacred hiddenness. The empty tomb is the first sign that something completely new has happened in the world. The longer I am with Adam, the less my hope is built on the possibility that one day he may smile, walk, or recognize my voice. If that were to happen I would be filled with joy, but I already know that it is his hiddenness that gives me life. Where he is most poor, there God dwells; where he is most silent, there God speaks; where he is most empty, there I find the signs of the resurrection. Adam is gradually explaining to me the meaning of the most used expression in liberation theology: "God's preferential option for the poor." Adam tells me that God dwells with the poor, not there where I can still connect my talents with what is left of theirs, but there where they are so completely empty that there is nothing for me to cling to and I am completely dependent on my faith.

"The Lord is risen, risen indeed." That is not a statement made by someone who finally had to give in to an argument. It is a statement of faith. When John entered the empty tomb and was faced with the linen cloths lying there, "he saw and he believed" (Jn 20:8). Seeing the poor like Adam and believing, that is the gift of L'Arche to the world.

What has the story of Adam to do with the big suffering of the world? It gives us a glimpse of the mystery that all suffering has a hidden quality, a quality of strangeness. Our temptation is to look at suffering as big, spectacular, noisy, and very imposing, the suffering that impatiently screams out: "What are you doing about it?" But in the center of all the hunger, homelessness, violence, torture, war, and the nuclear threat, there is a hidden anguish, a silent agony, an invisible loneliness, that nobody wants to touch. Jesus touched it, lived it, and carried it into the grave where he lifted it up to new life.

When we do not recognize this hidden quality of suffering, we might easily be seduced into taking on the posture of problem-solvers who, in a great eagerness to help, add violence to violence. There is an enormously seductive quality to the big sufferings of the world. They can even have a great fascination for us. Countless generous people, wanting to be of service in the world, have been overpowered by the forces they tried to conquer. The anger, resentment, rivalry, and even revenge among many peace-people are a painful reminder of this.

The Adams among us, who live a silent anguish that we cannot reach with our need to help but only with our own inner poverty, keep revealing to us the suffering beyond all suffering. It is the voiceless suffering of a broken humanity that cannot be identified with any group, race, nationality, or culture. It is the suffering that is hidden not only in the heart of the poor and oppressed of Latin America, but also in the hearts of the wealthy businessman, the successful lawyer, and the famous movie star. It is the suffering that is hidden not only in the hearts of the malnourished children of the young towns at the outskirts of Lima, Peru, but also in the hearts of the lonely depressed students at Yale and Harvard. It is the suffering that is hidden not only in the hearts of those who live in the concentration camps in Siberia, the refugee camps along the Cambodian border, and the prisons spread out all over the world, but also in the hearts of those who live in large monasteries, splendid estates, and spacious city apartments. It is the suffering that is hidden not only in the hearts of those who are violently kidnapped, tortured, and executed, but also in the hearts of the young gay men desperately longing for affection, the divorced women searching for a new beginning, and the old people waiting long hours for a visit.

Yes, it is that deeply hidden silent suffering that does not leave any human being untouched. Only by acknowledging this hidden suffering that binds our heart to the heart of all human beings can we become truly compassionate people who do not add violence to violence by good intentions, but who reverently bow before that sacred empty space where God chose to lay down his broken wounded body and from where he was raised up.

L'Arche is given to the world to remind us of the hidden quality of all suffering and to call us to live our small lives in compassionate solidarity with all humanity, a humanity destined to be raised up as a new creation.

I have an intuition that by reaching out to the suffering beyond all suffering we come in touch also with the source of joy, precisely because joy is not the opposite of suffering but hidden in the very center of it. Therefore, true joy is always found where we move to the very heart of the empty tomb of humanity.

THE INTIMATE FRIEND

The stranger reveals himself to us as the most intimate friend. When Mary of Magdala hears the stranger calling her by her name, she knows it is her Master. When Cleopas and his friend see how the stranger takes bread, blesses it, breaks it, and hands it to them, they know it is their dear teacher. When the disciples see the pierced hands and feet of the stranger, they know that their friend has returned, and when John the beloved disciple sees all the fish they have suddenly caught, he knows who that stranger at the shore is and says to Peter: "It is the Lord."

This knowing is much more than a simple recognition of a familiar person. It is a rediscovering of a long intimate relationship that has grown during years of listening, speaking, eating, and sharing the joys and pains of everyday life. Those who recognized Jesus were the ones who had lived with him and their recognition brought them in touch with that intimate, all-embracing love that had reshaped their lives in the most radical way. Knowing him again meant loving him again with a love that pervaded every fiber of their being. The stranger revealed himself as an intimate friend because he already was an intimate friend. The resurrection stories make one thing very clear. Only those who saw him in sweat and tears see him in his new body. Only those who knew him in the days of the long hard journey know him as the Lord of peace. Only those who loved him in his brokenness love him in his glory.

It is this deeply personal bond nurtured over the long years of faithful presence that forms eyes and ears that can see and hear the One who is risen from the grave.

I am explaining this to you with so much emphasis because the world keeps forgetting that it is the intimate personal connection that allows us to live in the midst of countless burning issues without losing heart and being swept away in defeatism, fatalism, sarcasm, skepticism, and cynicism.

During the past few months I have developed a friendship with one of the handicapped men in my house. His name is Bill.

At first he seemed simply interested in the many little things I could do for him. And he used me well. Intuitively he knew about my guilt-driven desire to help and he let me help him as much as possible. He let me pay for his beer, wash his dishes, and clean his room, even though he himself could do all of those things pretty well. I certainly didn't feel at home with him.

But as the months went by and we came to experience many joys and pains together, something started to change. One morning he gave me a generous hug. One afternoon he proudly took me to his room and showed me his new shirt. One day he took me out for a beer and paid for it himself, and on my birthday he bought me a lovely gift. During dinner he wanted to sit close to me and during Mass his joking interruptions of my homily were replaced by heartfelt words of love and concern. Thus we were becoming friends.

For me, coming home after a day of hard work became a completely different thing. It was returning to a safe place where I was held in love. And going out on a trip to plan something, teach something, or lecture about something became a light burden, an easy yoke, because of the knowledge that Bill was waiting for me and wanted to see me back and hear my story. And gradually I realized that I was coming to see the world through the eyes of the one who loves me. I recognized in the midst of the darkness of my world that there were signs of light, signs that I could see only because of the love with which I was sent into the world, signs that I could take into my heart and carry home to deepen the love that had begun.

What has this to say about L'Arche's gift to the world? L'Arche is there to remind us that the intimate personal relationships developed over months and years of faithfulness allow us to be in the world without being destroyed by its countless urgencies and emergencies.

What I want to say is simply this: Issues don't save us, people do. As long as our energy is completely invested in finding solutions to the burning issues of our time, whether they are social issues, church issues, racial issues, political issues, or sex issues, we are in constant danger of ending up in factions or parties fighting each other with a vengeance, in the name of justice and peace.

My own journey to L'Arche is directly connected with this movement from an issue-oriented life to a person-oriented life. I have seen the church in Holland being destroyed by increasing division over issues of authority, sexuality, and feminism. The larger the issues become, the smaller the place where people can return to affirm their love for each other and pray together for God's mercy. And at different theological schools in the United States I have witnessed a tragic loss of faith. Those who came with a desire to serve soon found themselves entangled in such a complex network of theological and sociological issues that an intimate uniting communion with God seemed increasingly impossible to find. A desire to love turned into a need to express indignation, a desire to pray turned into an endless battle for the right words, a desire to know God turned into a desperate feeling that there were no longer any safe names with which to address God.

None of the current issues that occupy the minds and hearts of men and women in church and society are without importance. They do need attention. But they can give birth to something new and life-giving only when they remain anchored in the personal bond that we as people of faith have with each other.

I came to L'Arche to re-establish and deepen that most personal connection. Without that connection I may win many minds, but lose many more hearts. L'Arche is given to the world to call us always back to that place of friendship and love from whence we can go out and recognize that the Lord is risen, risen indeed.

The Teacher

We now come to the third way in which the risen Lord appeared to his followers. He manifested himself to them not only as a stranger who became known to them as their most intimate friend, but also as their teacher who taught them the new meaning of suffering. In fact, the mysterious transition from stranger to friend was made possible because of the radical new teaching.

Jesus teaches his disciples that suffering and death are no longer connected with sin and punishment, but with the glory of God. Before his crucifixion Jesus had already indicated this. Facing a man who had been blind from birth, his disciples had asked him: "Rabbi, who sinned, this man or his parents?" and Jesus had said: "Neither he nor his parents sinned; he was born blind so that the works of God might be revealed in him" (Jn 9:3). Now walking as a stranger with Cleopas and his companion, who considered Jesus' death an incomprehensible failure, he reveals to them the fullness of the good news: "Was it not necessary that the Christ should suffer and thus enter into his glory?"

It is hard to grasp the revolutionary character of this teaching. All through the Hebrew Bible a connection is made between suffering and sin. And we keep making that connection. The questions: "Why did this happen to me, why did my house burn down, why torture, violence, and war, why this immense human suffering?..." have another question connected with them: "What did I do wrong?" The enormity of human suffering is caused not only by physical and emotional pain, but also—and maybe more so—by the deep sense of guilt attached to it. The destructiveness of human suffering is rooted in the guilt and deep self-rejection that underlies it.

Jesus radically and definitively disconnected suffering and death from sin and guilt. He did this in his own person. He who was without sin suffered most and so broke the fatal bond between suffering and sin. That is the great news. "Didn't you know that the Christ had to suffer and thus enter into his glory?" With that announcement Jesus reinterprets for his friends all they knew. "Starting with Moses and going through all the prophets, he explained to them the passages throughout the scriptures that were about himself" (Lk 24:27). Shortly after his appearance to Cleopas and his companion, he manifested himself to the apostles. "He opened their mind to understand the scriptures," Luke writes, "and said to them: 'So it is written that the Christ would suffer and on the third day rise from the dead'" (Lk 24:46).

If we want to understand the darkness of our world, we have to realize that the world continues to see suffering and death as ways to destruction to be avoided at all cost, and refuses to see them as ways to glory to be embraced without fear. L'Arche's gift to the world is the new Gospel teaching that the sting of guilt and sin has been taken out of suffering and death.

Living a daily routine in a house with handicapped people brings us in direct confrontation with our resistance to living our suffering as a way to glory. For me this is a daily reality. One of our handicapped men, Raymond, has, after many years in an institution, defined himself as the guilty one. He simply cannot believe that there is anything good in him and thus has become incapable of giving thanks. When I say, "Good morning Raymond," he says, "I am not awake yet." When I say, "I will miss you when you are gone for the weekend," he says, "I won't miss you for sure." When I call him long distance to say hello, he says, "Don't bug me. I am eating." When I bring him a nice gift, he says, "My room is too full for new things." It is not easy to live with such a voice close by, but it is the voice of our broken world saying: "You are to blame for your suffering. You got what you deserved and if you got a broken body or a broken mind, you are the one who is the guilty one." The endless chain of Raymond expressing self-rejection, self-blame, shame, and guilt brings the challenge of the new teaching of the risen Lord right into the heart of our life together.

Once, after a long litany of negativism, I shouted at Raymond in desperation, saying: "But Raymond, you are a good man." And with a most emphatic voice he shouted back: "No, no, I am not!" And suddenly I realized that he was clinging to his deep sense of guilt as the only way to make sense out of his immense suffering. All the violence that rips our world apart became suddenly visible in the "No, no, I am not!" shouted by my own brother.

Raymond is such an important member of our family. I see my own guilt, shame, and self-rejection in his anguished face. I hear my own self-complaints, self-accusations, and self-condemnation in his screams and I cannot run away. It is not the hiddenness of Adam or the intimate friendship of Bill that is the greatest challenge to my spiritual growth, but the merciless self-flagellation of Raymond who cannot yet believe that the sting has been taken out of death and who makes me realize that I still do not believe it either.

A friend of mine once defined community as the place where the one you least want to live with always lives. How true! But the one you least want to live with always is the one who reminds you of that part of yourself that is most wounded and most in need of healing. He makes you aware that you have not reached your destination yet, but have to keep moving on in an unceasing process of confession and forgiveness.

L'Arche is such a gift to the world because L'Arche wants to proclaim to the world that suffering is no longer in the way of glory, but the way to it. L'Arche wants to proclaim this not first of all by words, but by faithfulness to those for whom suffering and guilt are so hard to separate. And those are not only the handicapped men and women in our communities, but the assistants, priests, directors, and board members as well. Oh, how much do you and I and all our brothers and sisters in the human family need to hear the words: "Oh, foolish people, don't you know that our suffering has been freed by God from the demonic power of guilt and has been made into the way to glory?" But we keep forgetting it. We keep flagellating ourselves. We keep giving in to self-rejection and depression. We have to be taught over and over again the true meaning of the scriptures so that our hearts can start to burn again and our eyes and ears can be opened to the greatest message of hope ever brought to us.

Walking on the streets of New York City, Boston, Toronto, Paris, Amsterdam, or Rome, I don't see many radiant, joy-filled faces. Most people look tired. Their eyes stare away into empty space or are cast down to the ground. They carry newspapers in their hands that speak about corruption, blackmail, crime, violence, war, and impending catastrophes. Their burdens are heavy, their yokes very hard. With their whole being they cry out: "Why do we live and why do we keep living?"

L'Arche is a gift for this guilt-laden world by simply saying quietly: "All you who labor and are overburdened, go to the poor and there you will find him and he will give you rest...his yoke is easy and his burden light." (See Matthew 11:23-30.) It can be said in a smile, a flower, a dance, an embrace, or a gentle touch. It is far from easy to let go of our guilt and make our burden light. Since I have been at L'Arche, I have discovered how much I desire to control my own suffering and cling to my own dark powers which declare me guilty. Raymond and others like him confront me daily with that morbid desire.

But L'Arche holds on to its people and keeps teaching the hard liberating truth that the risen Lord has revealed to us that suffering is now the way to glory.

This brings me to the conclusion of this reflection about the daily life of L'Arche and the great struggles of the world.

The resurrection stories in which Jesus appears as stranger, friend, and teacher have helped me to articulate three ways in which L'Arche is given to the world. L'Arche reveals the hidden quality of all human suffering. L'Arche reminds our world that great issues can only divide us unless we are deeply rooted in personal friendships. L'Arche finally proclaims the truth that the sting of guilt and sin has been taken out of suffering and death. Adam, Bill, and Raymond are there to witness to these three ways in which L'Arche is given to the world.

As people of L'Arche, people of the resurrection, we must connect our small daily lives to the great struggles of our contemporary world. Without that connection, L'Arche loses its vocation. Concretely that means hard choices. It means a choice for hiddenness, a choice for friendship, and a choice for hard learning. If we keep making these choices, we will gradually discover that we are safely held in the heart of the risen Lord and that, in that divine heart, the heart of L'Arche and the heart of the world are one.

V

COMPASSION
IN THE
TIME OF AIDS

14

Our Story, Our Wisdom

I am really very grateful to be here with you this whole week. But I must confess that being at this conference has been a little bit like jumping into the unknown. It has not always been comfortable or easy, because I don't know what it will do to me. But it's very important for you to realize that I am in a place that challenges me, and that I am here to learn something new.

One thing I have learned is that this pandemic that we have been talking about is not God's curse or God's grace. Rather it is a time of opportunity, a privileged time. It is the reality in us and around us, and the way we choose to live in it is going to determine whether it reveals God as a vengeful God or as a healing Lover. We must remember those words of Jesus: "Why were those people killed when the tower of Siloam collapsed? Or those others, when Pilate mixed their blood with the blood of their sacrifices? Were they greater sinners than you are? No, none of that. It was for your conversion, for the conversion of the church, the world, our hearts."

What I am saying is very much a reflection of what I have heard and seen here. You have heard and seen the same things during these days, but maybe looking at it from a slightly different perspective can help you to say yes or no to it. When I was asked to speak of what I had learned here, I felt like saying, "Why do you want me to talk right after the conference? Give

A talk given to the National Catholic AIDS Network at Loyola University, Chicago, Illinois, July 26, 1994.

me about four weeks to think about it, and I might come up with something." But here I am. I have had to learn fast, or at least try to find some words for what I have not yet fully integrated. I have just three words that have really touched me here: community, body, and death. So we'll talk about the movement in community from exclusiveness to inclusiveness, the movement in the body from metaphor to reality, and the movement that our mortality helps us to realize, from a successful life to a fruitful life. That's what I've been hearing here; that's what feels connected with my own experience.

I'd like to start by speaking a little about community. This has been an incredible community over the last few days! Sometimes it takes a few days or weeks to get into community, but here it took about ten minutes. Somebody said to me, "Aren't they hugging a little too fast?" I answered, "No, no, they haven't been hugged in a long time; they're catching up." There's community here. I realize that community always moves—from exclusiveness to inclusiveness. For me, in the past, community often meant a safe place where "those others" were not present. I came from a very Catholic Dutch family, where it was clear that "they" were not believers. "They" got divorced and did all sorts of strange things. But "we" were OK because we were together in a safe place. It is frightening when boundaries are pushed out and broken down, because it doesn't feel safe any longer. I might have started in community, or in the church, or in the seminary, or in my family, in a safe, clearly-defined place. And then, bang, bang, bang—all those hedges and fences kept falling away. Suddenly, the non-believer might be more believing than the believer, the outsider might have something to teach the insider. Suddenly, the difference between Catholic and Protestant, Christian and Buddhist, religious and secular isn't the kind of difference I thought it was. When I went to Daybreak, my community now, I realized that the difference between handicapped and non-handicapped just wasn't there anymore. I realized that I could love the handicapped only because I was handicapped, that I could be close to people in pain only because somehow they revealed my own pain to me.

Coming to this conference was like being invited to let some other walls and boundaries tumble down, for instance those between caregivers and care receivers. We are all together. The pandemic brings us together. Client or helper, male or female, young or old, married or celibate, white or person of color, homosexual or heterosexual—all the distinctions that seemed so important—suddenly the pandemic throws all those differences away. Suddenly you realize that your heart is expanding and there are no limits to that expansion. It is community, it is inclusive, and there is nobody who cannot be invited to that community of the heart. We start experiencing and feeling that we are all human and belong to the same family.

But the great mystery here is that in community we find a new loneliness, and it creates a new intimacy. Paradoxically, if I'm well-embraced, well-held, well-kept by my friends, then suddenly, by the very intimacy of that embrace, I know that I am alone in a very deep way, in a loneliness that I didn't know before. It is pecisely the love and intimacy of the other that reveal my deepest loneliness, which I couldn't get in touch with before I entered into community. I feel that I've seen that here. In this wonderful freedom to hold, to touch, and to be close, we also realize how deeply alone we are and should be, alone for God. Alone I will die, even when I am surrounded by friends. It's my unique journey. I want to live it with others, but life is still my lonely journey. Yet when I discover that aloneness in a new way, I also realize a new intimacy. As we come together, we suddenly realize that we can be bonded like this only because we were loved long before we met each other. Long before we were born, we had already been seen, loved, and held safe. Long before we could say to each other, "I need you, hold me, touch me, heal me, care for me," there had already been a voice that said, "You are my beloved daughter, my beloved son, and on you my favor rests." We are here to say that to one another. Out of that reality we form community. And so the intimacy we are so freely expressing to one another is rooted in a sense of belonging that transcends all of us. We want to go back to that original place and hold each other there, so that we can be safe. I'm trying to say something I lived while I was here, the incredible beauty of being together in God. It is a unique mystery that in this assembly we can feel our aloneness, with one another, in the presence of a Voice that calls us "beloved."

I think that's exactly what Jesus was all about, what the cross is all about. Jesus lived in a very particular territory and time, with very particular people. But through his death he broke out of the boundaries of time and place. He became for all people the Jesus who came to create a covenant with humanity, made visible through his death. "When I am lifted up, I will draw all people unto myself," Jesus said. He also told us, "When I die, I can send my Spirit and the Spirit will blow where it wants." That's the mystery of the cross, that place from which all energy bursts forth and Jesus becomes the lover of all people. On the original cross, the vertical beam and horizontal beam were equal. And if you write Jews on one arm, Gentiles on the next, then God on the top, and Cosmos on the bottom, you will see that the cross of Jesus brings everything into one circle of love. Over the centuries we made the vertical beam longer and longer. Now perhaps this pandemic that we are living through is also a struggle all over the world to reclaim that cross with equal beams, so that we can be a community that does not exclude anyone. After all, the God we believe in is the God who has entered into communion with the human race as the compassionate mother of all humanity.

Next I want to talk about the body, which is sort of a scary thing for me to talk about. What I have learned here is that the body is indeed not just a metaphor, though that is very much how I have experienced it through most of my life. I'm increasingly afraid to live in my body as a reality, as a real place of being. I know that I have to discover what it really means to be a body, to be in the body, to be incarnate. I need to learn to be at home in myself, a temple of the Spirit, and therefore fully intimate with God, at home in my home where God dwells. At this conference I've become aware of the incredible beauty of the body. This whole pandemic has asked us to look into the innermost and most intimate places of our bodies, all the way into the cell structures, and really see this incredible, mysterious work of God.

Someone at this conference said that our bodies hold our sorrow and our joy, sometimes in the same places, and that precisely in our bodies we discover that joy and sorrow are never really separated. If you discover that in your body, you will probably discover it in other people's too. One of the great mysteries of the Christian life is that we look at a body that is completely broken and we say, "Here is my hope and my salvation." We believe that the sadness and gladness are never separate, because one invokes the other. It's in the mourning that we write the choreography of our dance. There's probably more sorrow in this room than in most other places on earth, yet this gathering has been such an ecstatic comfort. That's great news! The world in which we live keeps separating gladness from sadness. But God wants us to live them together, and the moment that God became flesh, all sorrow and joy became connected.

In my own flesh, in my body, I discover this real presence. So perhaps this conference can give us a new view of the Eucharist. I'm not able yet to say what that is, but we have to start thinking about it. In the Eucharist we celebrated a few nights ago, I suddenly realized that Jesus never said, "Nibble and sip." He said, "Eat and drink." Eat and drink to the full! And all at once I saw people eating and drinking in all sorts of ways. I saw that I could use again a word I had been critical of for at least twenty years, the word *transubstantiation.* I understood that the very substance of our being was being transformed, and that the substance of who we are was giving new life to a body that could hardly contain its feelings of expression, strength, and vitality. You and I were made new when we were surrounded by the mysteries of the Word, the touch, the eating, the drinking, and the dancing. All was part of that one transubstantiation that made us new. I think, dear friends, that the Eucharist is one of the greatest gifts that we as a community have. It's so simple and so mysterious. That's the place of healing we have hardly discovered. It may have become for many a place of exclusion, ritual, magic, or anxiety, but in fact it is the place where healing happens if you want it. If there's anything I would like to know better, live and celebrate better, call more people into, it is precisely the mystery of that real presence in the word, the offering, the gifts, the eating and drinking, the being. It's precisely the Eucharist. We come together as very vulnerable people, yet new life is created. Jesus says, "Eat me up, drink me empty, take it all in, I don't want to hold anything back. I want to become you. I don't want to be separate anymore. I want to be within, so that when you eat and drink, I'm vanishing because I am within you." The disciples recognized him in the breaking of the bread and then he was gone, because he was right in the center of their being. We become the living Christ, the body of Christ.

Finally, that word, that certain reality that has been so much present here: death. It means our own dying, the dying of those we are living with, the mortality of all flesh. I hope that together we can deepen our understanding of death, because it is clear that the pandemic no longer allows us to hide our faces from death. And what does it mean? A large part of humanity is dying. Humanity is nailed to the cross again. Christ is crucified again. And as you look at that cross, listen to the voice that says, "Mother, behold your son. My beloved, behold your mother. Sister, behold your brother. Love, behold your friend." As we stand under the cross of dying humanity, we hear a voice that calls us together, calls the few who dare to stay, who haven't run off. It is a powerful image, as if Jesus were saying, "You are becoming family right under my cross. As you stand here and see my totally emaciated body, my totally destroyed being, crying out in abandonment, something is being given for you." We look up and see water and blood flowing from the pierced heart, as the evangelist John did, the signs of something new. Theology says that the church was born out of the broken heart of Jesus. Today we can say it again, that a new church is being born right from the cross under which we are standing. The church is always born out of the broken heart from which water and blood flow. You have to see it, as John did. You have to see it and claim it. It's here. It's happening. You don't have to say, "Well, after I'm dead, this and that will happen, and then things will be better."

Don't wait for any of that. Just start living! I want to say too that you don't need to be angry, because you are so blessed, so graced in this moment.

I see wonderful things happening right here for us to claim. We just have to say, "It's ours. We want to be this church." It's already here! It's like St. Francis, who gave the church new life. He went to Pope Innocent III because he didn't want to do something on his own that might divide the church. Francis wanted to maintain one church. There were struggles and setbacks, but his vision prevailed. Surely the movement growing now is as powerful as the Franciscan movement was in the thirteenth century. Our task is to keep connecting it with the church. It's so important for you to claim that new community, that new world that is happening in your hearts, because you are being sent out. When you have lived it, you have to proclaim it. There is no choice. If you believe that the Word became flesh, you have to believe that flesh becomes Word again.

What we have lived in the body is there to be proclaimed. That's what it's about, that we have lived something in our bodies, felt it, experienced newness in ourselves. Then we have to make it Word, so that it can give life—even out of our death. And I tell you, when your Word comes from your flesh, it will heal, whether you intend it to or not. Everyone who touched Jesus was healed. Everyone! It happened. You have to believe that. And everyone who touches you when your body is filled with the truth of who you are and has become that place where God chooses to dwell, the people you touch cannot but be healed. You don't have to define healing; others will do that. You just have to go everywhere you normally go. But go also to the leaders of our church and go with an immense love. One of the things I hope from this conference is that we will stop seeking to place blame, but really go and care, care for the leaders who are so very lonely, frightened, and paralyzed. And I really hope you have the courage in a very simple and gentle way to care for the community that you are part of. You can say to them, "Come, there's a place for you, too. Let's talk." Go out to your world, to all those people you meet. You are privileged to know so many people. Some are dying, some are in anguish, but they are the saints. Go to them and tell them that you stand under their cross, that you have seen the water and blood flowing from their side. You in this room are so empowered, so renewed in so many ways, that you can go to people and embrace them, not because you agree with everything they say, but because you see their loneliness and their immense need to be loved. And when you go out to people, then you can start talking about what you are living.

I want to leave with you, in the end, that very deep word that Jesus says about death: "It is for your good that I'm going, because unless I go I cannot send you my Spirit." That word has to be rediscovered. Jesus, who died in his early thirties and who spoke about his death from the very beginning of his proclamation, is saying that his death is not the end but the beginning. It is not something to be afraid of, but something that opens a whole new world. Death is the place that allows him to send his love, his Spirit, his deepest self. And somehow, preparing ourselves for our death, helping others prepare themselves for theirs, means that we realize that our spirits and theirs will touch generations yet to come. Yes, we have to die with Christ, but we will be raised with Christ so as to send the Spirit of Christ.

This morning's reading was from the book of Sirach, about those whom we have buried but who are here with us, continuing to send us their wisdom so we can live. Do we really believe that? It means that I will be around for generations because I keep sending my spirit, my spirit which is from God and isn't going to die. In fact, that spirit was given to me, not just for these thirty or fifty or seventy years, but so that it can bear fruit long after my life on earth is over. It is precisely my vulnerability, my brokenness, and my death which allow me to be fruitful. "Fruitful," not "successful." And therefore, the main question is not "How much can I still do?" although that's not unimportant. The main question is, "How I can make my life fruitful? How can my dying be not the end of fruitfulness but rather its fullest realization?" Jesus lived that way, and we are called to live that way too. Then we may be able, gently, to let people who are dying discover that they are going to bear fruit far into the future, beyond their lifetimes. I think that's good news, really good news! And I learned it in this community, these last few days, because we have been receiving here the fruits of those who have died, their wisdom and their love. They are still with us. They are the saints, and we need them to claim their fruitfulness. We are praying that they will give us their spirit so that we can carry the spirit further.

I have a little story to tell at the end of these reflections. We have reflected on community, on the body, and on dying. I hope that what I've said is connected with what we have lived here, and that I've also shed a bit of light on where you are going. But, as a sort of personal ending, I want to share this story. A few years ago, my eighty-nine-year-old father came to visit me in Germany. He wanted to do something fun, so I said, "Let's go to the circus." There were five South African trapeze artists there, three flyers and two catchers, and they danced in the air! I was fascinated and told my father that I thought I'd missed my vocation, that what I'd always really wanted to do was to fly like that. One thing led to another, and now I join them for a week or two every year, traveling with the circus. The leader recently said to me, "Henri, everyone applauds for me because when I do those leaps and back flips, they think I'm the hero. But the real hero is the catcher. The only thing I have to do is stretch out my hands and trust, trust that he'll be there to pull me back up." You and I have been doing a lot of flying at this conference. It's wonderful; you'll get a lot of applause and you'll enjoy it. This is all good. But finally, it is trust that remains. Trust that when you come down from the triple somersault, your catcher will be there to pull you right back up again. So just stretch out your hands and trust the God of life.

VI

SOLIDARITY WITH
THE HUMAN FAMILY

15

Social Compassion

What are you finding to be a central resource for social compassion?

The new resource for social compassion is in fact a very old resource, too: it is the poor. I went to Peru recently to spend some months living in a poor barrio. I lived in a room put up on the roof of a poor person's house, where I looked out over a sandy desert full of the houses of the poor. Rather than finding myself with lots of time to be helpful, as I had expected, I found that just surviving physically was an accomplishment, as it was for everyone else there.

I first thought that I had to share some of what my privileged environment had bestowed upon me with those who were obviously very poor. This assumption was turned around radically in that impoverished setting. I received more than I could give.

In the parish of a hundred thousand people, seventy percent were younger than twenty. The children came alive for me. When I walked down the road, they were so affectionate, loving, and numerous that I found each finger clutched by a different child wherever I went. They were full of excitement and directness, experiencing life right where they were. They and their parents in countless ways helped to cure the depression and other problems I found I had in my first weeks there. They literally

An interview from *Living with Apocalypse: Spiritual Resources for Social Compassion,* edited by Tilden H. Edwards (San Francisco: Harper & Row, 1984).

hugged me into health and taught me that life is now, to be shared, and to be thankful for. I found them all reaching out to *me* in concern for my mournfulness. These poorest of the poor *knew* a certain joy even in the midst of their suffering that was *amazing*. No one was going to take away their deep awareness of the giftedness of existence in the mystery of God.

How does that lively faith become a revolution?

When it is received! Then this faith is revealed as a gift that can have greater power.

One of the tasks of ministry is to show people their divine gifts. A gift becomes visible in the eyes of the receiver. As ministers, we awaken others to their own qualities by receiving, celebrating, and valuing them, by accepting those gifts and expressing our gratitude. This happens when we interpret something as the grace of God in the other. It becomes revolutionary when the poor can realize their giftedness and know that they have something to give the world. Liberation theology is about claiming that giftedness and setting it free.

One danger I see among nuclear and social protesters, although I support their work totally, is that they can become so dominated by their fear of tomorrow that they miss the gift of the hour. The reality of today does not become a source of liberation for them. They then can become tainted by the very demon they are fighting, and soon they can find themselves turning hateful, aggressive, and violent. You can fight against death only in the strength of life, in God's presence now.

The nuclear threat is not ultimate. We need to believe Jesus' words, "I have overcome the world." The world belongs to God. We need to heed the practice Jesus gives us for standing before the Apocalypse in Luke 21:34-36:

> But take heed to yourselves lest your hearts be weighed down with dissipation and drunkenness and cares of this life, and that day come upon you suddenly like a snare; for it will come upon all who dwell upon the face of the whole earth. But watch at all times, praying

that you may have strength to escape all these things
that will take place, and to stand before the Son of
humanity.

Then we can protest as a form of witness to the Living God
and not with an anxious soul desperate to change the mind of the
president at the last minute. Then our resistance will be an authentic liturgy: the "work of the people" (which is the literal
meaning of *liturgy*), making God visible as a God of the living.
Protest, then, is an effort to prevent the world from taking away
our God-given life. We need to protest all kinds of things that
threaten to do this, including the media's great fascination with
death. As a *community* of witness, we need to say no to such
things on many different levels.

There are many ways of being a peacemaker. We need to experience our own humble task as part of the Body of Christ and
encourage others to accept their task. Whatever it is we do, we
need to feel *sent* by the community rather than working as isolated individuals. And we need to pray for one another, for our
common life and for our common task. Such intercessory prayer
is basic to Christian community.

If we are to be peacemakers, it is essential that we take on
what I would like to call a mentality of abundance and put away
from us the mentality of scarcity. This sense of scarcity makes us
desperate, and we turn to competition, hoarding, and a kind of
parody of self-preservation. This greed extends not only to material goods but also to knowledge, friendships, and ideas. We
worry that everything we possess is threatened. This is especially
true in a society that grows more affluent, experiences more opportunities for hoarding and more fears of losing what has been
stored, and in the process creates enemies and wars.

We must be willing to give away everything rather than
hoard out of a fear that there will not be enough to go around.
That is what Jesus shows us in the story of the few loaves and
fishes, taken and blessed from an oppressed child, a divine gift
that became more than enough for a great crowd. Remember,
too, how Jesus told his fishermen disciples to leave everything

and follow him, after showing them a great catch of fish that startled them.

This means that we must die to the self focused on scarcity so that we may enter into life trusting in God's abundance. This becomes the basis of real community: We each give what we have to one another. This *fruitful* life is not the same as a *successful* life, though. Fruitfulness is the gift that is given us as a result of our trust in God's presence. Fruitfulness is, in a way, the very opposite of success, of a life focused entirely on *results* and on our attempts to control the future according to our little views and our little survivals.

How do you see the place of spiritual discipline in fostering social compassion?

Every encounter in life involves the spiritual discipline of seeing God in others and making known to others what we have seen. Since our seeing is only partial, we also need other people who will help us to see. Through each encounter, we will come to see more clearly.

Everyone is a different refraction of the same love of God, the same light of the world, coming to us. We need a contemplative discipline for seeing this light. *We* can't see God in the world, only *God* can see God in the world. That is why contemplative life is so essential for the active ministry. If I have discovered God as the center of my being, then the God in me recognizes God in the world. We also then recognize the demons at work in us and the world. The demons are always close, trying to conquer us. The spiritual life requires a constant and vigilant deepening and enlivening of the presence of God in our hearts.

This process includes the real tension of discerning with which eye I see God: my own eye that wants to please and control, or God's eye. Life therefore needs to be lived in an ongoing process of confession and forgiveness. This is the ongoing dynamic of community. The demons lose their power when we confess that we have been in their clutches. The more deeply we confess, the more we will experience the forgiving love of

God—and the more deeply we will realize how much more we have to confess. Community life encourages this confession of our demons and our enchantment with them, so that the love of God can reveal itself. Only in confession will the Good News be revealed to us, as the New Testament with its focus on sinners makes clear. One of the great problems with the United States is its refusal to confess its sins. What a great difference it would make, for example, if the president could admit mistakes. The dynamics of social compassion have much to do with both individual and communal forms of confession. It is this that gives us eyes that can see God and the Kingdom in the world.

Can you say something more about the essential place of contemplation, or the mystical life, in this process?

The mystical life is the life by which I grow toward what is real and away from illusion, the life that grows into true relationship. The future of Christianity in the West depends on our ability to live mystically, that is, in touch with that core reality that is the center of events. Without claiming this truth that everything is *in God*, Christianity loses its transforming power and becomes something like "behaving decently," a series of rights and wrongs.

Spiritual discipline involves following the Lord, in the sense of becoming who he says we are, making true what is true, that is, claiming our connected relationship with God and one another and living it out. This is something that is foolish in the eyes of the world, since the world makes us believe that we need all kinds of things that we really don't.

It is out of the privilege of realizing who we really are that we become relevant socially: we want to love more; we admit to evil more clearly in and around us; and we learn to live together in mutual confession and forgiveness. Our power of diagnosis (which literally means "knowing through and through") is deepened, and we can say yes and no to things with more discernment. We become ecumenical in the sense of knowing our connectedness. Indeed, spiritual development is the center of real ecumenism.

This connectedness lies behind the Orthodox Fathers' criterion of holiness: loving one's enemies. As we come to see others' real nature, we realize that God loves our enemies in the same intimate way that we are loved, and that we can forgive them as God forgives them, because it is God forgiving through us.

Ministry in a mystical sense involves an inner freedom that radiates and heals. It thereby means more what we are than what we do. If we give everything to God as scripture invites us to, then we will find out who our neighbor is and what is needed. We shouldn't worry so much about trying to influence and do good to each other which, without rootedness in God, can end up being not real ministry but simply a way of dominating one another. Rather, we should concentrate on being faithful and obedient to God, on being "all ears" only to God, listening to God through all things.

What does all this say about true identity?

Our identity is in the One who loves us. This saves us from our false self, which is anxiously dependent on others' opinions and leads us to sell our souls to the world and to the Evil One who rules the world. The spiritual task is to say that a self defined by other is illusion.

Our true self is in God. As we are told again and again in John's Gospel, we can love others because God first loves us. The spiritual life is coming into touch with that *first* love, which says that we belong to God. As Jesus said, "Just as I don't belong to the world, neither do you"—but you, rather, belong to the Lover who gives you to yourself. We can be a liberating and creative presence in the world only if we don't belong to the world, if we don't depend on the world for our real identity. This is the real paradox of ministry: that we can minister to the world only if we don't belong to it.

The depth of our belonging to God is revealed by Jesus. His relation with God through the Holy Spirit is one of total openness. Everything Jesus owns is a gift from the Father. He never claims anything as just his apart from God. He says that we are called to enter the same relationship with the Father that he has, doing all that he does. In sending us the Holy Spirit, he says that we will be led into a full, intimate relationship with God, so that we won't have to be victims of the world's spirit.

Spiritually we are *in* God, *in* the Lord, *at home* in God. Our true identity is that we are God's children. It is from that perspective—from God's perspective—that we perceive the world. We are called to see the world as God sees it; that is what theology is all about. Therefore, we are continually diagnosing the illusory quality of anything outside this perspective.

What other spiritual resources help us with this perspective?

Following the liturgical year, with its seasons and days of commemoration, can help us understand this, because it shows us God taking place in history as a continual event. It helps us answer the basic ongoing question, "What's happening?" What's happening is that God is in our midst, is born among us, is suffering in us, rising up with hope, sending the Spirit. This contrasts with the bored, empty answers we usually get when we ask each other that question on the street: "What's up?" and we hear, "Oh, nothing much."

Resources like scripture, the church, the Eucharist, individual spiritual guidance, and our own hearts also can tell us that what's happening belongs to God. And this includes ourselves. They can help us connect our own story to God's story. They can help us to see that we are an ongoing revelation of God and to claim our own suffering and joy as part of God's. Our great temptation is to *disconnect* our story from God's story. Compassion comes from *making* these connections.

How can we deal with the church community that does not respond to calls for compassion and a real awareness of God in life?

The value of the spiritual life is not in the *numbers* who live it. God loves everyone, but some are elected as a creative minority to witness with a burning love for God. Jesus never predicted that everyone would love one another. He said there would be persecution, but he also said don't worry—you will know what

to say when the time comes. Even death can't take life away
from you.

What do you say to people who ask why God lets us suffer?

I don't say anything. The question really means there is deep
personal suffering. Allow the question to be there. By your own
solidarity with the question, you reveal the solidarity of God
with that suffering. God loves us so much that he does not simply take our suffering away: he suffers with us. If we understand
God's solidarity, if we see God as the One who did not cling to
power but gave it up, who did not cling to the ability to solve
everyone's problems, we have the mind of Jesus Christ. Be present to each other and experience in the depths the gift of life!
Christ didn't fall into solutions or solving problems—that's the
temptation of the desert. That's our temptation—to solve people's problems, to cure, not care. To care means being where the
suffering is. It's a way of living together so the mystery of life is
revealed.

There is joyful solidarity with humanity. You are part of the
human struggle. I am so human I can struggle with others. That
is the strength revealed by the people in Latin America—to be
connected with humanity and thus to be connected with Christ.
Be part of that salvific event! You can take it all on! Jesus said,
"Shoulder my yoke...my yoke is easy and my burden light."
That's what the mystical life is all about.

16

Thomas Merton's Call to Contemplation and Action

A reading from the Second Letter of Peter:

> This point must not be overlooked, dear friends. In the Lord's eyes, one day is as a thousand years and a thousand years are as a day. The Lord does not delay in keeping his promises—though some consider it "delay." Rather, he shows you generous patience, since he wants none to perish but all to come to repentance. The day of the Lord will come like a thief, and on that day the heavens will vanish with a roar: the elements will be destroyed by fire, and the earth and all its deeds will be made manifest.
>
> Since everything is to be destroyed in this way, what sort of men and women must you be! How holy in your conduct and devotion, looking for the coming of the day of God and trying to hasten it! Because of it, the heavens will be destroyed in flames and the elements will melt away in a blaze. What we await are new heavens and a new earth where, according to God's promise, the justice of God will reside. So, beloved, while waiting for this,

A sermon preached at St. Paul's Church, Columbia University, New York City, on December 10, 1978, the tenth anniversary of Thomas Merton's death.

195

make every effort to be found without stain or defile-
ment, and at peace in God's sight. (2 Peter 3:8-14)

Peter calls us to look for the coming of the day of God and to try
to hasten it. It is a call to look, to keep our eyes open, to be
awake, alert, attentive, and always watching. But it is also a call
to act, to become engaged, to try hard, to work strenuously without giving up. Thus Peter's call is a call to contemplation and action in the service of the coming of the day of the Lord.

Thomas Merton, whose life and death we celebrate today,
made this call his own and tried, through his numerous writings,
to show that this call belongs to the core of the life of every
Christian.

We are called to be contemplatives, that is *see-ers,* men and
women who see the coming of God. The day of the Lord is indeed always coming. It is not a coming that will occur in some
distant future, but a coming here and now among us. The Lord's
coming is an ongoing event around us, between us, and within
us. To become a contemplative, therefore, means to throw off—
or better, to peel off—the blindfolds that prevent us from *seeing*
his coming in the midst of our own world. Like John the Baptist,
Merton constantly points away from himself to the coming One,
and invites us to purify our hearts so that we might indeed recognize him as our Lord.

What is it that blinds us? Merton says: our illusions. If there
is any word that Merton uses repeatedly and with a certain
predilection, it is the word *illusion.* We could call him a specialist in illusions, not because he tried to uphold them but because
he sought to unmask them. The many illusions that Merton dis-
cusses can best be summarized in these two: the illusion that we
can know ourselves and the illusion that we can know God.

The illusion that we can know ourselves puts us on the road
to a frantic search for selfhood through self-fulfillment, self-real-
ization, and self-actualization. It is the illusion in which we become so concerned with a self-acquired identity that we constantly worry about how we are doing in comparison with others
and preoccupy ourselves with our own unique distinction. It is

the illusion that sets us on the road to competition, rivalry, and finally violence. It is the illusion that makes us conquerors who will fight for our place in the world even at the cost of others. This illusion leads some of us to nervous activism fueled by the belief that we are the results of our work. This same illusion leads others to morbid introspection born of the assumption that we are our own deepest feelings and emotions. All of Merton's writings on contemplation attempt to unmask this deep-seated illusion. We are not who we know ourselves to be, but who we are known to be by God. We are not what we can acquire and conquer, but what we have received. We are not the money we earn, the friends we make, or the results we achieve; rather, we are who God made us in God's infinite love. As long as we keep running around, anxiously trying to affirm ourselves or be affirmed by others, we remain blind to the One who has loved us first, dwells in our heart, and is indeed our true self.

The second illusion is that we can know God, that we can say with precision who God is and what God's will is for ourselves and for others. This is the great illusion that sets us on the road to self-righteousness and oppression. It is the illusion that makes whites think they know what is good for blacks, the rich think they know what is good for the poor, and men think they know what is good for women. It is the illusion of control, the illusion that we are masters of our own destiny and can therefore exercise unlimited power and ask for unconditional obedience. It is the illusion that leads to Auschwitz, Hiroshima, and Jonestown.

Thomas Merton invites us to an always deeper awareness of the incomprehensibility of God. He continually unmasks the illusion that we know God and so frees us to see the Lord in always new and surprising ways. All of Merton's prayers, studies, and meditations led him to both a humble recognition of the great abyss between the "allness" of God and the "nothingness" of human beings, and a grateful awareness that God in God's mercy reaches out over this abyss and embraces us in God's love.

Thus we are called to peel off the blindfolds of our illusions that lead to violence, oppression, hatred, and greed. In so doing, we become contemplatives, people who see the Lord's coming in the midst of everyday life.

But there is more. Peter calls us not only to look for the coming of the day of the Lord, but also to try to hasten it! This is one of the great paradoxes of the Christian life: knowing full well that God is coming in God's time and not in ours, on God's terms and not on ours. Peter nevertheless urges us to work hard with great fervor to hasten the Lord's coming. Here it becomes clear that our action is part of God's coming, that in a mysterious way the realization of the new heaven and the new earth depends on us, that our waiting is not a passive waiting but an active waiting, and that God's promise is not hanging above us in the air, but is deeply embedded in our everyday life.

No one in our time has understood this so well and articulated this so clearly as Thomas Merton. For Merton, contemplation and action can never be separated. The *see-er* acts. Merton has rightly become the guide for those who search for a Christian response to the great pains of our day: hunger, poverty, oppression, exploitation, war, and the threat of nuclear holocaust. He teaches us that action to hasten the coming of the Kingdom is the concrete working out of repentance and gratitude.

Action is first of all repentance. Peter writes: "The Lord does not delay in keeping his promise—though some consider it 'delay.' Rather he shows you generous patience since he wants none to perish but all to come to repentance." And what is repentance? It is to feed the hungry, to visit the sick, to liberate the oppressed. All of Merton's writings on social action make the same point: as long as you act to prove yourself, to justify yourself, or to get rid of your guilt-feelings, you will quickly lose heart and do more harm than good. Merton even goes so far as to say that work for others that does not lead to deeper purity of heart is little more than the imposition of our own compulsions on our surroundings. Why, then, should we act in the civil rights movement? So the whites will be converted by the blacks. Why, then, should we act in the peace movement? So we can discover the source of violence in our own hearts. Why act to alleviate hunger? So we can unmask our own greed. Thus all actions for others can become acts of repentance that bring us to a growing solidarity with our fellow human beings and so establish the basis for all reconciliation. To a friend Merton wrote: "The real hope is not in something we think we can do, but in God, who is making something good out of it in some way we cannot see." Indeed, God is the one who acts, and by our repentance we can hasten God's action. That is why Jesus said: "The time has come to its fullness, the Kingdom of God is at hand; repent" (Mk 1:15).

Action, however, is not only repentance. It is also, and perhaps even more, gratitude. Action is a grateful response that flows from our awareness of God's presence in this world. Jesus' entire ministry was one great act of thanksgiving to his Father. It is to participation in this ministry that we are called. Peter and Paul traveled from place to place with a relentless energy; Teresa of Avila built convents as if she would never get tired; Martin Luther King, Jr., preached, planned, and organized with an unquenchable zeal; and Mother Teresa of Calcutta is fearlessly hastening the coming of the Lord with her care for the poorest of the poor. But none of them tried to solve the problems of the world or sought to gather praise or prizes. Their actions were free of their compulsions, and consequently were spontaneous responses to the experience of God's active presence in their lives. Thus our action can become thanksgiving, and all that we do can become Eucharist.

Here we touch the core of Merton's life and work. It is the Eucharist, the eternal act of thanks given by Christ to his Father, an act of thanksgiving in which we become participants. Merton's life as a Christian, a monk, and a priest was anchored in the Eucharist. What really counted for him was not his books and articles, his name and fame, but the Lord Jesus Christ who came to make all of life a Eucharist. For in the Eucharist, all is God's action.

When Peter speaks about the coming of the Lord, he does not paint a sweet picture. "The heavens will vanish with a roar, the elements will be destroyed by fire, and the earth and its deeds will be made manifest." Merton saw that this fearful reality is in fact taking place. He was a witness to two wars, and lived in a period of racial violence, economic oppression, and political assassination. With Peter he asked: "Since everything is to be destroyed in this way, what kind of people must we be?" And to this he answered, "We must be holy in our conduct and devotion, looking in contemplation for the coming of the Lord and trying to hasten it by acts of repentance and gratitude."

17

The Journey from Despair to Hope

The passion of the Lord did not end at the cross. After the cross Jesus entered the tomb. The tomb is the place of disintegration, where the body rots, falls apart, and vanishes into dust. Jesus chose not only to die for us and with us, but also to enter this place of ultimate despair.

From this place of despair Jesus speaks to us about hope. From this place of rotting, of bad smells, of darkness, he emerges to accompany us as we journey. Even though we are often downcast, Jesus always speaks about hope. And this hope is different from optimism. Jesus is not an optimist. He is not a pessimist.

Optimism arranges reality in a way that enables us to say things will get better. Pessimism arranges the same reality so that we can say things will probably get worse. When it rains, the optimist says, "How wonderful! Things will grow." Seeing the same rain, the pessimist says, "Everything will drown."

Being neither an optimist nor a pessimist, Jesus speaks about hope that is not based on chances that things will get better or worse. His hope is built upon the promise that, whatever happens, God will stay with us at all times, in all places. God is the God of life.

As his followers, we are called to be people of hope and to build communities of hope in a world where the options are usually confined to a limited optimism or an unlimited pessimism. To do that we must enter the tomb from which Jesus speaks to us about hope. I want to enter with you into that tomb. This means honestly facing the despair we are dealing with in the world today. We cannot go around despair to hope. We have to go right through despair. We will never know what hope is until we have tasted real despair. We have to be able to look at the despair of this world in order to have an inkling of the hope that Jesus offers to us.

Currently, we are dealing with three levels of despair: in interpersonal relationships, in a global sense throughout the world, and in our church. I want to look at each of these levels of despair and then, drawing upon the hope Jesus offers us, try to say a word of hope in response.

Despair in personal relationships is becoming more and more visible. We all struggle with loneliness. We feel disconnected. We seem to have no home. We search within our marriages, within our friendships, within our communities. Anxiously, we look for a sense of belonging, rootedness, togetherness. This cry for acceptance very often is expressed in violence. "Please love me," we say, "I can't live without you. You have to fill the hunger in me. You have to close the painful gap I can no longer live with."

The need for some kind of satisfaction, some sense of belonging, is enormous. The ache is so deep we are willing to do anything to fill it. Often, we end up not only hurting but destroying each other. Much crime and violence and battering seem to be a perverted way of expressing our deepest need to be loved, to be held, to be embraced.

Marriage, friendship, sexuality, intimacy—all are in very deep crisis. Sometimes I have the sense that life between people resembles tightly interlocked fingers. People, so hungry for each other, want to get closer and closer, tighter and tighter. "You seem to fulfill my needs. Let's get closer. Let's live together. Let's merge into one body." Then suddenly we reach a point where we can go no further. Finally we say to one another, "We have been friends a long time and still feel lonely." Or, "We have been married for many years and I still feel you don't really understand me." "We have been living in community so long and we don't feel at home with one another." Then real pain develops. People say, "Maybe we should get some distance from each other, then try again." So they do. But still it does not work.

Eventually, this kind of friction leads to a breakup, bringing even deeper loneliness, precisely because we have tried so hard. Now that's despair. Your greatest desire is to have a home but the harder you try, the more you find everything falling apart. And you don't know what to do about it. People end up killing themselves out of sheer loneliness and depression.

Out of that grave of despair, Jesus comes to us, as he came out of his place of despair, the tomb. He encounters us. He says something we keep forgetting, the core of his message: "Love one another because I have loved you first." Jesus proclaims the first love. Jesus proclaims that God loved us long before we could ever begin to love one another. This love is total. It is full and unconditional. "I love you with all my divine heart. I embrace you with all that I have. I send you my inmost self. I want you to breathe my breath. I want you to live in the endless embrace of my love. Here you can find your home. I have made my home in you. You can make your home in me."

Real love results from the coming together of people who are deeply rooted in this first divine love. This love enables each of us to recognize the other as brother or sister. Love God with all your mind, heart, and soul, we are told. You will discover your neighbor within that love. With that as a foundation you can come together with others and build a home together.

Sometimes we are quite far from one another, sometimes very close. In either case, we have a home if we are anchored in divine love. We don't have to solve our own loneliness if we are rooted in God's love. We don't just love one another because we desperately need each other. Rather, we can be together in faithfulness because we are both rooted in that first love. Our love for one another thus becomes a witness to each other of that first divine love.

I am a limited, partial, broken reflection of a love that is unlimited, impartial, whole. If I say, "I love you," then what I am really saying is that we are communicating to each other in a broken and limited way a love that has no limit, that is not broken. You keep calling me back to that first divine love. I call you back to it. That is what marriage is about. That is what friendship is about. That is what community is about. In each case, we are calling each other back to that first love. We are saying to each other: "We are broken people. But we are embraced by one who says to us, 'Do not be afraid, I have loved you first. And that is where you are secure.'"

The whole spiritual life can be seen as a life in which we reclaim that first divine love. Prayer, contemplation, meditation, solitude, silence—they are all meant to develop an awareness of the voice in your heart that says, "I loved you long before you could have loved one another. I accepted you long before you could accept one another. I embraced you long before you could hold one another."

This is how we will find our freedom. Freedom comes when you know with your heart that you are loved. If you could accept and believe that you are unconditionally loved and embraced, you could go all over the world and never be lonely. This is a struggle, but if you experience it you will know what Jesus meant when he said: "You will be leaving me alone, yet I am not alone, because the Father is with me."

I have met people who have earned incredible acclaim, people who have been admired by millions and millions of other people—artists, writers, performers, preachers. Often I saw that the more well known they became the more lonely they grew. There is always an anxiousness in the heart that whispers, "Will they love me tomorrow, too? Is it for real? Is someone fooling me? Is someone using me?" If you are not free, that suspicion will always be there.

Freedom is the core of the spiritual life. It comes from claiming in your heart that unconditional first love that allows you to love your neighbors freely and unpossessively. Jesus shares this word of hope in our world full of violence—violence in our families, in our communities. In our personal relationships, a moral life is not enough. We must also live the mystical life, a life which is embraced by the God who says, "I love you fully and unconditionally."

The second level of despair is global, worldwide. Jesus lived through this despair in the grave also. For some time, I have been trying to find a way to pin down this despair. What I have finally come up with is the fact of our immense fascination with destruction and death. You see it everywhere. We spend billions and billions of dollars to build armaments that, if they are ever used, will destroy millions and millions of people, possibly the whole planet. There is enormous fascination with that power we have to wipe out life. Somehow, there may even be something in us that wants to push the button, to see what happens.

We see the same thing in entertainment. Look at what you see on television, hear on the radio, and read in novels. Mostly, we are entertained with death games. People sit in front of the TV and think, "Is he going to make it?" There's potential destruction everywhere. It's as if the whole world were high up in a circus tent without a net. "Are we going to make it or are we going to fall? My, how exciting!" People become millionaires by tickling us to death.

Sometimes it seems that we prefer the security of death to the insecurity of life. Death is fixed. It is definitive. It is sure. Life is unpredictable, open-ended. You never know where it will go. Something in us is tempted to choose death because at least we know what we are getting. I have seen people who live as if they were balancing on the edge of an abyss. They are nervous, unsure whether they are going to make it. Finally, they solve the dilemma by jumping. At least it is over; the tension is relieved. In a world like ours with so many tensions and insecurities, too many of us choose the security of death.

But Jesus says "no" to death. We can see that as he walked with his disciples to Emmaus. He was saying "yes" to life. He spoke about life at a time when his disciples' attention was fixed on death. You and I are called to say "no" to death all the time. This doesn't necessarily mean that we have to get into demonstrations and protest marches, at least not right away. As a starter, it means saying "no" to the small kinds of death that hang around us.

Almost always, these small deaths begin with judging. In judging, we deal with our own fears by putting other people into little boxes and, in effect, declaring them dead. "Oh, I know him," we say. "I know that type. He's not worth talking to." In doing this, we take the position that new life is no longer possible in our relationships with people. We have already decided who they are. We don't want to be bothered any more. That is why Jesus says, "Do not judge." Labeling people prevents us from seeing them as brothers and sisters and from developing community with them.

We must also stop judging ourselves. We put ourselves in boxes, too. "I have lived fifty years," we say. "Don't expect me to change. I can't do anything new or different." This self-rejection is really a step toward death. It can lead to suicide—physical, psychological, or spiritual.

This kind of judging goes on in ourselves, in others, in our communities, even among nations. We have already decided what the communists are up to. We have already decided what Nicaragua is all about. We deal with other nations as if we knew for certain that they are not to be trusted. It is decided by us ahead of time. And the same process goes on in the hearts of our "enemies."

Living without judgment is very difficult. It means trusting that new life can emerge even in a world full of distrust, violence, destruction, and war.

Life is always small. It is always vulnerable. It never shouts or screams. It always needs protection and guidance. Saying "yes" to it means being willing to look at the small life that seeks to be born in your heart, in your body, in your mind, among people. Death is always glamorous. Death shines; it is always big and noisy. Death goes bang, bang! Because life is very small, you can never see it happening. Have you every seen a tree actually grow? Can you see a child grow? Growth is too gentle, too tender. Life is basically hidden. It is small and begs for constant care and protection. If you are committed to always saying "yes" to life, you are going to have to become a person who chooses it when it is hidden.

I have a case in point from my own life. I live in a community with handicapped adults. Just after I moved in they asked me if I would be willing to take care of Adam. Adam cannot speak. Adam cannot walk. Adam is what some people might call "a vegetable." "Would you be willing to wash Adam?" they asked. "Would you be willing to dress him and give him breakfast?"

As I began to take care of Adam, I slowly discovered what life is about. Adam began to teach me about the smallness of living. As I bathed this twenty-five-year-old-man, washed his face, combed his hair, fed him and dressed him, I began to realize what an incredible gift life is. Adam spoke to me in a language I didn't know he could speak. He told me how hidden, vulnerable, and deep life is. Being with him gave me a sense of being closely in touch with living. After a while I felt an enormous desire to leave my office and my books and to be with Adam, because he would tell me what life was about.

I began to realize that every time people say "yes" to life in whatever form—the unborn life, life on death row, the life of the severely handicapped, the life of the broken and the homeless—they start to give hope to each other. I had never experienced hope so concretely until I began to wash Adam. Adam strengthened my hope. It wasn't optimism. Adam is never going to get better. But he offers hope. This hope can form a very strong bond among people who are willing to go where life is fragile and hidden. And, it brings us to the core of Christianity: proclaiming life together as we move closer and closer to the broken and the poor.

The third level of despair is in the church. I find it hard to discuss this despair, but I feel I must. We could, perhaps, tolerate the world in chaos, the world struggling with pain and violence. There would always be the church to fall back upon, to give us joy and hope. But in recent times, I have come to realize that some of the most difficult despair comes precisely from being part of that church. I have heard people say, "I can tolerate loneliness, I can tolerate great anxiety in the world, but what I cannot deal with is the fact that in the church people are always fighting, divided, in conflict. You expect the church to be a source of hope. And here all its members are in struggle with each other."

I come from Holland. Over the last thirty years the Dutch church has been deeply wounded by the conflicts among its members. People are no longer willing to stay within it; they walk away. But in leaving this broken and divided church they end up being more lonely than ever and often find themselves walking without Jesus.

I have a friend, a priest, who lives in Guatemala. He said to me, "I can deal with persecution by the military and the state. But the fact that some of my fellow priests are against me hurts me more deeply than anything else." The most painful persecution always seems to come from within, from places where it's least expected.

Jesus suffered that despair also. In the darkness of the grave he embraced the despair that existed among his own followers, among his own people, in his own body. We are tempted to run away and say, "I don't want to be connected with that body because it is all broken and it's too much to deal with."

But we are called to be a community. We are called to be together, in a fellowship of the weak, to proclaim Jesus as Lord. We must not romanticize this. It is a humble task. Quite simply, we must call our brothers and sisters together—there may only be three, or ten, or fifty—and say, "We want to come together as people in prayer in our common anguish."

We are called to be people of hope. Together, we can face our despairs—personal, global, or ecclesiastic. Together, too, we can find the risen Lord, emerged from his tomb of despair, ready once again to love us first. In embracing us, Jesus gives us the hope we need to find and live the life he has hidden in us and in the world.

18

The Prayer That Embraces the World

When St. Francis Xavier died on a small island off the coast of China four centuries ago, it took a few years before his superior, St. Ignatius Loyola, received the "news" of his death. Today we not only hear about faraway tragedies on the day they take place, but we often see them happen on our television screens. Thus hunger in Ethiopia, tragedy in India, terror in Central America, conflict in Northern Ireland, poverty throughout the world—all of this and much more enters our consciousness in rapid succession and affects our thoughts and feelings day after day.

The question I want to raise is: Do we pray more for our deeply wounded world since we know so much more about it? Do we pray more for those who try to heal these wounds? I'd like to explore why praying for the world and the missions has become so difficult and propose a way to make prayer the solid basis of all mission work.

Praying requires us to lift up the world's pain into God's presence, asking God to touch and heal it. But when we are bombarded daily with so much human misery, we are tempted to treat such tragedies as apartheid in South Africa or the "covert" war in Nicaragua as "too heavy a burden."

Many people withdraw into their own familiar, safe circle with the argument that the problems are simply too many and too great to face. Others face the issues, but these issues become heavy burdens dominating their lives. For both groups prayer is no longer possible; increasing knowledge of the darkness has paralyzed rather than mobilized them. Faith falters when guilt replaces hope and shame dissolves solidarity, or when our rage consumes hope and hatred displaces love. Then our task to make disciples of the nations degenerates into a sentimental dream with very little sense of mission.

Why has the world become such a heavy burden? We can't simply blame the media. I suspect that while we become more informed about the world, we become less transformed by the living Christ. The strategy of the power of evil is to make us think of life as a huge stack of very complicated issues, too many to respond to, too complex to understand, and too frustrating to deal with. The more entangled we become in issues the harder it is to recognize Jesus as the saving Lord of history.

As long as issues dominate our lives, whether they are Third World issues, hunger issues, nuclear issues, or women's issues, we cannot pray. Prayer is not directed to issues; it is not meant to unravel complexities or solve problems. Prayer is directed to a personal God who loves us and hears us: it is a cry from heart to heart, from spirit to spirit.

Issues easily imprison; a person can set free. Issues easily divide us; a person can unite. Issues easily exhaust; a person can give rest. Issues easily destroy; a person can offer new life. Despair is caused by orientation toward issues, but hope emerges when we direct ourselves with heart and mind to the person of a saving God. That is prayer.

Jesus leaves little doubt about the meaning of prayer when he says: "Apart from me you can do nothing; those who dwell in me as I dwell in them, bear much fruit" (Jn 15:5). Dwelling in Jesus is what prayer is all about.

Life becomes an unbearable burden whenever we lose touch with the presence of a loving Savior and see only hunger to be alleviated, injustice to be addressed, violence to be overcome, wars to be stopped, and loneliness to be removed. All these are *critical* issues and Christians must try to solve them; however, when our concern no longer flows from our personal encounter with the living Christ, we feel an oppressive weight.

Most of us try to get out from underneath by saying: "I have enough problems in keeping my own family and work going. Please do not burden me with the problems of the world. They only make me feel guilty and remind me of my powerlessness." We no longer participate in the full human reality, choosing instead to isolate ourselves in that corner of the world where we feel relatively safe. We may still say our fearful prayers, but we have forgotten that true prayer embraces the whole world, not just the small part where we live.

Here arises a key question: "Can we see Christ in the world?" The answer is, "No, we cannot see Christ in the world, but only the Christ in us can see Christ in the world." This means that through prayer the Christ within us opens our eyes to the Christ among us.

That is what is meant by the expression: "Spirit speaks to spirit." The Spirit of the living Christ dwelling in our innermost being gives us eyes to contemplate the living Christ as God becomes visible in the concrete events of our history. Thus, Christians who become involved in Central America, for example, do not move from prayer to politics but from prayer to prayer.

To relearn what praying for the world means, we have to realize that the burden of the world has become a light burden because of Jesus. When God saw how humanity's sin made the world an unbearable burden—a burden of painful birth and hard labor, competition and rivalry, anger and resentment, violence and war, sickness and death—God showed us infinite mercy in sending Jesus, not to take our burden away but to transform it.

The mission of Jesus was not to wipe out all human sorrow and take away all human pain, but to enter so fully into our world of sorrow and pain that nothing human would remain alien.

Jesus gathered up the human suffering of all times and places. He destroyed its fatal power by offering it to God through his voluntary death on the cross. Thus Jesus made an unbearable burden bearable. We now have a companion who has tasted the agony of humanity more fully and deeply than any other person in history.

We have an inkling of this mystery when we experience comfort through the simple presence of a friend in moments of inner darkness. Even though friends cannot take our darkness away, their presence often prevents the darkness from destroying us.

Jesus' total, unlimited, unconditional participation in the suffering of the world has opened to us the possibility of living in this world and facing its painful realities without becoming its victim. This is what Jesus meant when he prayed for his disciples: "I do not ask you to take them out of the world, but to guard them from the evil one" (Jn 17:15).

How then do we deal with the flood of problems we now know but would prefer not to know? The answer is simple, but difficult. We have to discover the suffering of the world in the heart of Jesus. There we can face it and stay alive. Apart from Jesus, the agonies of our world make us run away and hide. But when we are connected with Jesus we can come to the recognition that all that we see—though painful—draws us always to a more intimate communion with God.

"Come to me," Jesus says, "all you who are weary and find life burdensome, and I will refresh you. Take my yoke upon your shoulders and learn from me, for I am gentle and humble of heart. Your soul will find rest, for my yoke is easy and my burden light" (Mt 11:28-30).

Here the deeper meaning of prayer becomes manifest. To pray is to unite ourselves with Jesus and lift up the whole world through him to God in a cry for forgiveness, reconciliation, healing, and mercy. To pray, therefore, is to connect whatever human struggle or pain we encounter—whether starvation, torture, displacement of peoples, or any form of physical and mental anguish—with the gentle and humble heart of Jesus.

Thus, every bit of "news" about people makes us understand Jesus' suffering in a new way. We can even say that the unfolding of human history is at the same time the unfolding of the depth of Jesus' heart.

Prayer is leading every sorrow to the source of all healing: it is letting the warmth of Jesus' love melt the cold anger of resentment; it is opening a space where joy replaces sadness, mercy supplants bitterness, love displaces fear, gentleness and care overcome hatred and indifference. But, most of all, prayer is the way to become and remain part of Jesus' mission to draw all peoples to the intimacy of God's love.

Through death and resurrection, the heart of Jesus has become one with the heart of the world. The deeper we enter into the heart of Jesus, the deeper we enter into the heart of the world. This mystery is the basis of all mission and of all prayer. Once we have clearly heard the invitation to come to Jesus with all our burdens and be refreshed, mission as well as prayer become an obvious response.

Those on mission will find support in the knowledge that a worldwide network of prayer supports their work, and those who pray will find consolation in knowing that their prayers are lived out in a worldwide network of mission.

19

God Is Waiting for Us to Respond

What does it mean to keep watch for Christ in the world?

The spiritual life means that the Spirit of Love is given to us so that we can live with that Spirit within us. With that Spirit in us, we are able to recognize that same Spirit in the world. The Spirit blows where it wants, so the Spirit is everywhere. It's in people who are dying, people with AIDS, people who are broken, and people with disabilities.

To watch for Christ in the world is to see that the spirit within us recognizes the Spirit among us so that spirit speaks to Spirit, heart speaks to Heart, love speaks to Love. To watch for Christ is to be attentive to the presence of Christ in the world and in our heart. It's not a kind of emotional or intellectual gymnastics. If we carry God in our hearts, we see God in the world.

Are there disciplines that can help us keep watch?

The first discipline is the discipline of solitude. It's only in solitude that we can get in touch with the Spirit of God in us. Solitude is an important discipline in a busy world. Solitude involves prayer, spiritual reading, and being alone with God.

The second discipline is the discipline of community. Out of solitude we go into community. Community is not just a place where we do things together, but a place where together we recognize the presence of God. So, for instance, marriage involves

An interview with Henri Nouwen published in *Alive* magazine, November/December 1994.

two people forming community together, two people who have discovered God in their solitude. They are not together to cling to each other in loneliness. It is the same with friendship.

Friendship can sustain itself only if it is two pillars rooted in God and standing straight, so they can support the roof. Together, friends can build a home.

Community, whether a parish, a family, or an intentional community, is where people live together and want to discover in each other the presence of God.

The third discipline is ministry, reaching out to others. It's important to reach out to others because we want to share from the abundance of our life, not because we have a need to be good helpers or because we have something to prove. Jesus never healed anyone in a laborious way. Anyone who touched Jesus was healed. He was so full of the God whom he met in solitude, he was so in communion with people, that wherever he went, life went out from him. If you are living a life with God in solitude and in community with others, then without too much effort, you can be there for others.

It's easy to hear about the events of the day and get dragged down. How can we stay aware of what's going on in the world without losing grounding in faith?

There is no promise that everything will be rosy. The first thing is not to play savior of the world but to keep living in the world as a child of God. I see all these things happening, but I do not allow them to seduce me into the darkness. I live in the world but belong to God.

Secondly, if you live a life of watching and waiting, you will know what kind of call you have. You are not called to solve every problem in the world. Jesus was not called to go all over the world. He was called to be faithful to his own people. Every human being has a call. I work with mentally handicapped people. Sometimes I spend hours with one person, and we barely speak. Does that help people in Bosnia, does that help people in Northern Ireland, does it help people in Somalia? I don't know, but I think it does. I think that when I am faithful to one person who is given to me, when I am convinced that's my vocation, then I am doing more than when I am anxiously trying to put out all the fires all over the world. And that gives me peace.

I think newspapers are very seductive things—they surround us with the misery of the world without our being able to do anything about it. We have to do what we are called to do. Vocation is not just individual revelation. It grows in light of community—other believing Christians who have affirmed your call. Ministry is a response, an obedience, a listening with great attention to what God tells us to do. If we're trying to do everything in the world, it's to satisfy our egos.

What is the role of worship and the liturgical year in keeping watch?

The liturgical year is Advent, Christmas, Epiphany. It's Lent, experiencing Christ as a suffering servant; and Easter, the Resurrection. It's Pentecost, the sending of the Spirit. The liturgical year is living the life of Christ through the year—not just the life that Christ lived, but the life that we are living as the Body of Christ. We take a whole year to lay out the richness of the Christ-like life.

Worship is coming together as a community of God to claim the presence of Christ. So we listen to the readings, we break the bread, we share the cup, we sing songs. They are all gestures in which we remind each other that no matter what we are experiencing—whether it is joy or pain or suffering—God is there. The world around us is trying to pull us away from that. It wants to say that nothing is happening here so why don't you buy this or go here or find your happiness there? The worshiping community is saying God is right here with us. You stand around in a circle with people—one person just had a baby, another just lost her mother, another is happy over a new job—and you realize that everything is here. You want to thank God that we are never alone. The worship life of the church over the year is bringing Christ back into the center of our lives and realizing that we as a body of people are representing the living Christ in our world.

To whom do you look as models for watching for the Advent of Christ in the world?

If you think of all the prophets in our modern times—Martin Luther King, Jr., Cesar Chavez, or Dorothy Day—they are people who began by doing small things. I'm talking about small in the sense that what they did did not change everything overnight. They opened a soup kitchen or worked for the migrant workers or labored for the liberation of black people. Even when they knew their efforts were imperfect, these people created signs in the midst of this violent world, signs of the coming of the Kingdom.

After a lot of prayer, some friends of mine—John Dear and Philip Berrigan and a few others—went out to an Air Force base and began hammering on airplanes that were capable of dropping nuclear bombs. They hammered symbolically on the planes. Anyone who would do something like this must believe that God is a God of peace. They didn't perform such an action to do away with the military. They performed it as a symbolic act to remind people of what the Kingdom of God looks like. They were put in prison for their acts. There they prayed with prisoners and had Bible studies. They lived with poor people, the poor whom God loves so much.

They tried to apply what the prophet had said: to beat swords into plowshares. It sounds very poetic, but when taken quite seriously, it can lead to very fervent Christians ending up in prison. And that's their way of watching and waiting.

What ways can we as the church encourage the world to watch?

I don't think we can encourage the world. I think we can encourage our fellow Christians and everybody who believes in God. It's important to pay attention to what Gandhi was doing. We have to be a sign, a witness. I can have wonderful ideas, but finally people are going to look at how I'm living. Each individual Christian and each community of Christians has a unique call. Everybody can't do everything.

You get out and do what the gospel is saying. Jean Vanier is a prophet for me. He did something that I could relate to—working with mentally handicapped people. There are some people who go to prison, who develop a whole nonviolent strategy around that. There are people who live very simple lives of prayer. Some live in monasteries, some as hermits, some in families. There are doctors and lawyers who live as witnesses. There are people who use their wealth to bring about things that otherwise wouldn't be possible. We have to get in touch with what is our unique vocation, to be a sign of hope in the world without being fanatical and thinking that everyone should do what we do. I need to trust that God will do God's work through me if I am faithful to my vocation.

You spoke earlier about the importance of solitude in getting in touch with God. Solitude is difficult for Westerners. Could you talk about keeping the discipline of solitude?

Solitude comes from the word *solus*, meaning to be alone. People have an enormous number of things to do in life. Many of us are driven. Solitude pokes a hole in that drivenness and helps us stop for a moment and ask: "What is it all for?" It means spending a little time with God to listen to the voice who says, "You are mine, I am yours, I love you. You don't have to prove yourself. You are fine."

One simple way to practice solitude is to take a simple prayer like, "Lord Jesus Christ, have mercy on me." Sit down, light a candle, look at an icon, be in front of the blessed sacrament or the Bible, depending on your tradition. Simply be there and repeat the prayer for five minutes. Let each word sink from your mind into your heart and then carry all of them through the day.

Or take a simple sentence like, "The Lord is my shepherd." Repeat it very quietly so that gradually it is no longer an intellectual statement but becomes a truth for the heart. Some people can do this for five minutes, ten minutes, or even half an hour. Or before you go to work, spend a few moments with a book of meditations. Read the text for that day, so that the word stays with you when you go into your office, your work place, and throughout your day. It's like a painting that remains in your inner room and reminds you, "The Lord is my shepherd" or

"God is my Rock" or "You are my beloved." These words are not just thoughts. They create an interior space.

People who do this discover that they can discern what they can let go of and what they have to do. It's a way of sorting out the garbage with which we fill our minds. We think we are busy, but if we look closely, we find we spend hours doing useless things that are not at all critical.

Solitude is a way to get a little control over our own inner life. It's not easy. Once we start spending time alone, we discover how chaotic our minds are. We start thinking about thousands of other things—what we should do, whom we are mad at. If these thoughts come up, gently return to the center. Gradually if you really discover, for instance, that the Lord is your shepherd, you might be able to let go of a few things and be a lot more at peace. You don't have to be filled with garbage. You can be more centered.

From time to time we may want to do this discipline with someone else. Sometimes I spend a half hour with one person. We sit there and don't say anything, but we support each other's solitude. So, if there's something there that attracts you to practicing solitude, try it out.

We have been talking about watching for God, but is there a sense in which God watches for us?

God says, "I love you with an everlasting love," and Jesus came to tell us that. When Jesus was baptized, he heard a voice that said, "You are my beloved, on whom God's favor rests." That's a very important statement that Jesus wants us to hear. We are the beloved, not because we did anything, not because we proved ourselves. Basically, God loves us whatever we do. If that's true, these few years that we are in the world, we are sent to say, in the midst of our life, "Yes, God, I love you, too."

Just as God cares for us, it's very important that we care for God in the world. If God is born like a little baby, God cannot walk or speak unless someone teaches God. That's the story of Jesus, who needs human beings in order to grow. God is saying, "I want to be weak so you can love me. What better way to help you respond to my love than becoming weak so you can care for me?" God becomes a stumbling God who falls at the cross, who dies for us, and who is totally in need of love. God does this so that we can get close. The God who loves us is a God who becomes vulnerable, dependent in the manger and dependent on the cross, a God who basically is saying, "Are you there for me?"

God, you could say, is waiting for our answer. In a very mysterious way, God is dependent on us. God is saying, "I want to be vulnerable, I need your love. I have a desire for your affirmation of my love." God is a jealous God in the sense of wanting our love and wanting us to say yes. That's why in the end of the Gospel of John, Jesus asks Peter three times, "Do you love me?" God is waiting for us to respond. Life gives us endless opportunities for that response.